Current Developments in English for Acade
Purposes: Local Innovations and Global Pe

Edited by Prithvi N. Shrestha

Published by
Garnet Publishing Ltd.
8 Southern Court
South Street
Reading RG1 4QS, UK

www.garneteducation.com

British Library Cataloguing-in-Publication Data
A catalogue record for this book is available from the British Library.

ISBN: 978 1 78260 162 3

Production

Project coordinator:	Prithvi N. Shrestha
Editorial:	Matthew George
Design and layout:	Mike Hinks, Madeleine Maddock

Printed and bound in Lebanon by International Press: interpress@int-press.com

Contents

Foreword

The terms *local* and *global* – both key terms in the title of this volume – have at times been presented as opposing forces and at times presented as inextricably co-present, with the push towards the global frequently triggering or requiring a simultaneous pull towards the local. This has led to the creative conceptualization '*glocalization*'. In the context of business and consumerism, glocalization has generally referred to goods emanating from the developed world but which are modified for consumption in the developing world. Such a system thus promotes a flow of innovation in only one direction: from the developed to developing world.

In the educational contexts focused on in this volume, the terms *local* and *global* take on different inflections and meanings. Many of the chapters, for example, challenge the uni-directional movement of ideas and practices from the developed to developing world and instead exemplify how researchers, practitioners, ideas and resources flow from many different regions and combine in many different ways. Of particular significance is the linking of the term *local* with *innovation* and the term *global* with *perspectives*. As the linguist J. R. Firth put it 'You shall know a word by the company it keeps' (Firth, 1957: 11). And it certainly seems that, in the case of this volume, by ensuring *local* is in the 'company of' *innovation*, there is a strong valuing of educational practices which arise in specific communities and particular localities. Similarly, the linking of *global* and *perspectives* brings into view the value of reaching beyond the local in order to share theoretical viewpoints and practical experiences across regions and across nations.

In its carefully worded title, this volume thus communicates an important message. Both researchers and educators working in the context of English for Academic Purposes (EAP) and English for Specific Purposes (ESP) need to guard against the all-enveloping force of new practices and resources which emanate from only the more established sites of EAP/ESP research and development. Rather, new pedagogic designs and accompanying research arising from lesser known and less familiar locations and settings should also be acknowledged and valued. In other words, whilst local practices may benefit from global perspectives and connections, it is vital that pedagogical designs are allowed to flourish from the ground up in ways that relate to, and make sense of, their unique localities and contexts. Likewise, global perspectives can prosper from the invigorating challenges and critical reflections arising from local priorities and context specific implementation.

As Prithvi Shrestha – the editor of this volume – emphasizes in his introduction, local innovations and pioneering practices face many challenges and potential barriers. To innovate successfully in ways that have local relevance and resonance requires specialized understanding by those with a deep knowledge of local conditions. In the chapters making up this volume it is therefore encouraging to see partnerships forming between those with in-depth local knowledge and those with broader global experience. The studies and projects reported on in Chapter 4 (set in the Philippines), Chapter 5 (based in Pakistan) and Chapter 10 (focusing on Sierra Leone) are exemplary in this sense. It is in these contexts (all developing countries) that collaborations have formed between researchers, teachers and trainers and include those who are locals and those who are more globally based (from Europe and Australia). The chapters demonstrate how such collaborations, where the local and the global coalesce, lead to robust and creative bottom-up innovation, responding to local needs and local stakeholders. At the same time, the chapters show how global perspectives and experiences can enable team members to recognize and respond to features and aspects that traverse regional and national boundaries. In this sense they become part of a process of 'reverse innovation', whereby the local impacts on the global.

This volume presents a wide range of innovations in ESP and EAP which have been investigated by a diversity of local and global researchers, some well known and established, others in the process of becoming so. The projects respond to a wide range of needs that occur in a globalized economy where English may dominate but where cultural distinctiveness matters.

I am delighted to have been asked to write the foreword to such a pioneering volume, which brings out the value of small-scale innovations with wide-scale resonance.

Caroline Coffin, Professor in English Language and Applied Linguistics, The Open University

References

Firth, J. R. (1957). *Papers in Linguistics 1934–1951*. London: Oxford University Press.

Introduction by the Editor

Innovation – that is, new, beneficial ideas or practices – in English language teaching (ELT) has been a constant subject of academic discussion over the past few decades. This topic continues to be a concern to all ELT practitioners because, as teachers, we constantly invite new challenges into our teaching contexts, and these challenges must be addressed and resolved. However, innovation in the context of ELT is still under-researched (Waters, 2014), although areas of research are emerging in the fields of English for Academic Purposes (EAP) and English for Specific Purposes (ESP) (e.g., see Hyland & Wong, 2013). Despite the fact that both EAP and ESP are fertile grounds for innovation, pioneering practices are often limited to individual teachers or institutions. Therefore, there is a need for more research so that EAP and ESP practitioners across the globe can share and benefit from new ideas and approaches. In this context, this volume – the fourth book from the IATEFL ESP SIG – aims to bring together EAP and ESP practitioners from around the world to share their innovations and research into their novel practices.

Innovations in EAP and ESP are usually initiated locally to meet specific needs. Innovative practices, due to their small scale and local nature, may not flourish where there is a lack of institutional support or resistance to change (Waters, 2009). Even if the innovation is on a national or large scale, implementing it may still be challenging (Hu & McGrath, 2011). Despite these barriers, if local innovative practices in EAP and ESP can be shared with other practitioners, EAP and ESP learners from around the world stand to benefit, given the increasing demand for English language skills globally. Each of the 12 chapters in this volume aims to showcase local innovations from a global perspective.

In Chapter 1, Cope reports on an Australian study that examined how cultural differences can affect the presentation of similar content in three countries in which English is the first language (Australia, the UK and the USA). She employs a critical discourse analysis approach to analyze the language used, and presents a pedagogical approach (with practical techniques) for raising learner awareness of cultural differences in language use. Such a pedagogical approach can be applied to other ESP or EAP settings.

Chapter 2 (Knight and Candlin) concerns the teaching of business leadership skills following a 'nexus of practice' approach in Japan. Based on the findings of the evaluation of an ESP programme for undergraduate business students, the authors argue that such an approach allows the ESP practitioner to be more dynamic, reflective and responsive to the ever-changing needs of students. Such programmes are continually refined and involve real-life tasks such as projects and online forum discussions.

Lawrence in Chapter 3 addresses challenges she faced during an in-sessional EAP programme in a UK university. She presents an alternative approach to the existing in-sessional EAP provision with a cohort of mechanical engineering students. This approach is more inclusive because it does not separate students on the basis of whether they speak English as their first or additional language. The chapter shows that a more inclusive EAP provision needs effective collaboration with subject lecturers, offering the provision to all students and making assessment count towards the subject programme. For this to happen, institutional support is crucial.

Call-centre ESP is the focus of Chapter 4. Lockwood reports on an innovative approach used to develop an ESP curriculum and assessment for the call-centre industry in Manila. She describes how she collaborated effectively with the industry and developed innovative assessment tools to assess the impact of the curriculum on the business. The chapter also highlights potential challenges which may arise when working closely with industry.

Chapter 5 (Mansur and Shrestha) is concerned with challenges faced when trying to implement ESP innovations in a Pakistani university. In particular, this chapter explores how the programme was perceived by three key ESP stakeholders: MBA students, ESP teachers and administrators. The third stakeholder is powerful but their view is seldom represented in the EAP or ESP literature. The chapter shows how any conflict with administrators can have an adverse impact on any ESP curricular innovation.

In a Spanish context, Martín (Chapter 6) reports findings from a study that looked at English medium instruction (EMI) in higher education. She argues that subject lecturers who are learning to teach their subjects in English should be considered to be a new type of EAP or ESP learner. Martín proposes that the skills and knowledge of such teachers can be enhanced if the focus of their professional development is on the functional language required for EMI, rather than on qualifications.

In Chapter 7, Matheson and Basturkmen report on a study of EAP writing in a New Zealand university. They demonstrate how a generic EAP course can cater for the discipline-specific writing needs of arts and humanities students by drawing on a range of sources, including students' written texts. The genre-focused approach followed in this course can easily be applied to other genre-based disciplinary writing courses.

Reporting on a project that examined the use of mobile technologies in EAP, Shrestha, Fayram and Demouy (Chapter 8) explain how EAP learners' oral skills can be supported and assessed in an open and distance learning context. They describe how mobile technologies can be leveraged to enhance students' EAP listening and speaking skills when there is no face-to-face contact between students and tutors.

In Chapter 9, Tsuda and Furneaux focus on an ESP course for dieticians in Japan. Given the increasing role of the English language in the country, the authors argue that there is a dire need to develop appropriate ESP curricula and materials for Japanese dieticians. A number of recommendations are made which may be applicable to other contexts too.

Tully takes us to a novel area of ESP in Chapter 10: English language for trade union education in Sierra Leone. The author reports on how European ESP programmes for trade unionists' employability skills were adapted for Sierra Leone. She highlights the importance of working closely with various stakeholders for the success of the ESP programme in the country.

In Chapter 11, Velliaris, Willis and Breen present a study from Australia which investigated higher education pathway programmes and EAP and ESP for rapidly increasing numbers of international students. In their study, they draw on the reflections of academic staff in their institution. The authors make a number of recommendations for increasing the chances of international students' success through pathway programmes in Australia.

The final chapter (Zhou, Butler and Wei) is concerned with how we might better understand the trajectory of Asian (in this case, Chinese and Thai) graduate students' academic writing by tracing their cultural roots and considering the effects of these roots on the students' writing. The authors argue that it is essential for academic writing tutors to be aware of their students' cultural and educational backgrounds in order to be able to provide the right support.

Taken as a whole, these 12 chapters examine innovative practices in EAP and ESP which have been implemented in different parts of the world and considers how these practices may be applied to other contexts. I believe that readers will find this volume valuable in enriching their EAP and/or ESP repertoires, and find much food for thought among the array of research methods and innovative pedagogical approaches put forward.

This introduction would be incomplete without acknowledging the valuable contributions made by a number of people. First of all, I would like to thank all the contributing authors for trusting me with this volume and responding to all my requests in a timely manner. I am grateful to Professor Caroline Coffin who agreed to write a foreword to this volume. I am also indebted to the following colleagues who kindly helped me with the review and selection of the initial chapter proposals: Dr Inma Alvarez, Andy Gillett, Dr Kristina Hultgren, Dr Maria Leedham, Dr Ghanshyam Sharma and Dr Jackie Tuck.

Finally, the IATEFL ESP SIG is thankful to Garnet Education for enabling the publication of this volume. I am personally grateful to Matthew George and Mike Hinks for their patience and support throughout the writing process.

Prithvi N. Shrestha

References

Hu, Zhiwen, & McGrath, Ian. (2011). Innovation in higher education in China: are teachers ready to integrate ICT in English language teaching? *Technology, Pedagogy and Education, 20*(1), 41–59. doi: 10.1080/1475939X.2011.554014

Hyland, Ken, & Wong, Lillian L. C. (Eds.). (2013). *Innovation and Change in English Language Education*. Abingdon, Oxon: Routledge.

Waters, Alan. (2009). Managing innovation in English language education. *Language Teaching, 42*(4), 421–458. doi:10.1017/S026144480999005X

Waters, Alan. (2014). Managing innovation in English language education: A research agenda. *Language Teaching, 47*(1), 92–110.

From critical analysis to critical literacy in ESP: Developing skills for greater understanding of UK, US and Australian English texts

Jennifer Cope, The University of Sydney, Australia
Email: jen.cope@sydney.edu.au

1 Introduction

The importance of developing the critical literacy skills of English-language learners, so that they gain a greater understanding of texts, has been acknowledged in the literature (Hammond & Macken-Horarik, 1999). Similarly, the development of critical analytical skills in English language teaching to enable learners to gain a greater understanding of written texts, so that they can participate in the discourse (Cope, 2009), has become apparent. The relationship between critical analytical and literacy skills and their application to the sometimes complex and technical texts in the area of ESP, including EAP, can be considered particularly important. In line with Fairclough and Wodak's (1997) assertion that the ability to unpack critically texts so that ideologically loaded ideas are highlighted and understood will ultimately empower and enable learners to participate in that discourse, it is the aim of this chapter to show how this ability can be developed among ESP and EAP learners. Furthermore, the significance of analysing texts through the use of critical skills to unpack and understand meaning on different levels of a text has been confirmed as a major finding of a recent study (Cope, 2013). The study was carried out from an overall Critical Discourse Analytical perspective and Cope (2013) found that familiarity with – or at least an understanding of – culturally-specific contextual and intertextual references was a significant factor in understanding English language newspaper texts, from the differing cultural contexts of the United Kingdom, the United States and Australia.

The study, originating in Australia, analysed opinion texts on the global financial crisis. The texts were published, in English, in 2008 in English language broadsheet and specialised financial newspapers in the United Kingdom, the United States and Australia. Through critical analyses, the study identified a considerable number of culturally-specific references embedded within the texts. An awareness of the relationship between these references and the cultural contexts in which the commentaries were produced gave added meaning to the texts. The study is unique in that it examines how written English is used within the three different cultural contexts of the United Kingdom, the United States and Australia on the global financial crisis. Few previous studies have considered the impact of the cultural context on the production and understanding of English texts, or critically analysed and compared how the English language may be used within localised written texts from different cultural contexts in which English is the main language.

This chapter draws upon the cross-cultural English language comparative discourse study to inform the development of a pedagogical approach which can be used in ESP settings. It will discuss the quite considerable impact that a local cultural and political–economic context can have on a text's meaning, and how the meaning can be lost or diminished when the text is read by an audience in another context, even an audience with an advanced level of English language proficiency. A summary will be provided of effective methods used within the study's carefully designed integrated framework to analyse the data critically, and suggest how the study's framework can be modified for practical application as a pedagogical tool in ESP and EAP teaching contexts, outlining the development of critical analytical and literacy skills. Previous assumptions seem to have been made that an English text could be understood by English-language learners, whose proficiency levels were appropriate to the text, regardless of whether the text was published in the United Kingdom, the United States or Australia, and regardless of whether the student was based within or outside the country in which the text was produced. This chapter contests this assumption and presents a critical method for use in ESP and EAP instruction which enables learners to understand localised newspaper opinion texts produced in contexts with which they lack familiarity or knowledge. Thus, the importance for ESP and EAP learners of understanding references to the cultural and political–economic context, which are embedded within texts and often assume the familiarity of readers, is highlighted.

2 Background

Studies which have looked at cross-cultural media discourse have done so mainly through examining spoken or written texts from cultures and countries with different first languages (for example, Bhatia, 2006; Simon-Vandenbergen, White & Aijmer, 2007; Wang, 2007), and only a few have provided comparative discourse of countries in which English is the main language, for example, Fairclough's (2000) study of the political discourse of Blair's New Labour in the United Kingdom in relation to Clinton's US discourse, and Lauerbach's (2007) study of election nights on television in Britain, the United States and Germany. Bednarek and Caple (2012a) focus on examining how news values are constructed in English language Australian news stories on the Queensland floods, and discuss the potential for comparative studies. In *News Discourse*, however, Bednarek and Caple (2012b) consider the active construction of news stories and the meaning made by language and images in English language media from around the world. Apart from this study, virtually no others have examined the impact of culture and language use in the construction of opinion texts from the United Kingdom, the United States and Australia. Situated within the inner circle of Kachru's (1988) concentric circles – that is, countries in which English is the primary language for the majority of that country's population (Kirkpatrick, 2007), it is possibly assumed that these three countries, which all share English as their main language, also share cultural contexts. While cultural similarities in the inner circle countries occur, owing to common ancestry of a proportion of the people within these countries, as the countries and people evolve away from their common ancestry, differences in language and social practices will have occurred too. Consequently, the English language in the countries of the United

Kingdom, the United States and Australia is likely to have continued to develop too, as asserted by Kay (2004), due to contact with other languages or varieties, and because of social and cultural changes within these differing contexts. It should not be assumed, therefore, that an English-language learner, who lives in one country in which English is the first or main language (such as the United Kingdom), and communicates with a person from another context whose first or main language is English (such as the United States), will necessarily grasp the full meaning of what is being said or written.

It has been found that in spoken or written transactions, which take place in different cultures where the first language is different, events can be sequenced in a similar way, even though the language use can be seen to vary from one cultural group to another (Paltridge, 2006), while Huth and Taleghani-Nikazm (2006) put forward that it is the cultural norms which strongly influence the variety in language use. Moerman (1988) similarly states that writers and speakers can be seen to reflect their cultures and roles, which means they are able to assume certain things about a situation and its participants during interactions. These examples illustrate the impact that cultural factors play in interactions. Yet examining the role and impact that culture might exert on English language texts does not seem to have previously been an important consideration for understanding fully the meaning of texts produced in one English-speaking cultural context, and transferred to an alternative English-speaking context.

In view of globalisation, the number of English-language learners in both foreign language and second language learning contexts is predicted to be around 2 billion people within the next few years (Graddol, 2006). Since a large proportion of these 2 billion people are estimated to be learning English in schools, colleges, as independent adults or in their workplace, this has enormous implications for the learning and teaching of ESP. In particular, one underlying motivation for the study was to teach ESP learners to read critically and understand the contextual references of the texts they are reading, in relation to both their general understanding of the texts and their awareness of how writers can reveal their own alignment with certain ideas and also attempt to align the readers with their position. In ESP instruction, there needs to be an awareness that understanding a text is more than just knowing the meaning of the words and attention should be paid to the effect that context has on the discourse.

Genres of power, or professional genres (Bazerman, 1988, 1994; Halliday & Martin, 1993) – for example, scientific reports and legal documents used only by members of certain technical and professional activities (Lemke, 1995) – are relevant in ESP and EAP instruction. An acknowledgement of these genres contributes to furthering an understanding of how English first language in addition to second language learners can be affected by them. Scholars such as Kress (1982) and Martin (1989) argue that language learners should be taught how to critique genres of power so that they may engage in them, while van Dijk (1998) believes that critiquing texts will enable challenges to be made to the texts' underlying values. Pennycook (1997) argues strongly that there is the need for a more critical approach in EAP, which simultaneously enables learners to access the important language and culture of academic practices, while promoting cultural differences in the way things are done. However, while Pennycook's (1997) perspective is somewhat different to that of developing critical literacy skills of ESP and EAP learners, it does support the position that language is social practice and thereby needs to be taught in relation to the sociocultural context from which it comes.

Hultin and Westman (2013), furthermore, apply Janks' (2010) critical literacy approach to education and highlight how language and power are related: '… to contribute to an understanding of the use and production of text genres as a power-embedded practice.'(Hultin & Westman, 2013, p. 280)

Hence the development of ESP learners' critical analytical skills will help to improve their literacy skills so that they will be encouraged to become more confident about engaging in and responding to texts. This will be a positive outcome, as they are likely to have their own valuable experience to contribute to the discourse or genre of power. Developing critical analytical skills and hence the overall critical literacy of ESP learners requires readers to interact with, and negotiate, texts. Although the negotiation is primarily for the purpose of understanding the meaning of what has been written, it should, however, also involve the development of skills for the secondary purpose of identifying acts of positioning. The notion of positioning comes from the social psychology field. It is a dynamic process which takes place in discourse and reflects our beliefs (van Langenhove & Harré, 1999). In other words, by extending reading skills in the ESP context beyond comprehension of main ideas and details of a text, to develop critical analytical skills, so that readers become aware of how writers, and speakers position or align themselves with certain ideological, political or other beliefs, learners will become aware of how writers attempt to align readers and listeners with their points of view or positions. Previous studies have examined positioning in discourse in a variety of contexts, and include Arkoudis (2005) and Cooke (2009). However, no cross-cultural study of opinion texts from the United Kingdom, the United States and Australia on the global financial crisis has been found which examines positioning and its impact on writing choices.

The apparent lack of literature on the effect of cross-cultural differences on English newspaper texts, and the extent to which different contexts can impact how a text is understood, created a space for the study described in this chapter. I, therefore, investigated the impact of the broader cultural contexts of the United Kingdom, the United States and Australia, in conjunction with the immediate contexts, on the discourse in opinion texts from these three countries. I also examined the linguistic devices the writers used which related specifically to the contexts of the United Kingdom, the United States and Australia in which the opinion texts were produced.

3 Local context: Examples from the local context of Australia and English-language use

The following example taken from the Australian context will illustrate the impact that knowledge of the broader sociocultural and historical–political contexts can have on the meaning and significance of the word 'sorry'. While the word 'sorry' carries the same semantic meaning as varieties of English in other countries, the poignancy it is given within the Australian context, because of the historical background, is quite different. In the Australian context, there had been calls for an official apology to the Aboriginal people to acknowledge the atrocities committed against them ever since the Europeans arrived in Australia in the late 1700s, and by successive governments ever since. Because officials had refused to say 'sorry', the word itself became increasingly emotionally and politically charged. Thus, when Kevin Rudd, a former Prime Minister of Australia, said 'sorry' in the first ever formal Apology to Australia's Indigenous Peoples at the opening of Parliament in early 2008 (Rudd, 2008), it was a highly significant moment in Australia's history. Leaders and people from all walks of Australian life were relieved that the word had finally been uttered in an official capacity.

This scenario would probably contrast quite strongly with that of the North American or British context, where the utterance of a single word of apology such as 'sorry' for having committed such atrocious acts is likely to be construed as too little, too late – a more expansive apology would be required. For English-language learners in Australia to understand the significance of Kevin Rudd's speech, therefore, they would need to be aware of the relevant historical and cultural factors in Australia surrounding the debate, as well as the associated political and contentious issues surrounding the reconciliation campaign.

In addition, further evidence of specific Australian patterns of social relations and cultural values have been found by Wierzbicka (1997), who examined the word 'mate' – used extensively in Australia – and stated that the Australian variety of English includes a socio-category of the word 'mate' not found in other varieties of English, such as British and American English.

4 ESP/EAP issues which need to be addressed

4.1 Context matters

The examples outlined above in relation to Australia highlight the effect that contextual factors can have on the use and meaning of the English language across cultures and how the meaning can vary according to the cultural context in which it is written or spoken. This interdependence of context and meaning is important for ESP instruction. In line with Wodak's (2007) position, highlighting and distinguishing features of the context, so that hidden and coded meanings in texts can be analysed, must be taken into account in addressing the needs of ESP and EAP learners. The ability of ESP learners to unpack meanings within texts thus weighs quite heavily on developing their skills, so that they can identify the relationships, and make connections, between the language of the texts, intertextual references and references to contextual features, all of which can be particularly relevant to understanding a text such as a newspaper opinion piece.

4.2 Contextualising ESP teaching materials

Experience of English language teaching in Australia over a number of years, including ESP, revealed a prevalence of teaching materials which were published in an English-speaking country outside Australia, and automatically deemed suitable for use in Australia. This includes the use of non-localised ESP and EAP materials, which have generally been published by and for the larger markets of the United Kingdom and the United States. By way of example, I was part of a team which developed an ESP course for Vietnamese bankers in Australia. Due to a lack of Australian materials and time constraints, we had to rely on adapting British English-derived teaching materials for the Australian context. In addition to the somewhat mundane task of changing all pound sterling signs to Australian dollars, the materials also had to be recontextualised for Australian banking and economic conditions. This was necessary because the materials, originating from the United Kingdom, contained a surfeit of references to the banking industry in Britain, and consequently, lacked relevance to the Australian banking industry. Having reflected on this experience, I now approach the development of materials differently – that is, I select (and adapt if required) authentic materials from subjects or topics which best address the needs of students. Materials are analysed in advance of instruction to find out what assumed knowledge is contained in the text, and what features can be found which relate to global and local coherence of the texts (Celce-Murcia & Olshtain, 2000). Appropriate strategies can then be devised to help ESP learners to situate the text within the cultural context. This may be through identifying references which relate intertextually to other texts or evoke certain cultural or social worlds (Bazerman, 2004), and thereby relate to cultural contextual factors, the meaning of which could be essential for a deeper understanding of the text. As Gillett (2014) remarks: '… it will always be necessary for the EAP teacher to be able to analyse contexts and language, understand learners' needs and develop materials that suit those contexts and needs.'

Both teachers and learners of English need to be able to identify the effect that contexts might have on writing strategies and language use in a text and be aware of how these can affect the text's meanings and the way in which it is understood. A surprising amount of assumed knowledge can often be present in English language texts and identification of all the names, institutions, events and dates referred to is an effective way of contextualising ESP materials for learners.

4.3 Enabling ESP learners to participate in the discourse through critical literacy skills

Understandably, there seems to be a general tendency among learners from many disciplines, including ESP and EAP, not to want to engage in or challenge an opinion which an authoritative person has expressed in speaking or writing. This may perhaps be due to lack of confidence, cultural constraints or unfamiliarity with the variety of English in which the text is published or the cultural context from which the text is derived. Yet, as Basturkmen (2010, p. 8) notes: 'In ESP the learner is seen as a language learner engaged either in academic, professional or occupational pursuits and who uses English as a means to carry out those pursuits.'

Thus, generally motivated by external goals, ESP learners want to be able to function in the real world. Depending on the field they are in, they would benefit to some extent from being provided with the skills of critical literacy, so that they are able to participate in the discourse to achieve their real-world goals, be that in an academic or workplace context.

It is well known that assessing needs of learners is considered to be a fundamental concept in designing ESP courses (Belcher, 2006; Dudley-Evans & St. John, 1998; West, 1994). The notion, then, of addressing learners' needs in programme design could be expanded to include developing critical literacy skills as a necessary component of ESP instruction. This would encourage learners to be aware of how language is used within certain and specific contexts, and have the confidence themselves to apply it appropriately and engage in the discourse. Hirvela (2012, p. 77) points out that '… reading is at the heart of much of what ESP students do, both in acquiring knowledge of target community discourse and in conjunction with the use of another skill, such as writing.'

Thus, in conjunction with teaching reading comprehension skills, students could be shown how to link references in the text to the surrounding contexts, identify strategies the writer might be using to try to position them, and understand that they are active participants in reading. Developing these skills should contribute greatly to enabling ESP language learners to engage with, and participate in, the discourse.

5 Methodology

5.1 Research design

The discourse study was carried out from an overall critical discourse analytic perspective. Data was analysed qualitatively to investigate how contextual, intertextual and textual factors impact and affect the meaning of opinion texts on the global financial crisis in 2008 from the United Kingdom, the United States and Australia.

Several factors motivated the study and influenced its design: firstly, English language teaching experience in Australia revealed a somewhat heavy reliance on ELT materials from the United Kingdom and, conversely, a scarcity of contextually appropriate Australian materials. Secondly, the researcher – who was originally from the United Kingdom – had visited family in the United States on several occasions and, currently based in Australia, found that even though English was the first language shared by her family, differences in understanding and using the English language were perceived between the United Kingdom, the United States and Australia, largely as a result of the varying sociocultural, political, economic and legal contexts. Additionally, despite the study being a discourse study which focused on analysing texts within their diversified cultural contexts, the researcher always intended that the implications of the study would relate to English language learning, in particular ESP, because of her professional background.

5.2 Data collection methods

Given that the study was a cross-cultural comparison of newspaper opinion pieces from three countries, Connor & Moreno's (2005) notion of *tertium comparationis* – or comparative platform – was adhered to as far as was practically possible. This meant that in selecting the final sample, texts were chosen for their equivalence in terms of the contexts in which they were produced, the content of the opinion texts and the timeframe (from

September to December 2008, at the outset of the global financial crisis). In addition, the writers were influential or authoritative commentators and there was some attempt to balance the professional roles of the writers so that connections between their identity and language use could be made. To limit the variables, the newspaper sources were not a factor, with opinion texts selected from general broadsheet newspapers and specialised financial newspapers in each country. For the purpose of this chapter, examples are included from texts which appeared in *The New York Times, The Sydney Morning Herald* and the British newspaper *The Independent.*

5.3 Data analysis methods

One of the aims of the study related to the impact of the cultural contexts of the United Kingdom, the United States and Australia on the language of the texts from these three countries. For this reason, an assessment was made of the relevance of contextual factors at the time of the outset of the global financial crisis on the texts in each of the three countries. The contextual level was approached in two ways – for each country a timeline of events, key institutions and personnel was drawn up. Next, since the study was done from a critical discourse analytical perspective, a contextual analysis was carried out using an adapted version of van Dijk's (2008, 2009) sociocognitive 'context model'. This required looking at the spatiotemporal setting of the text in terms of where and when it was published, giving details of who the writer was in regard to their professional role and known ideologies, and what the ongoing social action was at the time of publication, constructed through analysing the themes of the texts.

To address the second aim of examining linguistic devices which writers used, and which seemed to be specific to the contexts of the United Kingdom, the United States and Australia, aspects of Bazerman's (2004) techniques of intertextuality were drawn upon to analyse direct and indirect quotations, and language resources which were specific to a particular place or time. A further part of my study, outside the scope of this chapter, focused on how blame and responsibility for the crisis were expressed in the texts. The integration of these methods of analyses helped to strengthen the analytical framework.

Since the data for the study consisted of texts, which were accessible through the public domain, no ethics approval was required.

6 Findings

Initial results from the analysis reveal that – perhaps not entirely unexpectedly – a large proportion of references relate specifically to the cultural contexts of each of the countries of the United Kingdom, the United States and Australia. These include institutional references, names of enterprises, bankers, politicians, economists and so on. To a lesser extent, there are references which relate to countries, events or people, outside of the country in which the newspaper text is published. In each of the data sets, a considerable amount of phraseology was found which would seem to be specific to the country context in which it was published. While it could probably be understood by people from different cultural contexts, they would require a high level of proficiency in standard English to understand it fully.

The following extracts provide examples of references and other features from each of the three countries. The text extracts are briefly contextualised and then subsequently analysed to identify the different types of reference used. Some additional features of the extracts are also assessed, such as how the writers' use of words with positive and negative connotations might contribute to the positioning of the writer and their audience.

6.1 UK example

The sample extract is from an opinion text which was published in the United Kingdom in *The Independent* newspaper on September 23, 2008. The author was George Osborne who, at the time of writing, was the Shadow Chancellor of the Exchequer for the British Conservative Party which was in opposition to the Labour government. The title of the commentary was 'Labour is in denial over its role in this financial crisis' and the main topic revolved around the issue of how the Labour Party had forgotten its role in reducing the regulation of financial institutions and had allowed the British economy to become heavily reliant on debt. The text sentence examples are followed by some further analysis:

A   This is the same Ed Balls who as Chief Economic Adviser to the Treasury for eight years boasted about the "light touch" regime of City regulation he had designed.

B   The star player of Labour's football team has scored a spectacular own-goal.

C   The current system of (deposit) protection did not command confidence over Northern Rock, but still remains in place over a year after we saw queues on our high street.

In sentence order, those references which are specifically related to the UK context are: Sentence A which contains 'Ed Balls', 'Chief Economic Adviser to the Treasury', and 'City'; Sentence B which mentions 'Labour's football team'; and Sentence C which contains 'Northern Rock', 'we' and 'our high street'. Thus, in just three fairly typical sentences (out of 35), there are references to politicians, the centre of the London financial district, a political party, a British bank, the first person personal pronoun 'we' referring to the British population and newspaper readers, and the possessive pronoun 'our' implying ownership by readers. The use of both these pronouns signals inclusivity to the British audience. While these terms will be understood by some readers, they could well cause confusion for English-language learners who are unfamiliar with the UK cultural context. Sentence B additionally uses the imagery of football, the sport itself being of particular pertinence to Britain's sociocultural context, as a way of highlighting how inept the chief economic adviser had been in scoring a goal for the opposing team. By using the word 'spectacular', which has positive connotations, Sentence B serves to enhance even further the ineptitude of Ed Balls and his team. This description of the Labour Party appears to be employed by the writer, who is in the main opposing political party to the government at the time, as a means of stating his position and as a device to try to persuade readers that the crisis occurred as a result of the chief economic adviser's previous actions.

6.2 US example

This sample text extract from a US opinion text was published in *The New York Times* on September 24, 2008. The writer was Barbara Ehrenreich and her professional role is given in the byline as an author. The title of the opinion text is 'The Power of Negative Thinking'. The text was about how the concept of positive thinking had infected the United States, including its finance industry and had, therefore, become one of the culprits of the financial crisis. Further analysis follows these text sentence examples:

D   Positive thinking is endemic to American culture – from weight-loss programs to cancer support groups – and in the last two decades it has put down deep roots in the corporate world as well.

E   The once-sober finance industry was not immune. On their Web sites, motivational speakers proudly list companies like Lehman Brothers and Merrill Lynch among their clients.

F   Americans did not start out as deluded optimists.

G   When it comes to how we think, "negative" is not the only alternative to "positive."

References to US culture include: in Sentence D – 'American culture'; Sentence E – '(the) finance industry', 'their Web sites' and 'their clients' which are all implicitly situated within the US context, whereas 'Lehman Brothers' and 'Merrill Lynch' are named American banks; Sentence F 'Americans'; and 'we' in Sentence G. Thus, references are made to the general American culture, the specific and general finance industry, financial institutions and things that they possess, the general people of America and an instance of the first personal pronoun 'we', indicating inclusivity. Imagery relating to disease is apparent in some sentences, such as 'endemic' in Sentence D as well as named support programmes, 'not immune' in Sentence E, while Sentence F contains a subtle allusion to a possible mental impairment in the word 'deluded'. Since disease generally has bad connotations, these associated words would seem to have been used by the writer to strengthen her viewpoint and create a fairly strong negative impression of 'positive thinking' in the minds of the readers.

6.3 Australian example

Looking at an example from the Australian context, the following sentences have been extracted from an opinion text in *The Sydney Morning Herald*, published on September 24, 2008. It was written by Chris Bowen, an Australian Labor Party politician who was the Assistant Treasurer to the Australian federal government at the time of writing. Entitled 'Good place in an economic storm', the main topic of the opinion text centred on the reasons why Australians should have confidence in the Australian economy and may even prosper in the challenging global economic crisis. Text sentence examples are followed by further analysis:

H   As some of the world's biggest banks go under, Australians can take some comfort from the fact each of our Big Four banks has an AA credit rating.

I   As the US Treasury Secretary, Hank Paulson, was casting around for a new financial services regulation model early in the year, he settled on what was known as the "Australian model".

J   And the actions taken by the Reserve Bank and the (Australian Prudential Regulation) authority in recent months were as well calibrated as those of any central agencies in the world.

K   Countries running a budget deficit have a limited number of tools with which to combat this crisis.

References related to the Australian cultural context can be seen in the sentences as follows: Sentence H contains 'Australians', 'our Big Four banks'; Sentence I – 'the Australian model'; Sentence J – 'the Reserve Bank' and 'the authority'. Thus, there are references to the ordinary Australian people, 'our' as a possessive pronoun to imply ownership of some sort by all Australians of the four major banks in Australia, the implied success of the Australian financial system as a role model, the central bank of Australia, and the Australian financial regulatory authority. In addition, several references relate to specific or unspecified places or cultures outside of Australia. These include the unspecified cultures in Sentence H's 'some of the world's biggest banks go under', a specified place in 'the US Treasury Secretary, Hank Paulson' in Sentence I and unspecified 'countries running a budget deficit' in Sentence K. By comparing the Australian situation with elsewhere, these references serve to confirm the security of the Australian financial system. The writer therefore seems to position himself to take credit for the success of Australian banks and the economic situation in 2008 in his role as assistant treasurer, while at the same time sharing some of the credit with the Australian public in order to position them as well.

Overall, the references and imagery contained within these extracts exemplify how the meaning of texts can vary according to the amount that readers understand and, to some extent, the understanding is based on readers' familiarity with the cultural contexts and their English language proficiency.

7 Pedagogical approach for ESP and EAP settings

It is recommended that the following pedagogical approach be used as it is or modified according to the needs of ESP learners. It is not a prescriptive method of teaching critical analytical and literacy skills, rather a series of suggested steps to follow in order to facilitate learners to understand and discover deeper or 'hidden' meanings in texts.

A grid could be drawn up which includes questions or features related to contextual and textual features of the newspaper opinion piece. Some work or discussion could take place before reading the text, and the remainder while reading and after reading the text.

Step 1: Broader contextual level

- What country is the newspaper published in?
- What do you know about the events, institutions, people who were involved in the subject matter (such as the global financial crisis) at that time?

Step 2: Immediate contextual features

- When was the newspaper article published?
- Who is the author?
- What is the author's professional role?
- Who would be the intended audience?

Step 3: What is the title of the text?

- Is there a subtitle, and if so, what is it?
- From this information, what do you think the text will be about?
- What point of view or belief do you think the author might have about the topic?

Step 4: Discuss these answers in pairs or small groups or as a whole class.

Step 5: Read the text and complete the items below:

- Identify names of buildings, organisations or people.
- Which names are you familiar with?
- Which names are unknown to you?
- Highlight phrases or words of whose meanings you are unsure.

Step 6: Key words and phrases

- Which words or phrases in the text, such as names or adjectives, do you think are important to your understanding of the whole text?
- Why do you think the writer uses these words?
- What effect do these words have on you?

Step 7: Discuss your answers from Steps 5 and 6.

Step 8: Writer and reader viewpoints

- What point of view or belief do you think the author is expressing on the topic?
- How has the author made their opinion clear?
- What opinion do you have of the topic?
- Has the author managed to make you have the same opinion?
- What words or phrases did the writer use to try to make you have a similar opinion?

8 Considerations of the ESP and EAP approach

The approach outlined above correlates in part with the assertion that readers are active participants: while reading and listening are considered to be receptive skills, they are not passive. Readers and listeners need to actively participate in quite complex interactions to negotiate meaning from texts (Clark, 1995). This can be partially achieved by situating a text within the cultural context in which it was produced, in order to try to understand the meaning of the text on a number of levels. The approach is considered to be especially appropriate and effective for use in ESP instruction to enable learners to develop their critical analytical skills, and hence improve their overall critical literacy skills. In devising this tool, certain factors pertaining to materials development and the needs of the learners have been taken into account:

1. The tool is an extension of the more commonly taught reading skills of identifying main ideas or locating specific details, usually taught for comprehension purposes, which are of course very valid. However, this tool, as illustrated in the findings section of this chapter, is intended to go beyond comprehension of the texts and look for hidden meanings and how writers are positioning themselves and readers. Certain shades of meaning may only be understood if you are a first language speaker of English and are familiar with the context in which the text is published.

2. ESP's strong focus on 'situated language use' (Basturkmen, 2010, p. 8), and the value of 'genre-based instruction in ESP settings' (Paltridge, 2012, p. 358) has contributed to the development of how this tool can be applied, so that connections can be made between the contextual aspects of the texts, and the impact these can have on the language choices of writers. Both the 'situated' and broader contexts of the newspaper texts, and their impact on the language use and references within the texts, have been reflected in my study.

3. Specialised and technical terminology is often used in ESP courses and texts. In addition, learners need to be able to understand the contextual factors surrounding the production of the texts in order to make connections and understand meaning of the texts. It is therefore acknowledged that in these regards, demands on ESP teachers will be higher (Basturkmen, 2010), as they will need to spend some time preparing the materials for the classroom through analysing the texts themselves (Celce-Murcia & Olshtain, 2000). Teachers may need to provide glosses for words that learners would not be able to understand from the context.

4. In general, this approach is discourse-based and concurs with Belcher's (2006) perspective that analysing whole texts, looking at example texts and subject-area specialist viewpoints, in addition to specific understanding of language use, is now more significant. Previously it was considered more important to understand only how language was used in specific contexts (Dudley-Evans & St John, 1998).

5. The critical analytical skills being developed could be for reading texts on their own or lead learners into using the writing strategies themselves. It is possible, though perhaps less likely, that the goal would be to replicate a newspaper opinion piece after reading it. It could, however, be followed by a written or oral response, used as input for a discussion, expressing opinions, or writing comments online in response to written commentaries.

9 Global implications for ESP and EAP teaching

Based on the study, the amount of intertextual and other references which are related to the cultural context and embedded within texts from the United Kingdom, the United States and Australia, could make the understanding of these texts difficult for those who are unfamiliar with the surrounding contextual factors. This could impact even on those who may be proficient in English, as they might struggle to understand meaning in sections of the text. With references being difficult to interpret, and because of a probable lack of knowledge of the context, learners would have difficulty in interpreting the writer's position, and how the writer might be trying to position the reader. It would seem that for a fuller understanding of opinion texts produced in different cultural contexts, contextual clues and a glossary of terms and events should be provided.

The intention of the researcher in the design of this study was to link the findings to English language learning, a priority being to develop a pedagogical approach for ESP. The implications of the selected texts being complex and dense, as well as the subject-specific topic of the global financial crisis, suggested the development of a tool which could help learners to develop their skills of critical analysis, and thereby act as a valuable supplementary tool for ESP courses. It is suggested that this tool can be used in such ESP settings as English for media, banking, finance or economics, business, public relations, crisis management and so on. The pedagogical approach suggested incorporates a simplified version of the framework for practical application in ESP teaching contexts, which can be further modified to make it appropriate to individual ESP or EAP settings.

Acknowledgements

The author wishes to thank the Editor for his invaluable guidance, and the reviewers of this chapter for their constructive feedback. She would also like to acknowledge The University of Sydney for her research scholarship and generous support provided during her PhD study.

References

Arkoudis, S. (2005). Fusing pedagogic horizons: Language and content teaching in the mainstream. *Linguistics and Education, 16*, 173–187.

Basturkmen, H. (2010). *Developing courses in English for specific purposes*. Basingstoke: Palgrave Macmillan.

Bazerman, C. (1988). *Shaping written knowledge: The genre and activity of the experimental articles in science*. Madison: University of Wisconsin Press.

Bazerman, C. (1994). 'Systems of genres and the enactment of social intentions'. In A. Friedman & P. Medway (Eds.), *Genre and the new rhetoric* (pp. 79–101). London & Bristol: Taylor & Francis.

Bazerman, C. (2004). 'Intertextuality: How texts rely on other texts.' In C. Bazerman & P. Prior (Eds.), *What writing does and how it does it: An introduction to analyzing texts and textual practices* (pp. 83–96). Mahwah, NJ & London: Lawrence Erlbaum Associates.

Bednarek, M., & Caple, H. (2012a). 'Value added': Language, image and news values. *Discourse, Context & Media, 1*, 103–113.

Bednarek, M., & Caple, H. (2012b). *News discourse*. London: Continuum International Publishing.

Belcher, D.D. (2006). English for specific purposes: Teaching to perceived needs and imagined futures in worlds of work, study, and everyday life. *TESOL Quarterly, 40*(1), 133–156.

Bhatia, A. (2006). Critical discourse analysis of political press conferences. *Discourse & Society, 17*(2), 173–203.

Celce-Murcia, M., & Olshtain, E. (2000). *Discourse and context in language teaching*. Cambridge: Cambridge University Press.

Clark, R. J. (1995). Developing critical reading practices. *Prospect: A journal of Australian TESOL, 10*(2), 65–80.

Connor, U., & Moreno, A. I. (2005). 'Tertium Comparationis: A vital component in contrastive research methodology.' In P. Bruthiaux, D. Atkinson, W. G. Eggington, W. Grabe, & V. Ramanathan (Eds.), *Directions in Applied Linguistics: Essays in Honor of Robert B. Kaplan* (pp. 153–164). Clevedon, England: Multilingual Matters.

Cooke, D. (2009). *Managers' positioning in the workplace: Acquiring participation strategies*. Paper presented at the 1st Combined Conference, The Applied Linguistics Associations of NZ and of Australia, Participation & acquisition: Exploring these metaphors in applied linguistics.

Cope, J. (2009). Accessing the vocational college from an ESL perspective: A system of genres analysis. *University of Sydney Papers in TESOL, 4*, 21–55.

Cope, J. (2013). *From critical analysis to critical literacy: Gaining a deeper understanding of US, UK and Australian English discourse.* Paper presented at The 4th International Conference on English, Discourse and Intercultural Communication, Macao, 4–7 June 2013.

Crawford, J. (2002). 'The role of materials in the language classroom: Finding the balance'. In J. C. Richards & W. A. Renandya (Eds.), *Methodology in language teaching: An anthology of current practice* (pp. 80–91). Cambridge & New York: Cambridge University Press.

Dudley-Evans, T., & St John, M. J. (1998). *Developments in English for specific purposes: A multi-disciplinary approach.* Cambridge: Cambridge University Press.

Ellis, R. (2003). *Task-based language teaching and learning.* Oxford: Oxford University Press.

Fairclough, N. (2000). *New Labour, new language?* London & New York: Routledge.

Fairclough, N., & Wodak, R. (1997). 'Critical discourse analysis'. In T. A. van Dijk (Ed.), Discourse as social interaction (pp. 258–284). London: Sage.

Gillett, A. (2014). *What is EAP?* Retrieved March 2, 2014, from http://www.uefap.com/bgnd/whatfram.htm

Graddol, D. (2006). *English next.* British Council Report. Retrieved February 21, 2014, from http://www.britishcouncil.org/learning-research-english-next.pdf

Halliday, M. A. K., & Martin, J. R. (1993). *Writing science: Literacy and discursive power.* Pittsburgh: University of Pittsburgh Press.

Hammond, J., & Macken-Horarik, M. (1999). Critical literacy: Challenges and questions for ESL classrooms. *TESOL Quarterly, 33*(3), 528–544.

Hirvela, A. (2012). 'ESP and reading'. In B. Paltridge & S. Starfield (Eds.), *The handbook of English for specific purposes* (pp. 77–94). Chichester: John Wiley & Sons Ltd. doi: 10.1002/9781118339855.ch4

Hultin, E., & Westman, M. (2013). Literacy teaching, genres and power. *Education Inquiry, 4*(2), 279–300.

Huth, T., & Taleghani-Nikazm. (2006). How can insights from conversation analysis be directly applied to teaching L2 pragmatics? *Language Teaching Research, 10*(1), 53–79.

Janks, H. (2010). *Literacy and power.* New York: Routledge.

Kachru, B. (1988). The sacred cows of English. *English Today, 16*(4), 3–8.

Kay, C. J. (Ed.) (2004) *Macquarie International English Dictionary: Complete and unabridged edition.* 2nd ed. Sydney: Pan MacMillan Australia Pty Ltd.

Kirkpatrick, A. (2007). *World Englishes: Implications for international communication and English language teaching.* Cambridge: Cambridge University Press.

Kress, G. (1982). *Learning to write*. London: Routledge.

Lauerbach, G. E. (2007). 'Presenting television election nights in Britain, the United States and Germany: Cross-cultural analyses'. In A. Fetzer & G. E. Lauerbach (Eds.), *Political discourse in the media: Cross-cultural perspectives* (pp. 315–375). Amsterdam & Philadelphia: John Benjamins B.V.

Lemke, J. (1995). *Textual politics: Discourse and social dynamics*. London: Taylor & Francis.

Martin, J. R. (1989). *Factual writing: Exploring and challenging social reality*. Oxford: Oxford University Press.

Moerman, M. (1988). *Talking culture: Ethnography and conversation analysis*. Philadelphia: University of Pennsylvania Press.

Paltridge, B. (2006). *Discourse analysis*. London & New York: Continuum.

Paltridge, B. (2012). 'Genre and English for specific purposes'. In B. Paltridge & S. Starfield (Eds.), *The handbook of English for specific purposes*. Chichester: John Wiley & Sons Ltd. doi: 10. 1002/9781118339855.ch18.

Pennycook, A. (1997). Vulgar pragmatism, critical pragmatism and EAP. *English for Specific Purposes, 16*(4), 253–269.

Rudd, K. (2008). *Apology to Australia's Indigenous Peoples*. Retrieved April 4, 2013, from http://australia.gov.au/about-australia/our-country/our-people/apology-to-australias-indigenous-peoples

Savignon, S. (2001). 'Communicative language teaching for the Twenty-First Century'. In M. Celce-Murcia (Ed.), *Teaching English as a second or foreign language.* (pp. 13–28). Boston: Heinle & Heinle.

Simon-Vandenbergen, A.-M., White, P. R. R., & Aijmer, K. (2007). 'Presupposition and "taking-for-granted" in mass communicated political argument: An illustration from British, Flemish and Swedish political colloquy'. In A. Fetzer & G. E. Lauerbach (Eds.), *Political discourse in the media: Cross-cultural perspectives* (pp. 31–74). Amsterdam & Philadelphia: John Benjamins B.V.

van Dijk, T. A. (1998). *Ideology*. London: Sage, 1998.

van Dijk, T. A. (2008). *Discourse and context*. Cambridge: Cambridge University Press.

van Dijk, T. A. (2009). 'Critical discourse studies: A sociocognitive approach'. In R. Wodak & M. Meyer (Eds.), *Methods of critical discourse analysis*. 2nd ed. (pp. 62–68). London: SAGE Publications Ltd.

van Langenhove, L., & Harré, R. (1999). 'Introducing positioning theory'. In R. Harré & van Langenhove (Eds.), *Positioning theory: Moral contexts of intentional action*. Oxford: Wiley-Blackwell.

Wang, W. (2007). *Genre across languages and cultures: Newspaper commentaries in China and Australia*. Saarbrücken, Germany: VDM Verlag Dr Müller.

West, R. (1994). Needs analysis in language teaching. *Language Teaching, 27*(1), 1–19.

Wierzbicka, A. (1997). 'Patterns of "friendship" across cultures'. In *Understanding cultures through their key words: English, Russian, Polish, German, and Japanese* (pp. 101–123). New York: Oxford University Press.

Wodak, R. (2007). Pragmatics and critical discourse analysis. *Pragmatics & Cognition, 15*(1), 203–225.

Leadership discourse as basis and means for developing L2 students into future leaders

Kevin Knight: Kanda University of International Studies, Japan
Christopher N. Candlin: Macquarie University, Sydney
Email: krknight1@hotmail.com and christophercandlin@gmail.com

1 Introduction

Bargiela-Chiappini, Nickerson and Planken (2013, p. 3) write that 'business discourse is all about how people communicate using talk or writing in commercial organisations to get their work done.' In this chapter, we focus on how findings from a study of *leadership* (not exclusively business-focused) discourse were applied innovatively in the leadership development of undergraduate L2 students in the International Business Career (IBC) major in the Department of International Communication (IC) at Kanda University of International Studies (KUIS) in Chiba, Japan.

Although 'societies around the world are crying out for more and better leadership' (Nohria & Khurana, 2010, p. 3), Carroll and Levy ask what is this 'often mysterious and complex concept called "leadership"'? (Carroll & Levy, 2010, p. 212). In the research project on which this chapter is based, narratives concerning the leadership beliefs and communication experiences of 20 leaders drawn from the fields of business, law, government, medicine, sports, counselling and academia were collected through a process of semi-structured interviews (Grindsted, 2005) by Skype (audio only), telephone and face to face. The responses of 15 of those leaders were subsequently shared with groups of Japanese undergraduates who were taking part in organisational leadership seminars as part of their English-medium International Business Career (IBC) studies. Students added to the 'archive' of such leadership accounts via a Google group (i.e., an online forum). In the online forum, the students posted their own responses to the questions, commented on the interview responses of the leaders and posted further responses from Japanese leaders they themselves had personally selected and interviewed. The data were then analysed following Talmy's precepts for such research interviews, viewing them in terms of a social practice (Talmy, 2011), which generated those personal narratives (Riessman, 2002) from the leaders that were then shared with the students.

In what follows we seek to describe and explain how the creation and implementation of such public domain online forums around a theme, as in those organisational leadership seminars we refer to above, can be said to constitute a 'nexus of practice' (Scollon, 2001) to be analysed in terms of Scollon's three-step discourse analytical methodology – that is, by 1) engaging the nexus of practice; 2) navigating the nexus of practice; and 3) changing the nexus of practice.

The analyses and findings presented draw upon data derived from the online forums. The chapter concludes with reflective discussion of how project-based learning (PBL) in the context of business case study programmes (Knight, 2014 a, b), when implemented prior to – and taught concurrently with – such organisational leadership seminars and online fora can serve as a productive approach to teaching leadership. In this regard, Knight (2013) notes that leadership can be seen as a process of both communicating to *create* a vision and communicating to *achieve* a vision.

Further, we demonstrate that since a typical needs-analysis is forward looking and goal oriented, while a nexus of practice approach is process oriented and reflective, the utilisation of both can enhance ESP programme development. In regard to a needs analysis specifically, a nexus of practice approach provides the opportunity to consider the reasons for, and outcomes of, the needs analysis.

2 Background

Knight (2014a, p. 8) discusses how specific courses offered to undergraduate students in the International Business Career (IBC) major in the Department of International Communication (IC) at Kanda University of International Studies (KUIS) in Chiba, Japan and 'aimed at preparing KUIS undergraduate students for success in internships overseas and as leaders in the global workforce upon graduation, were not created in a vacuum but were instead the result of various influences over time.' The table published in Knight (2012, p. 5) shows that the majority of KUIS students enter various fields of business (Table 1).

Table 1: KUIS Graduates' (March 2011) Fields of Employment

Industry	Breakdown of KUIS graduates employed
Services – Other	34%
Trading – Wholesale – Retail	28.8%
Transport – Logistics – Airport – Shipping	11.9%
Manufacturing – Construction	9.7%
Banking – Securities – Life Insurance – Property Insurance	6.0%
Travel – Hotel	5.1%
Teacher – Public Official	4.5%

From the perspective of course development, there was a need identified by the KUIS Career Education Center to provide training to develop the English-language communication skills of KUIS students in the area of business, with a focus on leadership. This course development is portrayed in Table 2.[1]

---

[1] The instructor, who was the creator of all of the courses listed in Table 2, was also engaged in research in the area of leadership discourse as introduced in the subsequent section of this chapter. The researcher/instructor/program creator/and first author of this paper are one and the same person.

Table 2: KUIS courses listed in order of development

	Course(s)	Department at KUIS	Reason for development
1	Business internship programme featuring simulated company where students acted as business consultants	Career Education Center	Internships in Japan did not provide students with substantial business/leadership experience using English.
2	English for Business Career courses (EBC 1, 2, 3, 4)	International Business Career major, Department of International Communication	The four EBC courses, which combine English language communication skills with business content, became a core component of the newly created IBC curriculum.
3	Organisational leadership seminars (1 and 2)	International Business Career major, Department of International Communication	As one of four core instructors of the IBC major, the instructor was required to teach seminars to second and third year students. In view of the business internship programme and EBC courses, the leadership seminars became capstone courses.

3 Conceptualisations of leadership

A review of the literature that is too extensive to cite in this chapter indicates that there are numerous conceptualisations of leadership. Leadership has been seen as a 'mystery' (Carroll & Levy, 2010, p. 212, cited above) and often involving influence. Glynn and Dejordy (2010, p. 121) credit Bass (1990, pp. 19–20) for '[cutting] through the bog' with the following 'integrative definition' of leadership:

> Leadership is an interaction between two or more members of a group that often involves structuring or restructuring of the situation and the perceptions and expectations of the members. Leaders are agents of change – persons whose acts affect other people more than other people's acts affect them. Leadership occurs when one group member modifies the motivation or competencies of others in the group.

The focus of research has often been on the process of leadership itself and not on how leadership has come to be conceptualised in a specific way (i.e., who is defining leadership and why?).

A primary objective of the research that informed the leadership training of KUIS students as described below was to obtain from 20 self-identified leaders[2] their conceptualisations of

---

[2] Interview data from only 15 of the 20 leaders was shown to the students.

leadership so that leadership could be isolated, analysed, understood and taught. To acquire this data, semi-structured interviews were conducted with the 20 leaders. The series of questions that were used at the start of the interviews are described in Knight (2014b, p. 204).

Nohria and Khurana (2010, p. 7) describe the state of research on leadership as consisting of 'a set of dualities that … seem to be at the heart of research on leadership.' These dualities were transformed by the first author of this chapter into pairs of statements that became part of a questionnaire used to conduct semi-structured interviews with primarily native English-speaking leaders in the public, private and academic sectors (Knight, 2011, 2012) (See Table 3). The leaders in the interviews were asked to identify which statement in a pair they agreed with more.

Table 3: Pairs of statements discussed in interviews and in leadership forums

1a	A leader's primary role is producing superior *performance* or results.
1b	A leader's primary role is making *meaning*.
2a	A leader is a special *person* (with unique personality and character traits).
2b	Leadership is a *social role* (defined as an influence relationship between the leader and follower).
3a	Leadership is *universal* (there is something in common among leaders across all situations and contexts).
3b	Leadership is *particular* (each person must lead differently depending on his or her own identity, understanding of leadership and particular situation).
4a	A leader has the ability to exercise *agency* (the power, influence, will and ability to do, to act, to change).
4b	A leader needs to attend to *constraints* (such as the organisation's history, myriad demands and stakeholders).
5a	Leadership development should be thought of in terms that emphasise leaders' capacity for *thinking and doing* (which puts an emphasis on various competencies).
5b	Leadership development should be thought of in terms that emphasise leaders' capacity of *becoming and being* (which puts an emphasis on an evolving identity).

The responses of the leaders to these questions informed the content of the organisational leadership seminars. Students were permitted to read the responses of 15 of the 20 leaders and were encouraged to address the questions themselves, before drawing on these questions when they interviewed selected Japanese leaders. Figures 1 to 4 from Knight (2014b, pp. 208–209) (reproduced below) highlight some of the findings of this process.

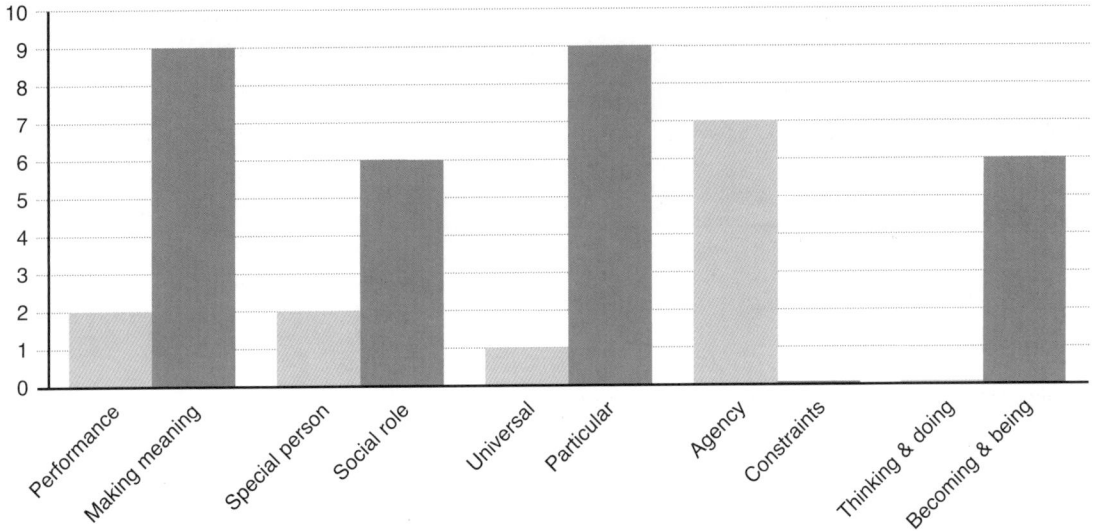

Figure 1: Group 1 students

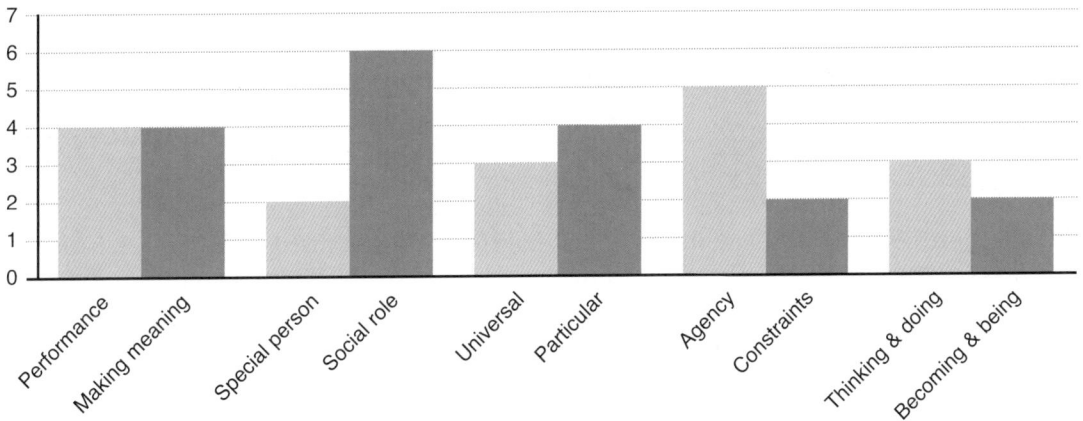

Figure 2: Leaders interviewed by Group 1 students

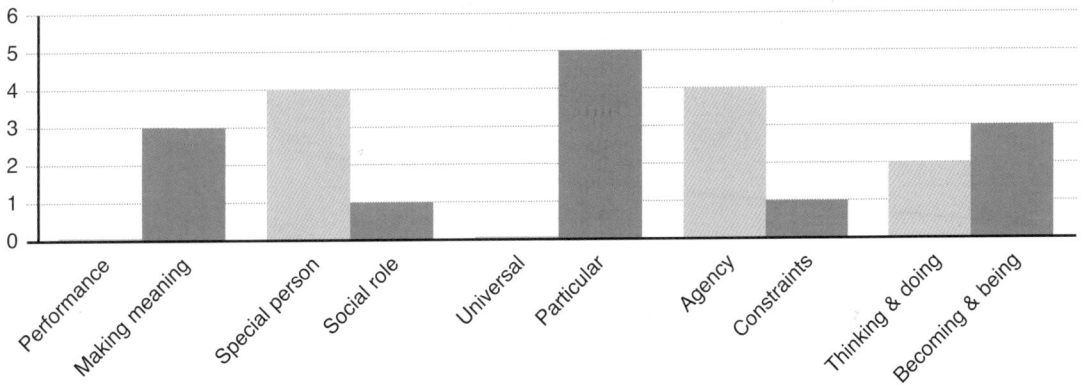

Figure 3: Group 2 students

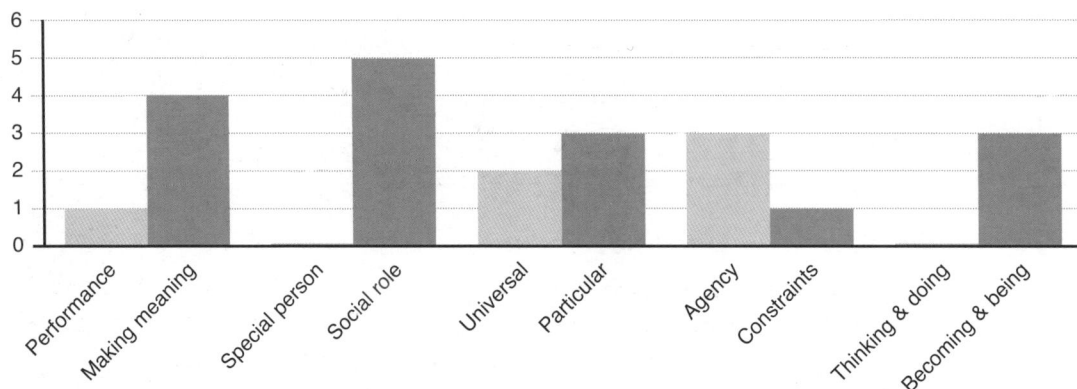

Figure 4: Leaders interviewed by Group 2 students

These tasks enabled the students to engage with how leaders conceptualised leadership. They began to understand the beliefs of leaders about the conceptualisation of leadership in relation to their own beliefs.

Identifying more specifically the characteristics of leadership following this initial exploration of leadership conceptualisation is the topic of the next section of this chapter.

4 Isolating leadership in narratives with STAR (Situation, Task/Problem, Action and Result)/CAR (Challenge, Action and Results) frameworks

In analysing the interview data, it was noted that the semi-structured research interviews (Grindsted, 2001, 2005) conducted with the 20 leaders resembled other interviews that focused on leadership ability (e.g., job interviews and MBA programme admissions interviews[3]). Specifically, the interviews with the 20 leaders culminated in two questions that could be labelled 'behavioural questions'. (See Table 4).

Table 4: Final two questions in questionnaire used to interview 20 leaders

Leadership communication

10) What are some specific communication challenges that you usually face as a leader in your job? (In answering this question, please identify the situation, the location, the people involved and the seriousness of the challenge/critical extent of the challenge.)

11) Consider a time that you strategically and successfully used communication as a leader to achieve a specific goal. I am interested in your story of that event (i.e., your personal account/narrative of that event).[4]

---

[3] The leaders were asked to talk about their leadership performances in their leadership roles.

[4] Question adapted from Fairhurst (2011, pp. 201–208).

11a. What was the opportunity or problem you needed to address?

11b. Who were the key stakeholders and why?

11c. What expectations did the stakeholders have of you as a leader? What expectations did you have of yourself as a leader?

11d. What was your basic message, idea, or case for change?

11e. What were important factors to consider in formulating your basic message to have the impact that you desired (e.g., different perceptions of the opportunity or problem, terms or arguments that should be avoided, constraints on resources, agreement from everyone needed, the need to regulate emotions, the importance of generating trust or believability, potential inconsistencies in the message that could confuse stakeholders, etc.)?

11f. What communication techniques did you use to formulate and deliver your message to have the impact that you desired (e.g., humour (including funny story or anecdote), use of metaphor or analogy, simplification of the message, repetition of certain phrases, method/place/time of delivery, nonverbal communication, physical appearance, use of technology, etc.)?

11g. What was the result of your efforts from the view of leadership communication?

11h. If you had to repeat the event, what would you do differently, if anything, to achieve better results from the view of leadership communication?

The identification of leadership in the responses to these behavioural questions was based on the following reasoning by the researchers:

1. The 20 individuals who were interviewed were self-identified as leaders.

2. They responded to behavioural questions about leadership in which they were asked to describe leadership performances.

3. The actions of the leaders set out in these responses served to identify characteristics of leadership in action – i.e., the leaders described actions undertaken as leaders in a response to a question about leadership.

4. These actions could be isolated by applying the STAR or CAR frameworks used to respond to behavioural questions where A refers to action.

5. In the context of the STAR or CAR framework, the A or action is leadership by definition; a leader engaged in the act of leading.[5]

In the Career Resource Manual in use at the University of California, Davis, there is a reference to the STAR method. (See Table 5.)

---

[5] It is important to note that it was the leaders themselves who were identifying what leadership meant to them through the self-selection of the A or action. The researchers were not labelling leadership a priori.

Table 5: Tips for the Behavioural Interview from UC Davis Internship and Career Center (Career Resource Manual, 2013, pp. 44–45)

Tips for the Behavioural Interview

Behavioural interview questions assess how you have acted in past situations, with the idea that past performance is a key indicator of your future efforts.

How to Prepare ...

Use the **STAR** method to help you form an example:

Situation • Task/Problem • Action • Result

Employers May Ask You ...

Tell me about a time when you were in a leadership position.

A further example is to be found in the Career Guide (2013–2014, p. 27) of UC San Diego, which teaches undergraduate students to use the CAR method to respond to behavioural questions in interviews for jobs or internships. (See Table 6.)

Table 6: The CAR Method

Employers use behavioural based questions to screen job candidates in interviews. The premise is that the most accurate predictor of future performance and competencies is past experience in similar situations. When responding to behavioural based interview questions use the CAR method:

Using the CAR method

Challenge

Briefly and specifically describe the challenge that you solved or developed an action plan to overcome. Describe a specific event or situation, not a generalised description of what you have done in the past. Be sure to give enough detail for the interviewer to understand, but keep it brief. This situation can be from a previous job, a volunteer experience, or any relevant event. Stay clear of personal stories or events that make you emotional.

Action you took

Describe the action or steps you took to solve the problem, overcome the obstacle or remedy the situation. Be sure to focus on what you did specifically. Even if you are discussing a group project or effort, describe what you did. Don't tell what you might do, tell what you did.

Results you achieved

What was the outcome? Were the results measurable? What were the benefits? What was learned? Did you gain any insights?

Sample response

Question: Tell me about a time when you used teamwork to solve a problem?

Answer

Challenge: Our student organisation didn't have enough funds to coordinate an ice cream social to welcome new members to UC San Diego.

Action: Rather than give up I coordinated a brainstorming session with members to identify funding sources: We developed a plan that included collaborating with another student organisation to make it a joint event, contacting local businesses for donations and outreaching to student organisation alumni to assist. I personally contacted and followed up with over 15 alumni members through LinkedIn.

Results: With the collaborative spirit of working with another student organisation, local businesses and alumni, I was able to secure enough funds to pay for the ice cream social while incorporating alumni networking to make it fun. As a result … new members felt welcomed and motivated to join our organisation.

By analysing the responses of the leaders in accordance with the STAR and CAR frameworks, the given *As* or actions could be isolated in relation to the identification of leadership performance. Leadership could therefore be clearly seen as being contextualised and situation-bound. Analysis of the leaders' responses also displayed how leadership, in their view, involved influencing others who may or may not have been their subordinates. For example, project leadership was clearly identified and described in leadership narratives.

5 Instructor's conceptualisation of leadership

In developing the leadership curriculum, proposals for the teaching of leadership were inevitably influenced by the instructor's personal conceptualisation of leadership. Figure 5 provides a visualisation of such a conceptualisation of leadership.

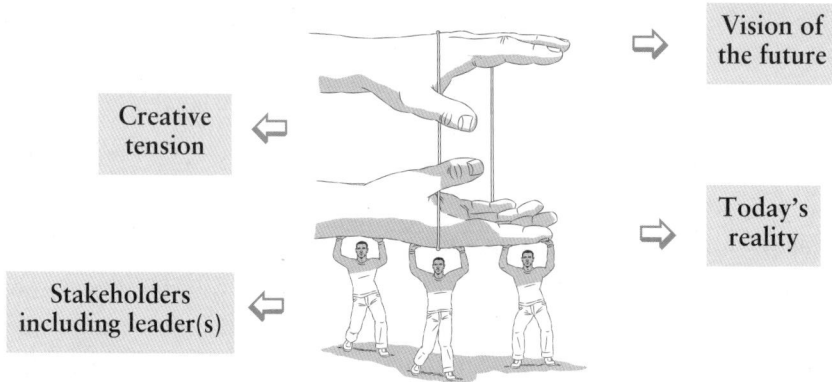

**Leadership is ...
making real a vision**

Vision of
the future

Creative
tension

Today's
reality

Stakeholders
including leader(s)

in collaboration with others

Note: This is my personal conceptualization of leadership. It is based on semi-structured interviews with 20 leaders in the public, private, and academic sectors, the creation of multiple online forums on leadership, and the experience of high-profile leadership roles in a study of the discourse of leadership.

Figure 5: Adaptation of reflective practice group contest submission at Macquarie University[6]

Figure 5 displays an adaptation of an entry to a contest held by the Reflective Practice Group at Macquarie University. As the footnote in Figure 5 explains, this personal conceptualisation was based upon the research of leadership forums and the teaching of the organisational leadership seminars. This personal conceptualisation of leadership also incorporated the instructor's understanding of and engagement in high profile leadership roles in TESOL International Association. These roles included the following:

- Chair of the TESOL English for Specific Purposes Interest Section (ESP-IS); and

- Member of the Board of Directors' Governance Review Task Force (GRTF).

As ESP-IS chair, the creative aspect of leadership was one intensely experienced by the instructor in the creation and implementation of five global online forums for month-long discussions related to the professional development of ESP practitioners. In this regard, the instructor, acting as a leader, had the vision and acted to realise it with the support of others.

As a member of the GRTF, the instructor was involved in the drafting of recommendations based on research findings. In this regard, the vision to be created derived from the analysis of data collected. The task of the GRTF was not to implement the recommendations.

---

[6] The original entry to the contest contained a photo of hands and stick figures. The "creative tension" section of the illustration in Figure 5 was influenced by and adapted from Senge (1990a), which the instructor had read around 20 years earlier. See also Senge (1990b, 2006)

Accordingly, the instructor came to view leadership as actions not only to create a vision but also as actions to achieve such a vision, and that these actions could overlap. In this connection, the instructor shared the following in a TESOL Blog post.

> As a researcher of professional communication, I recognise that many different conceptualisations of leadership exist. For me personally, however, I like to view leadership as a communication process consisting of two parts: 1) communicating to create a vision; and 2) communicating to achieve a vision. Leadership is considered by many to be an "influence relationship" and in my personal conceptualisation of leadership, leadership would involve influencing others through communication associated with the goals of Part 1 and Part 2.

> Viewing leadership in this way also facilitates the teaching of those communication skills that would be used to create a shared vision and to motivate others to achieve a shared vision.

> [See more at: http://blog.tesol.org/looking-at-communication-through-a-leadership-lens/#sthash.JX4FBf3s.dpuf]

This view of leadership communication aligns with the work of Fairhurst (2011). It should be noted that the concepts of framing and obtaining 'buy in' (or stakeholder agreement) were introduced to students in the organisational leadership seminars as set out in Table 2. Moreover, the importance of project leadership and online communication inherent in the instructor's personal conceptualisation of leadership was manifested in the activities in the organisational seminar used to teach leadership. These organisational leadership seminars and online forums are considered in the subsequent section.

6 Scollon's nexus analysis and its relevance

Knight (2014a, p. 14) writes of the creation and implementation of the four EBC courses (listed in Table 2) preceding the organisational leadership seminars as follows:

> This paper has also shown that the course design as well as the approaches selected and utilised to meet the needs of the learners may be significantly influenced by the experiences of the course creator and instructor in academic or occupational contexts. In other words, although ESP programmes address the needs of the participants, the approaches selected and utilised to meet those needs may be influenced by other courses that an instructor has created, taught, or experienced.

This section in the chapter concerns the creation and implementation of the organisational leadership seminars and related online forums at KUIS, drawing on the historical and mediated discourse analytical (MDA) perspectives outlined in Scollons' concept of a nexus of practice. Scollon and Scollon (2004, p. 159) describe the nexus of practice in the following way:

> A nexus of practice is the point at which historical trajectories of people, places, discourses, ideas and objects come together to enable some action which in itself alters those historical trajectories in some way as those trajectories emanate from this moment of social action.

A nexus analysis is conducted on a nexus of practice, which, according to Scollon and Scollon (2004), acts as a focus for exploring the particular issue under investigation, as here, for example, the leadership curriculum project, its inputs, participants and processes. As we outlined earlier, the three main activities in such a nexus analysis are: 1) engaging the nexus of practice; 2) navigating the nexus of practice; and 3) changing the nexus of practice.

> The sequencing of tasks begins by engaging the researcher in the key mediated actions that are relevant to the social issue under study, and then moves to navigating and mapping the cycles of discourse, of people, and of mediational means which are at the heart of the significant actions being studied. Although we discuss changing the nexus of [practice] as the third stage, a *nexus analysis* recognises throughout the analysis that the processes of change are the results of the activities of the researcher in recording the actions, engaging in discourses with the participants, and constructing new courses of action. (Scollon & Scollon, 2004, p. 152)

In this case, the issue (or focus of the nexus of practice) under investigation is the creation and implementation of the organisational leadership seminars and the related online forums on leadership. As noted above, the researcher/instructor/programme creator/and first author of this chapter are one and the same person.

Such a nexus analysis differs significantly from a typical ESP needs analysis. In this context, Knight (2014c) cites Abrar-ul-Hassan (2012, p. 6) in regard to the assessment of learning needs for developing an ESP programme.

> Needs are gaps between programme goals and the learner's proficiency at that stage, which is defined with reference to communicative functions and discourse communities.

> *Needs* or 'Target Needs' are comprised of necessities, lacks and wants (Hutchinson & Waters, 1989, p. 54). First, necessities are 'determined by the demands of the target situation'. This procedure involves the estimation of necessary skills required for the learner to work efficiently in the target situation. Second, lacks are the gaps between the target proficiency and existing proficiency of the learner. Third, wants are perceptions of the learners about their own needs (Hutchinson & Waters, 1989, pp. 55–57). A systematic NA is comprised of a diagnosis of necessities, lacks and wants …

In contrast to the above, in the case of the creation and implementation of the organisational leadership seminars and related online forums at KUIS, such a nexus analysis is more directed at addressing three questions which are continually relevant to the ongoing programme development:

1. Why is this programme being created and conducted in the way that it is?

2. Who are the stakeholders, including the researcher/practitioner, and what are their roles in the creation and implementation of the programme?

3. What is the role of 'communication' in the creation and implementation of the programme?

To address these questions, we need to consider programme development from the perspective of the researcher as well as that of the practitioner. However, although such programme development is a jointly constructed enterprise, we do not limit our perspective of programme development to that formulated in Kertzner, Knight and Swartley (2012) where such programme development is depicted as an ongoing cycle consisting of: 1) appraising stakeholder needs; 2) determining performance goals; 3) formulating course design; 4) devising lesson plans; 5) producing training materials; 6) delivering training; and 7) constructing assessment tasks. Rather we adopt the stance of Schön's (1983) reflective practitioner in the manner described by Finlay (2008, p. 3):

> [One] of [Schön's] most important and enduring contributions was to identify two types of reflection: reflection-on-action (after-the-event thinking) and reflection-in-action (thinking while doing).
>
> In the case of reflection-on-action, professionals are understood consciously to review, describe, analyse and evaluate their past practice with a view to gaining insight to improve future practice. With reflection-in-action, professionals are seen as examining their experiences and responses as they occur. In both types of reflection, professionals aim to connect with their feelings and attend to relevant theory. They seek to build new understandings to shape their action in the unfolding situation.

In an effective needs analysis, the 'workplace language training provider builds a strong client relationship,' determines 'client needs, expectations and goals' as part of an 'organisational needs assessment,' and '[designs] a programme' (Friedenberg, Kennedy, Lomperis, Martin, & Westerfield, 2003, p. vii). As reflective practitioners, on the other hand, our focus is on understanding how a curriculum is developed and taught dynamically. This means that the reflective practitioner must become aware of how that curriculum is transforming and being transformed by the various individual, institutional and societal forces acting upon it.

Scollon and Scollon (2004, p. 160) describe navigating the nexus of practice as follows:

> If we think of an action as a moment in time and space in which the historical bodies and the interaction order of people and the discourses in place intersect, then each of these can be thought of as having a history that leads into that moment and a future that leads away from it in arcs of semiotic cycles of change and transformation.

In the case of programme development, a nexus analysis enables us to see and give an account of why and how the programme is shaped and changed in specific ways, requiring participants to keep the overall shape and purposes of the curriculum in mind as well as focusing on the micro analysis of its content and practices as it unfolds.

Central to this process is an awareness of the discourses and their realisations in the texts of curriculum design and enactment. Scollon and Scollon (2004, p. 173) write that in a nexus analysis, discourses in the following forms can be analysed:

- speech of the participants in mediated actions (whether foregrounded or backgrounded)
- texts used as mediational means (whether foregrounded or backgrounded) such as books, magazines, train schedules, street signs, logos and brand names, directions for use on packages and other objects)

- images and other semiotic systems used as mediational means (pictures, gestures, manner of dressing, design of buildings and other places, works of art as focal points or as decorations)

- submerged in the historical body of the participants and in the practices in which they engage

- submerged in the design of the built environment and objects

- speech or writing or images of the analysts in conducting the nexus analysis (either within or apart from the moment of the mediated action)

In the case of the organisational leadership seminars and online forums at KUIS, becoming aware of such a set of discourses entailed examining documents such as the course syllabus and the online communications of the students. The questions in Table 7 facilitated the understanding of the reasons why the documents and communications appeared in their current forms.

Table 7: Guiding questions in nexus analysis (Scollon & Scollon, 2004, pp. 173–175)

	Types of interrogation of the data	Guiding questions
1	Critical Discourse Analysis	How are social power interests produced in this discourse?
2	Interactional sociolinguistics	What positions and alignments are participants taking up in relationship to each other, to the discourses in which they are involved, the places in which these discourses occur, and to the mediational means they are using, and the mediated actions which they are taking?
3	Linguistic anthropology	How are sociocultural or historical thought or cultural patterns in the language and its genres and registers providing a template for the mediated actions of participants in the nexus of practice?

The questions in Table 7 led us to address the following issues in regard to the development of the organisational leadership seminars and online forums at KUIS:

- Who creates and controls programme development?

- Why did the students participate in online forums?

- How was communication affected by various cultures?[7]

These questions are addressed in the following section of this chapter.

---

[7] 'Cultures' refers to that of urban Japanese youth, KUIS students, etc.

7 Analysis of online forums on leadership

In Table 2, we noted that the instructor was required, as a core IBC instructor, to create seminars but without needing to have the seminars focus on organisational leadership or to create online forums on leadership within those seminars. At KUIS, the seminar is usually the name of the instructor followed by seminar. For example, in project-related applications submitted to the Student Affairs Office, the students referred to the course as 'Kevin Seminar' although the family name would be used in the case of Japanese professors where family name is listed first. The seminars are selected by the students, and the core instructors each give a five-minute presentation to inform and attract students to a seminar. The organisational leadership seminar was the only seminar offered exclusively in English medium.

The course syllabus is set out in Table 8. Although parts of the syllabus are written to attract students, other parts of the syllabus are written for other purposes, including self-promotion of the instructor, a necessary entailment in an academic environment where the instructor is evaluated for promotion by his supervisor and peers (See Crichton, 2010). Research and portfolios were important discussion topics of faculty members. The reference to an 'American-style seminar' was intended to indicate that the students and the instructor would not meet outside of the class as might be more common in the case of Japanese colleagues.

Table 8: Organisational leadership seminar syllabus

IBC Seminar: *Organisational Leadership*

Overview: Leaders in companies are often considered to be successful members of society. This seminar will focus on understanding leadership in an organisation (e.g., a company):

1) What is leadership?

2) How do leaders practice leadership?

3) How do leaders communicate?

4) What are leadership skills?

5) How can leadership (skills) be developed?

6) What can we learn from leaders?

7) How can research on leadership be conducted?

This American-style seminar will be conducted in English only. All reading, discussion, and reports will be done in English. The seminar may focus on the material from various articles or from a book such as the following:

Nohria, N. & Khurana, R. (Eds.) (2010). *Handbook of leadership theory and practice: A Harvard Business School centennial colloquium.* Boston, MA: Harvard Business Press.

Liu, L. (2010). *Conversations on leadership: Wisdom from global management gurus*. San Francisco, CA: Jossey-Bass.

Fairhurst, G. (2011). *The power of framing: Creating the language of leadership*. San Francisco, CA: Jossey-Bass.

Research: The research in the seminar should be related to leadership (i.e., leadership in practice, leadership communication, leadership development, leadership identity, leadership and gender, etc.). For example:

- Interviews with leaders (original research, etc.) to understand leadership in different organisations/industries

- Examining the spoken and written communications of leaders (speeches, interviews annual reports, websites, etc.)

- Examining the communication in leadership teams

- Examining leadership development programmes/approaches (and/or their effectiveness)

- Investigating the difference between male and female leadership styles

- Investigating the difference between leadership in different types of organisations

Leadership portfolio: In order to learn more about leadership, the participants will engage in leadership activities and be the subjects of leadership research. The results of these efforts will be collected in a leadership portfolio.

Instructor: Kevin Knight (PhD Candidate, MBA, MPIA) is currently conducting doctoral research on leadership communication. He has completed interviews with numerous leaders (including CEOs, partners, managers, etc.) in primarily the United States and obtained examples of leadership in practice. His career includes work experience with private, public, and academic sector institutions including Sony and the Japan Patent Office.

Contact: knight@kanda.kuis.ac.jp

The first online forum was launched at the same time as the first organisational leadership seminar. There were forums for different groups of students and for different purposes. All five of the forums are displayed in Table 9. The online forums were created by the instructor and were available in the public domain. The forums were threaded discussions. The instructor was responsible for introducing the discussion topics and for providing timelines to students for posting comments (See Table 10). The students received an email when a topic or comments were posted and could also respond with an email or access the online forum directly. The instructor chose to conduct the forums in this way drawing on his own experience in participating in online forums in leadership roles. Moreover, it was important to make students aware that their posts would most likely be viewed by the public in leadership roles, so they should take care in choosing what they posted.

Table 9: Online forums on leadership

Order of creation	Name of forum	Participants	Primary purpose(s)	Instructor involvement
1	KUIS Leadership Discussion	Group 1 (sophomore year)	To discuss the beliefs of 15 leaders and to post related research data To discuss the narratives of leaders	Primarily posting instructions
2	KUIS Leadership Discussion 2	Group 1 (junior year)	To discuss leadership scenarios	Primarily posting scenarios
3	KUIS Leadership Discussion 3	Group 2 (sophomore year)	To discuss the beliefs of 15 leaders and to post related research data To discuss the narratives of leaders	Primarily posting instructions
4	KUIS Leadership Discussion (November 2013)	Group 1 (junior year)	To discuss leadership in English with invited Japanese leaders	Chair of discussion and active participant
5	Mystery Leader	Group 2 (sophomore year)	To discuss leadership in English with a native English-speaking leader whose identity was not revealed	Primarily posting instructions

Table 10: Sample postings in first KUIS Leadership Discussion

Posted by	Purpose	Content
Instructor	Timeline posted as topic	Question 4 (Please respond by May 9 at 6:00 pm)
Instructor	Instructions for posting after clicking on topic	4. Choose one statement or the other but not both. There is no right or wrong answer. Please explain the reasons for your choice. 1a A leader's primary role is producing superior *performance* or results. 1b A leader's primary role is making *meaning*.
First student to respond	Response to question	I support the statement of 1b. The reason why I decided to choose 1b is that the leaders have to control their own team and to let the members work efficiently as a group or company in order to get high sales or produce great performance. In my opinion, it is the leader's biggest duty. And I think even if the leader was great, he/she couldn't produce superior performance or results by they alone. So, their role is making meaning, inspiring their members to work well or encouraging them in order to get great results and produce superior achievement.
Second student to respond	Response to question	Hello. I support a statement of 1b, too. The reasons why I think that the leader need give first priority to team's goals and carry out one's beliefs bravely rather than individual profits. But, in actuality, there are many leaders who forget roles of the leader and pursue only one's own interests. According to maxim of the chairman of ITOCHU, 'Consider surrounding people's happiness first rather than your profits. It is the leader's conditions.' I sympathised with this maxim. I think that the leader who pursues mental nourishments rather than financial profits will probably be liked and relied on by everyone.

Table 10 contains sample postings from the first KUIS Leadership Discussion. KUIS Leadership Discussions 1 and 3 resembled research focus groups because the students were asked to respond to a particular question and could read any previous responses before responding themselves.

The questions in Table 3 were addressed in three ways:

1. Each student was asked to post a response to the same question.

2. In class, the students read the responses of 15 leaders to the question, and outside of class each student posted comments indicating which leader's response the student agreed with most and why.

3. Each student asked the question to a Japanese leader and posted the response.

After the questions in Table 3 had been addressed, students read the final narratives of some of the 15 leaders and posted online what they felt they had learned about leadership from those narratives.

However, in KUIS Leadership Discussion 2 (See Table 9), the focus of the discussions changed. The instructor created leadership scenarios from the interview data and asked students to post responses online (See Table 11).

Table 11: KUIS Leadership Discussion 2

Posted by	Purpose	Content
Instructor	Timeline posted as topic	Topic 3. SNS recruiting system - What would you say and do? (Post by May 8).
Instructor	Instructions for posting after clicking on topic	Topic 3. SNS recruiting system – What would you say and do? (Post by May 8). **Background:** You are the manager of an HR department in a big company. You want the employees in the company to use their social networks (SNS) to tell their contacts (friends) about job openings in the company. Some managers in the company are worried. The managers think that members of their teams will want to apply for the new jobs. **Activity:** How do you persuade the stakeholders (managers, employees) to support your idea for employees to use SNS to tell their contacts about job openings? Post your response. Comment on the responses of others.

The responses of the students to the scenarios made it possible to obtain individual students' conceptualisations of leadership (i.e., as action) and to compare it with the action in the STAR/CAR story of the original narrative or excerpt in the interview data. In addition, the Group 1 students were asked to create their own leadership scenarios. (See Table 12 which was adapted from Knight, 2014b, p. 213.)

Table 12: Sample leadership development scenario (Group 1)

Leadership action	Scenario
Motivate others to work harder	You work at Japanese bar and you're a part-time leader. You receive a great deal of trust from other staff and also your boss. You have to act as a buffer between all part-timers and formal workers including shop master. Your big role is to communicate with all staff and to keep their motivation at high level. But we caused a rift in the friendship between our boss and the other staff because our boss has made a small trouble. After that trouble, part-timers got down their own motivation and they goofed off their working. So, your task is to improve all staff's motivation. If you faced this kind of problem, what should you do?

Discussions of these scenarios were conducted in class with the author of the scenario responsible for supplying information to the other students. These scenarios were based on authentic situations so the discussions in class revealed what the students did not reveal in the online forum; for example, 'small trouble' in Table 12 was revealed in class to mean an affair between a married boss and part-time staff. It was interesting to compare what students said they would have done, to what was actually done in that situation. In this case, the scenarios functioned as business case studies with the students placed in the roles of leaders.

The KUIS Leadership Discussion (November 2013) was conducted at a very busy time for Group 1 students. The students were asked to invite Japanese leaders to participate in the discussion, but as the discussion was to be held in English, there was some trouble in finding leaders. In addition, the timing of the discussion was in conflict with the big leadership projects of the student teams. In addition, it was the case that the students were to begin job hunting from the ensuing January. The focus of the discussion became that of the leaders responding to the questions of the instructor. The students were encouraged to contribute their own leadership stories, but as the students had invited leaders, it did not seem to be the students' place to position themselves on the same level as those leaders. For all of these reasons, student participation in the discussion was almost non-existent.

In order to provide a discussion that encouraged students to ask questions of a leader, the Mystery Leader (ML) discussion was created. The students in this discussion were Group 2 students, and the discussion was held for a shorter period of time in December 2013. The Mystery Leader was based in Australia and had had a leadership role at the university. The students could only obtain information by asking questions. The ML was not allowed to offer information on his own. The students participated actively in the discussion.

8 Conclusion

How did the nexus of practice approach engage a different kind of process and produce a different kind of outcome from that of the traditional ESP needs analysis? As we indicate earlier, a traditional ESP needs analysis is forward-looking and places an emphasis on 'What must be done to give students the English language communication skills that they need in the immediate future?' In contrast, adopting a nexus of practice approach is reflective and dynamic, focusing on 'Why is a programme being conducted in this way and how could it be refined?'

In particular, adopting a nexus of practice approach caused the instructor to view actions in the organisational leadership seminars and online forums as contingent and interrelated. As a consequence, the instructor began to consider connections between the organisational leadership seminars, the online forums, the students' other classes, the students' activities outside of class, and the students' preparation for job interviews as central to the ongoing curriculum development and delivery process. From a reflective point of view, the combination of courses in Table 2 which featured project-based learning, business case studies, and exposure to leadership beliefs and accounts of leadership became a productive and dynamic approach to teaching leadership.

In any study of the nexus of practice, the complex roles of the instructor and students are highlighted. Although the students were still undergraduates, they were also already professionals in the business world. Further, the instructor was engaged in high-level leadership activities outside of his role as an instructor. Based on these realisations, the instructor looked for ways to enhance the synergy between coursework and activities outside of the classroom for the purpose of leadership development. To achieve such synergy, team projects and project-based learning were introduced.

Finally, the knowledge about leadership the instructor had acquired through the exploration and actions associated within the nexus of practice caused him to teach leadership differently. The instructor came to perceive leadership as creating and achieving a vision. In this way, the focus of the nexus of practice was transformed from trying to understand leadership to one of trying to encourage students to create and achieve visions. It became important not only to enable students to achieve a vision but also to enable them to share the story of that vision in a job-related interview. As one student recently noted in the online forum, the leadership class is very good for job-hunting.

From our point of view, a nexus of practice approach provides for an ongoing review of and reflection on a programme in progress. As such, it increases the instructor's awareness of the need for change. This enhanced awareness results in timely decision making, thereby making the instructor a better programme developer and leader. The ESP approach taken in this study may be applicable to other contexts where constant refinement of an ESP programme is needed.

References

Abrar-ul-Hassan, S. (2012). State-of-the-art review: Revisiting the ins and outs of ESP practice. *Professional and Academic English*, 39, 4–11.

Bargiela-Chiappini, F., Nickerson, C., & Planken B. (2013). *Business discourse.* 2nd ed. New York, New York: Palgrave Macmillan.

Bass, B. M. (1990). *Bass & Stogdill's handbook of leadership: Theory, research, and managerial applications.* 3rd ed. New York: The Free Press.

Candlin, C. (2013). Metaphors & methods in L2 classroom & language advising research. [Presentation]. Chiba, Japan: Kanda University of International Studies.

Carroll, B., & Levy, L. (2010) Leadership development as identity construction. *Management Communication Quarterly*, 24(2), 211–231.

Crichton, J. (2010). *The discourse of commercialisation: A multi-perspectived analysis.* Basingstoke: Palgrave Macmillan.

Finlay, L. (2008). Reflecting on 'Reflective practice'. *Practice-Based Professional Learning Centre. Retrieved December*, 27, 2012.

Friedenberg, J., Kennedy, D., Lomperis, A., Martin, W., & Westerfield, K. With contributions from van Naerssen, M. (2003). *Effective practices in workplace language training: Guidelines for providers of workplace English language training services.* Alexandria, Virginia: TESOL, Inc.

Glynn, M. A., & DeJordy, R. (2010). 'Leadership through an organisation behaviour lens'. In N. Nohria & R. Khurana (Eds.) *Handbook of leadership theory and practice: A Harvard Business School centennial colloquium.* Boston: Harvard Business Press.

Grindsted, A. (2005). Interactive resources used in semi-structured research interviewing. *Journal of Pragmatics*, 37, 1015–1035.

Hutchinson, T., & Waters, A. (1989). *English for specific purposes.* Cambridge, England: Cambridge University Press.

Kertzner, D., Knight, K., & Swartley, E. (2012). *Principled ESP – Best practices and case studies* [Webinar]. Alexandria, Virginia: TESOL International Association.

Knight, K. (2011). *Discourses of leadership as basis for developing leadership communication skills: Obtaining the insights of leaders through semi-structured interviews* [PowerPoint presentation]. Sydney, Australia: Macquarie University HDRO Showcase.

Knight, K. (2012). *Discourses of leadership as basis for developing leadership communication skills: Co-construction of online forum* [PowerPoint presentation]. Sydney, Australia: Macquarie University HDRO Showcase.

Knight, K. (2013). Looking at communication through a leadership lens. *TESOL Blog.* Alexandria, Virginia: TESOL International Association.

Knight, K. (2014a). Preparing undergraduate students in Japan for the global workplace through four EBC courses. *Professional and Academic English*, 42, 8–14.

Knight, K. (2014b). Creation of online forum for leadership development of KUIS students. *The Journal of Kanda University of International Studies*, 26, 241–269.

Knight, K. (2014c). Multiple perspectives on ESP needs analysis and research. *TESOL Blog*. Alexandria, Virginia: TESOL International Association.

Nohria, N., & Khurana, R. (2010). Advancing leadership theory and practice. In N. Nohria & R. Khurana (Eds.), *Handbook of leadership theory and practice: A Harvard business school centennial colloquium* (pp. 3–25). Boston: Harvard Business Press.

Riessman, C. (2002). 'Analysis of personal narratives'. In J. F. Gubrium & J. A. Holstein (Eds.), *Handbook of interview research* (pp. 695–710). Thousand Oaks, CA: Sage Publications.

Scollon, R. (2001). *Mediated discourse: The nexus of practice*. London & New York: Routledge.

Scollon, R., & Scollon, S. (2004). Appendix: A practical field guide for mediated discourse analysis. In *Nexus analysis: Discourse and the emerging internet*. New York: Routledge.

Schön, D. (1983). *The reflective practitioner: How professionals think in action*. New York: Basic Books.

Senge, P. (1990a, 2006) *The fifth discipline: The art and practice of the learning organization*. New York, NY: Doubleday/Currency.

Senge, P. (1990b). The leader's new work: Building learning organizations. *Sloan Management Review*, 32(1), 7–23.

Talmy, S. (2011). The interview as collaborative achievement: Interaction, identity and ideology in a speech event. *Applied Linguistics, 32*(1), 25–42.

University of California, Davis. (2013). *Career resource manual 2013*. Davis, CA: UC Davis Internship and Career Center.

University of California, San Diego. (2013). *Career guide 2013–14*. San Diego, CA: UC San Diego Career Center.

Discipline-specific language enhancement: Technical communication for Mechanical Engineering students

Alice Lawrence, University of Sheffield, UK

Email: a.lawrence@sheffield.ac.uk

1 Introduction

Since the mid-1990s, student mobility has increased as a result of globalisation and the growth of higher education worldwide (OECD, 2011, p. 30). The most recent data from the Organisation for Economic Cooperation and Development (OECD, 2011) shows that from 2007 to 2011, the mobile student population rose from just over 3.6 million students to over 4.8 million, roughly representing a 33% increase. In particular, English-speaking countries – mainly Australia, New Zealand, Canada, the United Kingdom and the United States – have seen increases in non-domestic students registered on their higher education (HE) courses. Countries where English is not the main language – for example, Japan, Spain and the Netherlands – also experienced a similar trend (OECD, 2011, p. 30). Furthermore, because English is increasingly viewed as an international language, HE institutions (HEIs) in non-English-speaking countries are also opting to provide HE courses in English (e.g., University of Nijmegen in the Netherlands and the Politecnico di Milano in Italy). The growth in the number of international students in English-medium programmes has increased the demand for English for Academic Purposes (EAP) support.

In the United Kingdom, it is not only international students who require language development: a report into UK native English student academic writing highlighted weaknesses in sentence structure, grammar, punctuation and spelling (Ganobcsik-Williams, 2004, p. 16). There is also a perception – somewhat sensationalised by the media – that standards in academic literacy are falling, although there is little solid evidence to confirm or refute this, as it is a relatively new area of research (Lillis & Scott, 2007). As writing is the most common means of HE assessment and is a permanent record, any weaknesses are very obvious – whether they be at the level of surface grammar, or of demonstrating one's ability to select appropriate reading material, synthesise ideas and comment critically – and can affect student progression. Finally, not only have changing sociopolitical conditions in the United Kingdom increased the number of HE students, who now come from a wider range of backgrounds, but also, new HE assessment genres have been introduced in response to industry requirements.

Recognising the range of student language needs, many UK HEIs provide language and study skills support for both non-native speakers (NNS) and native speakers (NS) of English. However, because the organisational and funding structure of HEIs differs, language and study support service providers may sit within different parts of an institution.

For example, some services may be provided by academic departments such as Education or English Language and Linguistics, while others may be provided by the Student Services Department.

Many NNS students are offered a place on an HE degree programme on the condition that they achieve a particular level on the International English Language Testing Service (IELTS) examination. While some NNS students prepare for, and take, the IELTS examination in their home countries, others choose to develop their language skills in the UK, registering on a 'pre-sessional' programme (PS) – that is, a programme that takes place prior to their academic subject programme. PS courses are not considered to be 'support' as they are full time and students must pay for them. The courses normally combine study skills (e.g., seminar practice, giving presentations, reading skills, paraphrasing, summarising, synthesising information, referencing, structuring an essay and so on) with grammar, vocabulary and IELTS exam practice. PS courses also familiarise students with UK academic culture.

Once NNS students have met their conditional language requirement and have started their degree, 'in-sessional' (IS) language courses are often provided. These courses are considered to be 'support' as they are offered alongside the students' academic degree programmes, and their main aim is to help students experiencing difficulty with language on their academic courses. IS support courses, therefore, are usually optional, part time and free of charge (although sometimes a nominal fee for materials is charged).

There are several reasons such language support is deemed necessary despite students having met the English-language condition required by an HEI, in particular for NNS students. The main reason is that the IELTS band (or equivalent) required by HEIs can range from 6.0 to 7.5, depending on the level of study (e.g., undergraduate, postgraduate, research) and discipline. IELTS (2011, p. 8) information for institutions states that students with a band of 6.5 or below on 'linguistically demanding academic courses … will need further English study'. Although IELTS states that a band of 7.0 is 'probably acceptable' (IELTS, 2011, p. 8) for such courses, the cautious tone suggests that even students with a band 7.0 may benefit from further English study. Further, although there is an Academic English IELTS exam, it does not include some of the linguistically challenging skills that students need on their UK degree courses – that is, summarising, paraphrasing and synthesising source materials. IS support is therefore provided to 'fill in the gaps' between what students have already achieved and what they need to be able to do with language on their academic courses.

IS language support courses may include grammar, general language skills (e.g., Speaking, Listening, Reading and Writing), EAP and English for Specific Academic Purposes (ESAP). Such English-language support is aimed mainly at NNS; however, NS students from a wide range of educational backgrounds, including those who are starting HE courses as mature students, may also have gaps in their language and study skills. For example, some UK science and engineering students may have had little prior experience of summarising, paraphrasing and synthesising source materials. Many HEIs therefore provide IS support aimed at all students – NNS and NS – such as information literacy, exam revision techniques and individual writing support tutorials.

This chapter considers an alternative to IS ESAP support: first, it discusses relevant literature, outlining approaches to curriculum design, ESAP, collaboration and issues relating to evaluation, assessment and feedback. Against this backdrop, it then describes the local context of the study reported here, outlining flaws in existing IS language support services and suggesting an alternative model of language development, the pilot module 'Technical Communication for Mechanical Engineering' (TC). This is followed by a description and evaluation of the writing component of the pilot TC. Finally, the chapter considers the implications for HEIs globally which choose to deliver courses through the medium of English.

2 Literature review

2.1 Curriculum design

Various approaches to curriculum design have evolved over time, with new features being added to those already existing. For example, two key features of Tyler's (1949) 'product' approach, which has influenced curriculum design greatly (Howard, 2007), are that students should acquire a specific body of knowledge, and that goals and outcomes of learning are specified. The 'process' approach (Stenhouse, 1975, cited in Howard, 2007) specified the inclusion of how learning and teaching would take place, and this included collaboration between learners and teachers to evaluate learning as a feature. The post-modern 'praxis' model of curriculum (Grundy, 1987) features 'emancipation' (Freire, 2006): by working with teachers and identifying their own needs and goals, students can overcome their own problems, such as barriers to learning. A more recent development is the 'inclusive curriculum' approach. Morgan and Houghton (2011, p. 5) state that:

> An inclusive curriculum design approach is one that takes into account students' educational, cultural and social background and experience as well as the presence of any physical or sensory impairment and their mental well-being.

Such an approach requires a 'proactive anticipatory approach to … learning and teaching' and should be founded 'on principles of equity, collaboration, flexibility and accountability.' (Morgan & Houghton, 2011, p. 5). They suggest that despite their good intentions, institutions who identify 'disadvantaged' individuals, or groups, as having a 'need' or 'deficit' and then provide a service to integrate them into the mainstream, thereby 'remedying' the situation, are discriminatory and can stigmatise the very students they are trying to help. Partly in recognition of this, and partly due to legal changes in the United Kingdom (Equality Act 2010), the discourse around terms such as 'need' and 'disadvantage' has changed, resulting in a more proactive approach to the learning and teaching of a diverse and changing student population. Developing and implementing inclusive HE curricula requires institutions to change their systems; this differs from the previous approach which focussed on change happening within the individual student. Indeed, Morgan and Houghton emphasise that responsibility for change lies with, and within, individual members of HEI staff (Morgan & Houghton, 2011) and what is afforded to one student should be afforded to all.

In light of this, and the principles cited above (Morgan & Houghton, 2011, p. 5), it can be argued that 'deficit models' are discriminatory and therefore inherently inequitable; to ensure equal opportunities for all students, inclusive models should be promoted. Cronin, Foster and Lister (1999) took an inclusive approach to address gender bias; they designed an HE curriculum for all students: it included collaborative learning and teaching methods, and communication skills. Student feedback showed that inequities between students decreased and student confidence increased. However, its success depended on the extent of departmental commitment and engagement to the inclusive curriculum; some departments did not engage, with the result that the changes were less effective. Cronin et al., (1999) conclude that to effect proper curriculum change, a change in institutional culture is necessary and should involve close collaboration between staff with diverse expertise, and also students (Cronin et al., 1999, p. 179; also see Morgan & Houghton 2011).

2.2 ESAP

A branch of English-language teaching, ESAP is considered an effective way of helping students learn the specific language and academic practices of the discourse community to which they belong (Dudley-Evans & St John, 1998; Hutchinson & Waters, 1987). Communication skills are valued by industry and employers; therefore, to ensure the needs of society are met, educational institutions confer with industry and employers when developing courses (Barnett, 2001). The professional body ensuring the quality of engineering education in the United Kingdom, the Accreditation Board for Engineering and Technology (ABET), specifies two engineering education outcomes directly related to communication: ability to communicate effectively and ability to work in multi-disciplinary teams (ABET, 2000). Communication skills are therefore embedded in the engineering curriculum. Indeed, in the early 2000s, embedding communication and other transferable skills in the curriculum was promoted by HE academic units of Learning & Teaching: Burke (2002) provides a range of examples and Ganobcsik-Williams (2004) also emphasises the importance of institutional culture change to achieve this. Sloan and Porter (2010, p. 204) and Baik and Greig (2009, p. 405) reiterate the necessity of communication and negotiation between staff, especially with reference to language-support modules. However, given the significant number of international students on UK PGT Engineering programmes, it may also be necessary to include a greater language component within the programmes. The TC module described further below explicitly develops the communication skills specified by industry while also focusing on the use of appropriate technical language as identified by a needs analysis.

2.3 Collaboration

Evidence shows that in order for ESAP courses to be effective, communication between subject lecturers and ESAP tutors should include negotiation about the content and its sequencing (e.g., Sloan & Porter, 2010; Baik & Greig, 2009). Students also negotiate their learning needs with the ESAP tutor, therefore influencing what is taught, and how and when it is taught. However, while learners and ESAP tutors often collaborate closely, communication between learners and subject lecturers, and/or ESAP tutors and subject lecturers, is not always as close as necessary; this can result in a less effective curriculum. Indeed, subject lecturers sometimes make assumptions about the knowledge and study skills international students have acquired in their previous education cultures. This can lead to a mismatch between the expectations of students and subject lecturers about, for example, the types of assessment that engineering students must produce.

2.4 Evaluation, assessment and feedback

The purpose of evaluating an education programme is to ascertain the effectiveness and efficiency of teaching, with a view to improving it (Robinson, 1991; Dudley-Evans & St. John, 1998). Measuring the progress of students on ESAP support courses is challenging because such courses tend to vary in length, and do not bear credit or include direct assessment. Also, when such classes are taught alongside subject content, other factors, such as student exposure to the language and discourse practices of their discipline, cannot be separated from the content and impact of support courses. Research into tailored language classes for students of Business and Management in two UK HE institutions (Sloan & Porter, 2010; Alexander, Argent & Spencer, 2008) has shown measurable changes in student module assignment marks; however, although the support classes contributed to the improvement in marks, it was not possible to specify the extent of this. The same conclusion was reached in a support course for Architecture students (Baik & Greig, 2009, pp. 413–414).

Further, an inherent difficulty in directly assessing language development is that the typical content (outlined further below) is inextricably linked to critical reading and writing, which are themselves reflected as better quality work, and marked as such by subject lecturers. Language is the vehicle which carries the message. The message in the context of HE assessment includes displaying knowledge, and demonstrating the ability to use evidence to support an argument. Therefore, what a student has learned in an IS language support course is demonstrated, and to some extent assessed, through the specific subject by the subject teacher.

Assessment can have a formative or summative purpose; these two purposes are complementary, and to some extent, interdependent (Purpura, 2004). Whichever type of assessment is used, it will be most effective if it is designed for a specific purpose (Bligh, 1990, p. 127). As will be explained later, the designs of two Engineering assignments were appropriate for TC assessment as they involved the production of sections of a laboratory report. Although the assignments were summative, TC assessment fulfilled a formative role, in that detailed feedback was given to students, and could be applied to their eventual third, and final, summative assessment – a full laboratory report.

Feedback in the ESAP context differs from that in a general English language classroom. In the general English context, teachers are trained to respond firstly to the ideas expressed in student writing and secondly to language use (Alexander et al., 2008, p. 209). However, this principle cannot be extended to ESAP as teachers are not usually subject-specific experts and student ideas about discipline-related content fall outside their remit. Even if they are discipline experts (e.g., Education, Applied Linguistics), their role as language teachers precludes them from giving feedback on academic content, as this could be seen as collusion and/or giving the student an unfair advantage. It could be expected that ESAP teacher feedback should focus on language use and information organisation. Teachers therefore need to be competent discourse analysts to enable them to identify the target discourse and comment usefully on IS ESAP student writing.

Considering the issues raised above, a study was conducted to determine whether attending the pilot TC module would make a significant difference to the writing of all the students. In order to evaluate the effectiveness of the Semester 1 writing component of the TC module, the following research questions were posed:

1. Did the writing marks of students who took the inclusive TC module improve at the end of Semester 1?

2. Did students who took language support courses in addition to TC achieve higher marks than those who only took the TC module?

3. Did the writing marks of students who *did not* take the inclusive TC module improve at the end of Semester 1?

4. Did students perceive the TC module to be useful?

3 Local context

The University of Sheffield (TUOS), UK, where this study took place, offers both full-time PS English courses and part-time IS language support, provided through the English Language Teaching Centre (ELTC), which is a section of the institution's Student Services Department (SSD). PS courses include General English and EAP courses. Once PS students achieve the required level of English for their degree programme and progress to TUOS, they are offered IS language support. All language support is free to students and funded by SSD, ELTC and academic departments. There are four in-sessional English language support services at TUOS, mainly but not exclusively, aimed at NNS: English Language Support (ELS); Departmental Language Support (DLS); Writing Advisory Service (WAS); and Online Language Support (OLS). Due to space limitations ELS, WAS and OLS are described very briefly below. DLS is described in more detail because it is an ESAP programme.

Briefly, ELS provides nine general English and EAP skills courses, the latter broadly aimed either at students on Science and Technology courses, or at those on Arts, Humanities and Social Sciences courses. Courses last 10 weeks and the weekly lessons are 90 minutes long: each course therefore provides 15 hours of class time over a semester. There is no formal assessment but there is a 'progress check' exercise at the end of each ELS course which is based on the syllabus and takes the form of simple 'can do' statements.

WAS is an individual writing advisory service, providing bookable 60-minute tutorials to which students bring a draft of their writing. There is no restriction to the number of tutorials an individual student can book, but they can only make one booking at a time. An online record is kept of writing advice and suggested resources; students have access to this so they can monitor their own progress and refer back to the advice given during the tutorial.

Available to all TUOS students, OLS provides online language support exercises, including Aspects of Academic Writing (e.g., describing a process, describing data) and Advanced Aspects of Academic Writing (e.g., synthesising information, writing a literature review). The exercises give immediate feedback to the student. IS support tutors refer both NS and NNS students to particular OLS exercises for homework or self study.

'DLS' is the TUOS term for 'ESAP' and has been provided since the early 1990s but underwent a major reform in 2006. DLS is provided in a variety of 'mix and match' formats (courses, workshops, individual tutorials) to academic departments who request it for their students. In 2013–14, over 35 departments received DLS. Each department is offered 50 hours of language support per year free of charge, to be shared among different groups of students. Additional hours of support can be provided at a charge to the department.

DLS is embedded into the requesting department's own timetable to ensure that students can attend and that the support is provided at the right time during the semester to be of use to students. Some departments request regular weekly support while others only request several short workshops (e.g., 'Scientific Writing' for 3rd Year Physics undergraduates). DLS is usually optional and mainly aimed at NNS student, some of whom may be singled out for support; it is, however, increasingly being extended to NS. Depending on these factors, class size can therefore range from 2 to 25 students. Approximately 70% of DLS is requested for taught postgraduate students, 20% for research students, and 10% for undergraduate students.

Each department nominates a subject lecturer to liaise with the English language teacher. DLS is embedded to a greater or lesser degree into the academic syllabus depending on the level of collaboration with the subject lecturer. It is recommended that it run alongside a subject specific module so language can be better contextualised. Initially working with the subject lecturer, the DLS teacher gathers information related to departmental needs (e.g., assignment genres that may be unfamiliar to students; assignment deadlines; comments/perceptions of subject specialists regarding student language needs; and anonymised samples of past student writing provided by the department). DLS teachers also often audit subject lectures and are given access to the subject resources in the TUOS virtual learning environment (VLE), including assignments and assessment criteria, in order to familiarise themselves with what students encounter. When the language teacher meets the students, he or she also undertakes a needs analysis with them; then, using all the information, a syllabus and course outline are created and shared with the subject lecturer and students, who are encouraged to comment and suggest changes if they wish. After the first DLS syllabus is created for a particular DLS cohort, it can often be amended for use with future similar cohorts in the same department.

Depending on the discipline and level (e.g., undergraduate, postgraduate, research), typical DLS content includes: pronunciation of subject specific vocabulary; seminar discussion skills; giving spoken and written peer feedback; nominalisation in writing; paraphrasing and summarising; constructing a logical, persuasive written argument; expressing author voice in writing; analysing assignment questions and briefs; analysing and answering exam questions; writing various reports (e.g., laboratory, design or environmental impact assessment reports); academic register; and grammar. As well as adapting materials provided in published ESAP resources, DLS teachers also create their own materials from subject-specific resources provided by subject lecturers.

As mentioned above, although it is difficult to attribute language progress directly to IS support, informal, formative assessment is undertaken, and feedback given by DLS teachers. Depending on the 'format' of DLS (e.g., tutorials, regular classes, etc) teachers may collect samples (spoken and written) of student language from the classroom; they may also undertake regular test–teach–test activities, to help students recognise their own progress; they may encourage student self-assessment of language performance to develop autonomy and self-monitoring of language.

Tailoring DLS by embedding it within a student's timetable; holding it within a department's own space; designing a syllabus to coincide/dovetail with the demands of a subject-specific module and the needs of a homogenous group of students; and contextualising language, results in DLS being more immediately relevant than ELS to students. Moreover, it is more inclusive as it is increasingly being requested for mixed NS and NNS groups.

Attendance at both DLS and ELS courses is high at the beginning of the academic year, and declines progressively as assignment deadlines approach; this is offset by an increase in demand for WAS appointments at peak assignment deadline periods.

Despite all these support provisions, there are three interrelated concerns with IS language support at TUOS. First, although TUOS (2007, p. 3) defines an inclusive curriculum as one that 'enables all [their] students from whatever background to achieve their full potential', IS support falls squarely within the Morgan and Houghton's description (2011, p. 5) of well-intentioned but discriminatory practices – that is, in this case, providing support for students who have performed poorly, on the basis of English language, on assessed work or during presentations and seminars and have been referred to support services; or who lack confidence in their own competencies, further exacerbated by being told 'IELTS 6.5 is not good enough'. The Morgan and Houghton perspective discussed earlier would place the current discourse used by TUOS and ELTC within a deficit and discriminatory model of learning. Also, some TUOS colleagues have voiced concern that IS support may appear discriminatory because it mainly 'targets' international students. To avoid this, some departments request that support be extended to all students so as not appear discriminatory. To be fair to TUOS, resources, while extensive, are not unlimited, so the current approach of IS support is related to funding, and therefore 'targets' home and international students who may need help, while recognising that their needs coincide in some areas, but differ in others.

The second concern is that, similar to most UK HEIs, TUOS language support is optional. Accordingly, it consists of relatively few contact hours, is not formally assessed and is not credit-bearing. The lack of formal recognition of their achievements may result in students not investing time or effort in enhancing their language and communication skills, or withdrawing from IS courses as pressure from their subject degree increases.

Third, at TUOS, anecdotal evidence suggests that uptake and regular attendance of language support by students with the weakest language skills is low, possibly because they are caught in a vicious cycle caused by not understanding course content or seminars as a result of their weaker language skills. It has also been suggested that they may be too embarrassed by their language skills to attend.

To address the concerns outlined above, the pilot TC module for a cohort of postgraduate Mechanical Engineering NS and NNS students was introduced as an alternative to DLS. Different from DLS in that TC was not a language support course; its goal was to enhance all students' language skills; it was formally assessed, credit-bearing and compulsory. It was inclusive in that it did not target students on the basis of culture, language or specific needs, representing a shift away from a deficit approach to language support. Although the pilot module included speaking skills, only the writing component is described below.

4 Course description

4.1 Aims and learning outcomes

Drawing on aspects of curriculum design outlined earlier, and thus more deeply embedded in the Mechanical Engineering curriculum, the 5-credit pilot TC module ran over two semesters (40-hours). Its overall aim was to equip NS and NNS students with professional communication skills for the workplace, specifically to:

- develop professional technical writing and speaking skills;

- enable students to communicate engineering concepts accurately and appropriately; and

- increase student knowledge of the discourse and genre conventions of laboratory reports and technical presentations.

The TC module is closely related to a core Mechanical Engineering module, Advanced Experiments and Modelling (AEM), which is designed to develop student knowledge and laboratory skills in preparation for more advanced laboratory and modelling work. AEM includes computational fluid dynamics (CFD); design, manufacturing and testing of solid structures; computer modelling and advanced mathematics.

Although the students had met the Department's English language entry requirements, either a General Certificate of Secondary Education in English (Grade A to C) or IELTS 6.5, or equivalent, subject lecturers had reported that many students submitted poorly written assignments, such as laboratory reports and 'final projects' (dissertations). They had identified grammar, sentence structure, register, paraphrasing, and citing and referencing previous research, as areas of weakness in writing for both NS and NNS students, although the NNS students had more difficulties in these areas. Accordingly, learning outcomes for writing were specified as:

- the ability to write a full, professional Laboratory Report, including an appropriately structured Abstract, Literature Survey, Data Description, Discussion and Conclusion in accurate technical English;

- an understanding of the following discourse and genre conventions of Laboratory Reports: obligatory and optional elements, text organisation, technical vocabulary, appropriate syntax;

- the ability to describe technical data accurately and clearly in writing;

- the ability to explain Engineering concepts clearly and appropriately in writing;

- an awareness of coherence and argumentation in writing; and

- an awareness of differences in spoken and technical written English.

4.2 Ethics

Because this was a pilot module, and there were limited resources, it was decided to extend the module to approximately half of the AEM cohort (described in detail later). This raised two key issues related to fairness: firstly, and somewhat ironically, the pilot module, designed to promote a model of inclusivity, was not extended equitably. Students not registered on the pilot module would not receive the same language input; however, they were encouraged to attend the DLS and other IS support outlined above. The TC students had two hours additional contact time, in an already busy timetable; however, as DLS and other support were optional, few opted to attend. Four AEM students who were not registered on the TC module asked, and were given, permission to participate in the TC sessions but not be assessed. When they became busy with coursework deadlines, they stopped attending. Secondly, the 5 credits that the pilot TC module afforded took students above the required level of credits required for their degree; therefore, those not enrolled on the module, still gained the necessary number of credits from their other MSc modules.

Despite these dilemmas, the pilot module was approved by TUOS Learning & Teaching Services and the study on the pilot module was approved by the Mechanical Engineering Ethics Review administration, on the basis that it was unlikely to cause harm to students.

4.3 Needs analysis

Technical writing content was selected on the basis of generic features of technical English (such as nominalisation, and describing and explaining engineering specifications); the language and discourse features required to fulfil the AEM assignment briefs (outlined below); and frequent student errors. In order to launch the TC module at the beginning of the academic year, a needs analysis was undertaken by ELTC staff on a previous cohort's assessed written laboratory reports and revealed numerous errors.

NNS errors tended to be subject–verb agreement; article use; distinction between countable and uncountable nouns; singular–plural formation; choice of word class; active/passive voice use and form; verb tense use and form; number of verbs used in a sentence; and use of relative pronouns. In addition, sentences tended to be rather long, often between 30 and 50 words. When describing the Experimental Procedure (EP), a detailed explanation of how the experiment was carried out, there was evidence that some NNS had copied and pasted laboratory instructions (e.g., '1. *Make sure you calibrate the spirit level so your measurements are accurate.*'), rather than describing their own actions in the laboratory in an impersonal style (e.g., '*First, the spirit level was calibrated to ensure accurate readings were taken.*'). NNS descriptions of data were sometimes imprecise, due in part to errors in the use of comparatives; also, comments on results tended towards over-confident generalisation or did not express causality effectively.

The writing of both previous NS and NNS contained errors in the structure and punctuation of defining and non-defining relative clauses and lacked nominalisation, and cohesion and coherence at the sentence and paragraph levels. It also included a number of features associated with informal spoken register, such as phrasal verbs (e.g., 'figure out' and 'find out' instead of 'calculate' and 'find') and inconcise vocabulary (e.g., 'a lot of', 'get'). Early diagnostic activities in the classroom confirmed that the same areas required attention.

4.4 Learning and teaching method and content

The pilot TC curriculum was mainly delivered through a 'weak' form of task-based learning, in that students usually had to work together to achieve a task involving a focus on meaning and providing a reason for student–student collaboration (Ellis, 2003). For example, one written task was a dictagloss activity on the topic of different types of eddy current sensor; students reconstructed the text together, using knowledge of both the topic and grammar. Students also wrote a section of a laboratory report (e.g., the literature review) and then peer reviewed each other's work, giving constructive feedback on accuracy of paraphrasing, citing and referencing. To enable them to do this, they had learned how to give constructive feedback in a previous TC session. Information sharing activities on topics such as Computational Fluid Dynamics (CFD) modelling of aerodynamic wingfoils on Formula 1 racing cars proved to be interesting and useful for the students, who were keen to learn more about such topics, with language being of secondary interest. Because there were both NS (or near NS) and NNS in the groups, the participants were able to help each other when selecting the language needed to achieve the task.

Taking a test–teach–test approach, the main language focus tends to follow the first attempt at a task. Because learning outcomes include the ability to write laboratory and design reports, there is a strong genre and discourse analytical flavour to taught sessions; for example, having attempted to write an Experimental Procedure (EP) section in class, students then focussed on the type of information included (e.g., description of the apparatus, description of stages of an experiment etc.); verb tenses and forms used; sentence length; and sequencing words and phrases (e.g., 'following this', 'prior to verb+*ing*') in a sample EP. They then tried to improve their own written work and finally peer-reviewed each others' writing.

4.5 Materials

Materials were related to discipline content; for example, activities to develop and practise reading, summarising and paraphrasing skills were created from authentic texts about CFD, Eddy Currents, Spot Welding and Buckling Behaviour. The texts were also used to create language exercises focussing on aspects of grammar (e.g., nominalisation; use of past passive to describe the Experimental Procedure; article use) and discourse (e.g., how to structure a report; how to express causality effectively; register). Students could access the TC session materials (e.g., PowerPoint slides, language tasks, answers/suggested answers to tasks and exercises, etc) in the VLE. Resources for each session were made available at the end of the session.

4.6 More collaboration

Once the module began, students were also invited to give regular, anonymous feedback and make suggestions for language-related content they felt they needed. This was done at the end of each session for the first four sessions, and less frequently thereafter. This proved a useful way of collecting immediate feedback on the usefulness of lesson activities and language-related content from a large class of students with varying language proficiency levels. Feedback and suggestions led to changes in how some of the activities were structured and the order of language content. It also generated discussion between the TC teacher and the students about their concerns, including their anxieties about AEM assessment. Taking immediate feedback regularly from the beginning of the module therefore led to collaboration between students and the TC teacher, and resulted in a closer tailoring of the pilot module to their needs.

4.7 Assessment

TC content was sequenced according to the order of AEM assessments: AEM and TC teaching staff discussed these during the TC syllabus design stage to ensure that TC assessment would be appropriate. AEM assessment required students to submit two partial laboratory reports of different lengths in Semester 1, and one complete report, and a formal presentation, in Semester 2. The written AEM reports were submitted electronically through the institution's VLE. Subject lecturers assessed the assignments for content, while the TC teacher assessed the same assignments for the language and discourse features outlined above and using criteria outlined below. This method was efficient for students because it did not increase their assessed coursework.

Following discussions, it was decided that the first partial report (350 words) would be the Results section, involving the description and comparison of data to be submitted in mid-November 2013. This was because previous cohorts seemed to have difficulty in describing and comparing data precisely and concisely, and repeated the same errors in many of their other reports. By focussing on the language required for this section early in the year, students would have time throughout their course to improve their ability to describe and compare data, which they were required to do on other Mechanical Engineering modules.

The second partial report (1050 words) on a CFD experiment would build on the first assessment by increasing the number of sections, to include: Background; Numerical Procedure (theoretical and mathematical reasoning); Experimental Procedure (EP); Results (i.e., data description and comparison); and Discussion and Recommendations. The complete report in Semester 2 would also include an Abstract and Literature Review. This approach would scaffold student development of genre knowledge and language skills.

The TC module also addressed other issues related to assessment (e.g., assignment genres; analysing the assignment brief). To enable materials to be tailored to discipline-related topics, the TC teacher was given access to the AEM module resources in the institution's VLE; this included access to all AEM assignments, marking criteria and guidance. If anything in the VLE was unclear, the TC teacher could seek clarification from the relevant member of AEM staff. For example, in order that the TC teacher could understand how students would undertake the CFD experiment, the subject lecturer took the TC teacher to the laboratory, showed her the apparatus, explained step-by-step the experimental procedure and described how students would undertake computer modelling of their results. Without this level of collaboration between the subject lecturer and the TC teacher, the materials, tasks and TC assessment criteria would have been less immediately relevant.

Although attendance was compulsory, it did not count to the overall module mark (see Appendix 1) so non-attendance would not result in failure of the module. The assessed writing component was weighted at 60% of the total TC module mark, and the assessed speaking component was weighted at 40%. As the speaking component was assessed during class time, non-attendance affected the overall module mark. If a student's combined coursework did not achieve an overall score of 45%, they failed the module. However, because the credits actually exceeded the number required for graduation this did not prevent the student from graduating. Credits signal that the academic department place a great deal of importance on TC, and making it compulsory re-iterated this to NS and NNS students. The credits are therefore symbolic rather than practical, but this is an aspect TUOS will need to reconsider if the TC model were implemented formally, and more broadly across the institution.

Each assignment had its own TC assessment criteria based on the discourse and language features covered on the module, Assignment 2 (A2) being longer and more linguistically complex than Assignment 1 (A1). The TC marking scale ranged from 0–10 marks for both assignments. Marking was blind, using specified marking criteria which were informed by the language and discourse content – for example, 'Appropriate sentence length', suggested as 15–25 words and based on what has been observed in their discipline. Detailed criteria are provided in Appendix 1 but these still require further development and refinement. A spreadsheet was created as a record of individual student language use, based on the module content and criteria. This enabled simple frequencies to be tallied, progress to be monitored and comparisons made. The TC teacher was the main marker but random blind second marking was also undertaken by a colleague to ensure consistency.

The TC curriculum therefore draws on several approaches to curriculum design outlined earlier, and aspects of it were informed by a needs analysis, collaboration with a subject lecturer, negotiation with students, and genre and language analysis of Mechanical Engineering texts.

5 Methodology

5.1 Subjects

The AEM cohort consisted of 118 students, 8 of whom were female. Native British students represented about 8% of the group. Non-native English-speaker students came from 20 different countries, Chinese students making up about 60% of the entire cohort. 58 of the AEM cohort were randomly selected for the pilot TC module: these formed the 'taught group' (TG) of this study. Two of the TG were British NS; 42 students were Chinese; 14 students were from other countries: India, Mexico, Saudi Arabia, Pakistan, Italy, Malaysia and Indonesia. The remaining 60 students formed a 'control group' (CG). Early in the first semester, several students withdrew, leaving 56 students in the TG, and 55 students in the CG. For comparison purposes, all CG student assignments were marked using the same TC marking criteria.

5.2 Data collection and analysis

Data was primarily collected as part of the normal process of monitoring module effectiveness and student attainment. However, because it was also to be used for this project, which resulted in a change in the original purpose of its collection, ethical approval was sought, and gained, from the Department of Mechanical Engineering.

Although quantitative and qualitative data were collected, this chapter only reports on the former. Impact was evaluated quantitatively by comparing marks for two assignments submitted in Semester 1. Student marks were collected in the normal course of marking the assessed work as explained above. These were subjected to statistical analysis in the form of unpaired and paired *t* tests, using GraphPad software©, to identify any significant differences between the marks of the taught and control groups.

Perceived impact was also evaluated using descriptive statistics through the normal 'end of semester' student module feedback process, using an online survey (SurveyMonkey©). Most of the 26 questions were multiple choice with a comments box for further information. There was one 'ranking' question and one question asking students to rate, on a Likert Scale of 1 to 5, the extent to which they agreed with statements.

Feedback was collected on attendance; level of sessions; usefulness, relevance and level of materials; usefulness and application of feedback; impact of the module on their understanding and ability to use specific language and discourse features covered in the module; use – and usefulness – of the TC resources in the VLE; transferability of TC content to writing in other Mechanical Engineering modules; use of TUOS language support services; perceptions of their own language improvement; reasons for language improvement; suggestions for Semester 2 content; biographical data about language background, including language of secondary and undergraduate education, English-language qualifications and professional work experience.

6 Findings and Discussion

6.1 Quantitative data

CG and TG student names were cross referenced with ELTC in-sessional support registration and attendance data in Semester 1 to identify which students had received this type of language support. This showed that seventeen CG students had registered for various types of support but only five students had attended four or more DLS, ELS Grammar or ELS Reading and Writing for Science and Technology sessions and none had attended a WAS appointment. Eleven TG students also registered for ELTC in-sessional support, however only 3 TG students attended 4 or more ELS sessions and two of these also attended DLS. None had attended WAS by Week 12 of Semester 1 (i.e., the deadline for Assessment 2).

For TC purposes, both assessments were marked out of 10 (see Appendix 1). The CG and TG mean marks for A1 were 5.0 and 5.65 respectively. For A2, the mean marks for the CG and TG were 5.5 and 6.25 respectively.

Unpaired and paired *t* tests compared marks between the CG and TG. The unpaired *t* test comparing marks for A1 for both CG and TG did not reveal a statistically significant difference between them (two-tailed P value = 0.1514). Students submitted A1 in Week 6 of their module so had not been 'immersed' in their studies for long. For this reason, neither group had had much language input, either from TC or IS support services. Even when students in both groups who had attended IS support had been removed from the analysis, there was no statistically significant difference (two-tailed P value = 0.2536) between the groups. This suggests that both groups were fairly homogenous and started from a similar baseline.

A2 was submitted in Week 12 of the AEM and TC modules (i.e., after 12 x 2-hour TC sessions). The TG achieved higher marks for A2 than did the CG. The unpaired *t* test comparing A2 marks for both groups showed that there was a statistically significant difference between them (two-tailed P value = 0.0373). Even when students who had attended IS support had been removed from analysis, there was still a statistically significant difference (two-tailed P value = 0.0409). It could therefore be cautiously assumed that the difference may be due to the pilot TC module.

The paired *t* test comparing CG marks for both A1 and A2 revealed a statistically significant difference between them (two-tailed P value = 0.0457). As the mean marks are higher for A2, this suggests that CG students performed better in A2. However, after students who had attended IS support were removed from the analysis, the difference disappeared (two-tailed

P value = 0.3097) suggesting that IS support may have made the difference, despite students withdrawing before the end of their course. It is also possible that because these students were motivated enough to register and attend IS support, compared to those who had not registered, despite withdrawing later, they still tried hard to write well.

The paired *t* test comparing TG marks for both A1 and A2 for the TG revealed an *extremely* statistically significant difference between them (two-tailed P value = 0.0008). Even when the marks of TG students who attended IS support were removed from the data, the paired *t* test comparing A1 and A2 showed a very statistically significant difference (two-tailed P value = 0.0093), suggesting that the pilot TC module may have contributed to their improvement.

Although it is not possible to measure the extent to which immersion in Mechanical Engineering study may have influenced their language development, all the students could be reasonably expected to have experienced a similar amount of immersion. In all the above cases, even when students who had taken IS support were excluded from the analysis, the paired *t* tests suggest that the increase in the TG marks may be related to the TC module.

6.2 Online survey feedback

Feedback was collected anonymously from the TG, at the end of Semester 1, using an online survey (SurveyMonkey©). The response rate was 41% (23/56 students). 20 of the respondents had attended regularly, i.e., 6 to 8 sessions, out of a maximum of 12 sessions. While the results cannot be generalised to the entire group, they nevertheless indicate several trends. The section below reports student feedback, beginning with those who did not attend frequently.

6.3 Infrequent attenders (N=3)

The least frequent attenders were those who attended fewer than 5 sessions out of a possible 12 in Semester 1. Two had worked in industry, outside the United Kingdom, before starting their Masters degree and one was a native speaker. They had had their secondary and/or undergraduate engineering education in English and used English at home or with friends. They also had GCSE English (Grade C or above) or IELTS scores of 8.0 or 7.0. These students were either experienced engineers, relatively proficient users of English, or both. Accordingly, the Technical Communication module was not perceived as useful to them so they rarely attended, despite the module being compulsory.

All three reported that TC had made them focus on grammatical accuracy, and two mentioned that it had helped improve their writing on other Mechanical Engineering modules. They all applied A1 feedback when writing A2 and found the TC session materials in the VLE useful. So, despite their reservations about the TC sessions, these students did still seem to draw some benefit from the module. This supports the idea of extending the module to all students; however, further development to make TC more interesting and challenging for the more proficient communicators is required. One possibility could be to make the first hour compulsory and more discourse based (e.g., what to include, and how to organise the Introduction or Literature Review of a report, giving a Presentation), and make the second hour optional and more language based (e.g., grammar, register, vocabulary, pronunciation).

6.4 Regular attenders (N=20)

These students attended between 6 and 8 sessions out of a possible 12. They generally thought the sessions were pitched at the right level (N=16), agreeing that the module helped them improve their technical communication (N=17). Most (N=18) agreed that the module made them focus on grammatical accuracy. In comments, they specified that the module had helped them improve technical writing, academic writing, report writing and speaking, and made them pay attention to their use of English. This is supported by the quantitative data described above, in that, generally, marks for TC increased from A1 to A2, reflecting an improvement.

Students were asked about the contribution of other types of language learning to their improvement. Responses show that a variety of language-learning types had helped them improve, TC being the most common, followed by language self study and immersion in Mechanical Engineering. They ranked TC as the most useful contributor to their improvement, followed by self study. This suggests that TC was perceived as the most effective means to improve their technical communication skills; it also suggests that although immersion was a common contributor, it was not perceived by these respondents to be as useful as self study. Institutional language support services did not rank highly, possibly because few of the students had used them. A few comments in the feedback suggested that because they already had two hours of TC, they did not have time for more face-to-face language study but this needs further investigation.

Students were asked about specific taught features or aspects of the TC module, which were presented in statements on a Likert Scale of 1 to 5 (Strongly Agree to Strongly Disagree) and for which they had to rate how far they agreed with statements (e.g., *'I have a better understanding of how to write the background/introduction section'*; *'I have a better understanding of how to present my data'*). Many of this group agreed they had a better understanding of how to write the background section (N=18); describe experimental procedures (N=15); and present their data (N=14). Nevertheless, responses suggest that more time should be spent on these areas. All regular attenders reported applying A1 feedback to A2, one commenting 'Really useful feedback'. They also accessed TC resources in the VLE and most (N=17) found them useful. These students reported that the TC module had helped them improve their writing for other Mechanical Engineering modules.

Two regular attenders found the sessions boring: both had been educated in English and had GCSE level English. Nevertheless, similar to the infrequent attenders, they applied the feedback from A1 to A2 and one found the module made him focus more on grammar, improve his technical communication, and he stated that he had applied what he had learnt to other Mechanical Engineering modules.

To summarise the above and to answer the research questions stated earlier:

1. Did the writing marks of students who took the inclusive TC module improve at the end of Semester 1? The quantitative data provides good statistical evidence that the pilot inclusive TC module increased student marks at the end of Semester 1.

2. Did students who took language support courses in addition to TC achieve higher marks than those who only took the TC module? There is some evidence suggesting that IS support may have had an impact on the writing marks of the TG group: when the TG data included students who had received IS support, the difference between their A1 and A2 marks was 'extremely statistically significant' ($P = 0.0008$), whereas when they were excluded, the difference was 'very statistically significant' ($P = 0.0093$). (See also Question 3 below).

3. Did the writing marks of students who *did not* take the inclusive TC module improve at the end of Semester 1? The evidence suggests that CG students who did not take TC or IS support did not improve as there was no significant difference between their A1 and A2 marks. When the data of those who took IS support was included, a significant difference was found ($P = 0.3097$).

4. Did students perceive the TC module to be useful? Survey findings show that students who attended regularly perceived the TC module as the most useful contributor to their improvement, reporting that it had helped improve their assignment writing for other Mechanical Engineering modules. Even native and near-native speakers reported that the TC module raised their awareness of their use of English, and that they applied feedback to their later coursework, despite perceiving TC as 'not useful'.

7 Global implications

Given the increase in the number of international students receiving their higher education through the medium of English worldwide, and changes in UK HE student profile, effective non-discriminatory modules, that enhance writing skills while not increasing coursework, would benefit students and staff.

As discussed earlier, research suggests that faculty members wishing to promote an inclusive learning environment, and to enhance the communication skills of all their students, require institutional support. Research has also shown that collaboration with discipline staff is a key contributor to the success of ESAP courses in general (Sloan & Porter, 2010; Baik & Greig, 2009). When a module bears credit and is formally assessed through discipline coursework, such collaboration is essential and also requires institutional support.

A shift from deficit-based ESAP support delivered to a proportion of students, to inclusive writing skills enhancement for *all* students, would therefore require, as Morgan and Houghton (2011) indicate, a shift in institutional strategy, as well as significant resources. To develop and embed inclusive ESAP modules within discipline-specific curricula, a considerable amount of practical strategic planning by both academic departments and language teaching staff would also be necessary, as was seen for the pilot TC module. For example, VLE access should be given to language teachers early enough for them to familiarise themselves with the subject content and seek clarification where necessary. For early access to be useful, content such as assessment briefs and deadlines for the upcoming academic year must be up-to-date; if not, the language teacher could waste valuable time preparing a syllabus and materials that may no longer be relevant. The onus is therefore on the academic department to ensure that subject lecturers have updated the VLE content early on in the summer, which may be difficult as they may be on leave, busy marking exam papers or engaged in their own research commitments. Finally, language teachers may also need further professional development to become competent, and confident, discourse and genre analysts; this would enable them to understand the variety of genres students are expected to read and write to meet their assessment requirements.

8 Conclusion

The findings suggest that the pilot, inclusive, tailored and formally assessed ESAP Technical Communication module was effective in enhancing the writing skills of all students who attended regularly. Embedding the TC module within a postgraduate degree and close collaboration between the language teacher and subject lecturer proved an effective combination for designing a relevant and useful curriculum. There were, however, several limitations to this study, specifically, the different levels of language complexity of the two assignments; relatively unrefined marking criteria; minimal standardisation of markers; and the relatively low survey response rate.

Several areas of the TC curriculum therefore require development. For example, language and discourse features for writing the Experimental Procedure should be made clearer and the module should be made more challenging for native/near native English speakers. Also, criteria used to assess the assignments require further refinement and marker standardisation should be increased. Another potential improvement is to offer students individual (or small group) tutorials to ensure they understand feedback and have an opportunity to ask questions. Although students were invited to talk to the ELTC teacher about their assignment, few took up the offer. A more formal tutorial system could be implemented. It would be also useful to give the students some training in interpreting and applying feedback.

Acknowledgement

The contribution to this pilot Technical Communication module by staff and students in the Department of Mechanical Engineering, University Sheffield, is much appreciated.

References

Accreditation Board for Engineering and Technology (2000) *Key Skills and Knowledge for Engineers*. Retrieved December 23, 2013, from http://wps.pearsoncustom.com/pls_1256647969_pwo/217/55692/14257392.cw/index.html.

Alexander, O., Argent, S., & Spencer, J. (2008). *EAP Essentials: A teacher's guide to principle and practice*. Reading: Garnet Education.

Baik, C., & Greig, J. (2009). Improving the academic outcomes of undergraduate ESL students: the case for discipline-based academic skills programmes. *Higher Education Research & Development*, 28, 4, pp. 401–416.

Barnett, R., Parry, G., & Coate, K. (2001). Conceptualising Curriculum Change. *Teaching in Higher Education*, 6, 4, pp. 435–449. Retrieved December 23, 2013, from http://dx.doi.org/10.1080/13562510120078009.

Bligh, D. (1990). *Higher Education*. London: Cassell.

Burke, P. (2002) *Resource Guide: The Development of Key Skills in Higher Education*. Retrieved on March 30, 2014 from http://www.heacademy.ac.uk/assets/hlst/documents/resource_guides/development_of_ke yskills_in_higher_education.pdf

Coleman, James A. (2006). English-medium teaching in European Higher Education. *Language Teaching*, 39(1), pp. 1–14. Retrieved December 23, 2013, from http://oro.open.ac.uk/5189/1/download.pdf.

Cronin, C., Foster, M., & Lister, E. (1999). SET for the future: Working towards inclusive science, engineering and technology curricula in higher education. *Studies in Higher Education*, 24, 2, pp. 165–182. Retrieved December 23, 2013, from http://dx.doi.org/10.1080/03075079912331379868.

Dudley Evans, T., & St John, M. J. (1998). *Developments in English for Specific Purposes: A multi-disciplinary approach*. Cambridge: Cambridge University Press.

Ellis, R. (2003). *Task-based Language Learning and Teaching*. Oxford & New York: Oxford Applied Linguistics.

Freire, P. (2006). *Pedagogy of the Oppressed*, 30th Anniversary ed. New York: Continuum.

Howard, J. (2007). *Curriculum Development*. Retrieved May 25, 2011 from http://ocw.tudelft.nl/fileadmin/ocw/courses/DevelopmentofTeachingandActiveLearning/ Article_Judith_Howard_on_Curriculum_Design.pdf.

Hutchinson, T., & Waters, A. (1987). *English for specific purposes: A learning-centered approach*. Cambridge: Cambridge University Press.

Ganobcsik-Williams, L. (2004). *A Report on the Teaching of Academic Writing in UK Higher Education*. The Royal Literary Fund. Retrieved February 28, 2014, from http://www.rlf.org.uk/fellowshipscheme/documents/TeachingWritingUKHE.pdf.

Grundy, S. (1987). *Curriculum: product or praxis*. London: Falmer Press.

IELTS Guide for Institutions and Organisations 2011. Retrieved April 5, 2014, from http://www.ielts.org/pdf/Guide%20for%20Institutions%20and%20Organisations%202011.pdf.

Lillis, Theresa and Scott, Mary (2007). Defining academic literacies research: issues of epistemology, ideology and strategy. *Journal of Applied Linguistics*, 4(1) 5–32. Retrieved March 22, 2014, from http://oro.open.ac.uk/17057/1/JAL_Lillis_and_Scott_pdf.pdf.

Morgan, H., & Houghton, A. M. (2011) *Inclusive Curriculum Design in Higher Education: Considerations for effective practise across and within subject areas*. The Higher Education Academy. Retrieved on March 30, 2014, from http://www.heacademy.ac.uk/assets/documents/inclusion/disability/ICD_introduction.pdf#page=1&zoom=auto,0,842.

OECD (2011). *Education at a Glance 2011: Highlights*, OECD Publishing. Retrieved February 02, 2014, from http://www.oecd.org/education/skills-beyond-school/48631550.pdf.

Purpura, J. (2004). *Assessing Grammar*. Cambridge University Press: Cambridge.

Robinson, P. (1991). *ESP Today: A Practitioner's Guide*. New York: Prentice Hall.

Sloan, D., & Porter, E. (2010). Changing international student and business staff perceptions of in-sessional EAP: using the CEM model. *Journal of English for Academic Purposes*, 9, pp. 198–210.

Stenhouse, L. (1975). *An Introduction to Curriculum Research and Development:* London: Heinemann.

The University of Sheffield (2007). *The inclusive learning and teaching handbook*. Sheffield: TUOS. Retrieved on March 30, 2014, from https://www.sheffield.ac.uk/polopoly_fs/1.18989!/file/The-inclusive-learning-and-teaching-handbook.pdf.

Tyler, R.W. (1949) *Basic Principles of curriculum and instruction*. Chicago: University of Chicago Press. Cited in Howard, J. (2007) *Curriculum Development*. Retrieved May 25, 2011.

Appendix

Module ELT6001 Technical Communication for Mechanical Engineers

(5 credits = 100%) 2013–14

Distribution of Marks

Semester 1: 2 x sections of a lab report (Total: 20% – 2 x 10%)

Semester 2: 1 x full-length report (Total: 40%)

Semester 2: 1 x presentation (Total: 20%)

Semester 2: Seminar participation (Total: 10%)

Semester 2: Pronunciation (Total: 10%)

Assignment 1: Presentation of theoretical results (Grade /10)

1. Presentation of results: data is introduced, described and briefly commented on /discussed (e.g., interpretation, comparison, implications).

2. Vocabulary and register: correct word forms are used. Formal academic written style used.

3. Grammar: Every sentence contains at least one main verb. The verb tense is appropriate. Verb formation is accurate. Appropriate choice of active and passive voice. S-V A is generally correct. The definite article is used consistently and appropriately.

4. Appropriate sentence structure: length, punctuation.

5. A range of sentence lengths is used, average length being 15–25 words.

6. A range of punctuation (comma, full-stop, colon and semi-colon) is used to perform several different functions. Sentences should include an appropriate number of clauses (2 or 3).

9–10: Very good/excellent presentation of results. Very accurate use of language and appropriacy in all areas (1–6 above). Formal features of language are used throughout. Good range of sentence lengths. Excellent use of a range of punctuation marks.

6–8: Generally adequate presentation of results. Good use of language, accuracy and appropriacy in most areas (1–6 above). Formal features of language are used and spoken or informal features of language are rarely used. Appropriate sentence length. Correctly used punctuation.

3–5: Weak presentation of results. Reasonable use, accuracy and appropriacy in some areas (1–6 above). Generally, formal technical or academic style is used with some lapses into spoken or informal features of language. Occasional long sentences. Some inconsistent use of punctuation.

0–2: Inadequate presentation of results. Limited use, accuracy and appropriacy in most areas (1–6 above). Spoken or informal features of language are used. Overly long sentences. Lack of, or incorrectly used, punctuation.

Assignment 2: Partial Lab Report comparing own lab results with modelled results (Grade /10)

1. Introduction, experimental method and presentation and discussion of data are included.

2. Presentation of results:
   - Data is introduced, described and briefly commented on.
   - Conventional data formatting is used.

3. Discussion of results: data is discussed (e.g., compared, interpreted, implications made).

4. Overall language use:
   - Correct word forms are used.
   - Formal, academic written style used and should be concise (e.g., including use of nominalisation).
   - The definite article is used consistently and appropriately.

5. Verbs:
   - Every sentence contains at least one main verb.
   - Appropriate choice of active and passive voice.
   - The verb tense is appropriate for the section.
   - Verb formation is accurate.
   - Subject–verb agreement is generally correct.

6. Appropriate sentence structure:
   - A range of sentence lengths is used, average length being 15–25 words.
   - A range of punctuation (comma, full-stop, colon and semi-colon) is used to perform several different functions. Sentences should include an appropriate number of clauses (2 or 3).

9–10: Very good/excellent presentation of experimental method, results and discussion. Consistently accurate forms and use of language in all areas (1–6 above). Formal features of language are used throughout, including correct nominalisation. Good range of sentence lengths. Excellent use of a range of punctuation marks.

6–8: Generally adequate presentation of experimental method, results and discussion. Generally accurate formation and use of language but some inconsistencies in some areas (1–6 above). Formal features of language are used and spoken or informal features of language are rarely used. Appropriate sentence length. Correctly used punctuation.

3–5: Weak presentation of experimental method, results and discussion. Reasonable use and accurate formation of language but with many inconsistencies in most of the areas (1–6 above). Generally, formal technical or academic style is used with some lapses into spoken or informal features of language. Occasional long sentences. Some inconsistent use of punctuation.

0–2: Inadequate presentation of experimental method, results and discussion. Limited accuracy in word formation and language use in most areas (1–6 above). Spoken or informal features of language are used. Overly long sentences. Lack of, or incorrectly used, punctuation and nominalisation.

The state of the art: Asian call centre ESP curriculum and assessment development

Jane Lockwood, Department of English, City University of Hong Kong
Email: lockwood@cityu.edu.hk

1 Introduction

The Business Processing Outsourcing (BPO) industry, and specifically those Multinational Companies (MNCs) domiciled in the United Kingdom, the US and Australia, have been rapidly expanding into the developing economies of India and the Philippines looking for quality work at significant savings. These countries have become preferred BPO destinations partly because of their colonial legacies where English was previously used in government, education and business, and where businesses believe there are existing linguistic and cultural affinities. These countries have positioned themselves therefore for a range of business services including call centres. However, the question is:

> What is the nature and quality of this English communication and how have communications training and assessment practices been developed to meet the needs of this growing industry?

This chapter provides an overview of the communications needs within the Asian call centre industry using a 'language audit' case study carried out in a third-party call centre in Manila. It provides an outline of the academic research completed to date showing where English communication has been found to break down on the phones and it will specifically focus on how such research and development has led to innovative development for English for Specific Purposes (ESP) curriculum and assessment for this industry. An important issue for call centres has been how to measure the business impact of its ESP training and assessment and there is a final discussion on how ESP applied linguists and business experts collaborate in order to achieve solutions that are not only pedagogically sound, but also positively affect the business bottom lines.

2 Asian call centre context

Western English-speaking countries such as the United Kingdom and the US have been sending work overseas to developing countries where the work can be completed cheaply and the quality of the work, they claim, is not compromised. This trend (Freidman, 2005) has become known as 'off-shoring', where companies set up localised branches, or 'outsourcing', where third parties act as middle men in delivering such services. This section describes the context and needs of English communication in Asian call centres.

A typical call centre in Asia hires local university graduates and places them in teams of twelve where they are supervised and mentored by a Team Lead. A call centre may vary in size from about 50 seats to 3,000 seats depending on the business and number of accounts. 'Third-party' call centres may have as many as 30,000 seats across different locations in the same country comprising a number of different businesses. In Manila alone, the call centre industry has grown rapidly over the last decade and the Philippines now employs approximately 500,000 Customer Services Representatives (CSRs).

Many have written about the call centre industry being metrics driven (e.g., Taylor & Bain, 1999; Friginal, 2007, 2009). Such measures include: Average Handling Time (AHT); first time resolution (FTR); and numbers of calls answered per day. These metrics comprise performance business indicators for individual CSRs and teams. In addition, external measures, commonly referred to as customer satisfaction surveys (Customer Satisfaction scores – CSats; Net Score Promoters – NPS) also provide quality target levels to be met as part of service level agreements. Good communication obviously plays a key role in achieving successful business metrics and I will come back to this later in this chapter as part of a discussion on the importance of linking ESP training and assessment to business targets and outcomes.

Whilst the Philippines has now overtaken India in the number of call centre seats provided (NY Times, 2011), it was India that first opened its doors to this industry almost 20 years ago. At that time, Western businesses were not only nervous about the political issues involved in sending this kind of work off-shore, but were also nervous about the quality of customer care delivered in English where employees did not speak English as their mother tongue. The prevailing business beliefs at that time, which persist to some extent today, were that customer services representatives (CSRs) needed perfect, error-free English grammar and pronunciation in order to be understood by English-speaking customers. This limited business view of what comprises English language communicative competence has spawned a plethora of courses on 'accent neutralisation' and the relentless testing of 'grammar and pronunciation accuracy'. In recent years, such approaches are increasingly questioned by the businesses as they have not delivered the business results and quality measures expected. This has afforded a unique opportunity for business stakeholders and applied linguists to work collaboratively on innovative ESP curriculum and assessment solutions that impact business outcomes.

3 ESP studies to date

The following section of this chapter reviews some key studies in ESP business and occupational curriculum and assessment development together with a review of studies relating specifically to the call centre industry.

3.1 ESP curriculum studies

As businesses increasingly require English to carry out globalised trade and communication (Nickerson, 2010) the demand for business ESP training curricula has grown. Two markets exist within the call centre industry; the first is a high volume 'pre-hire' call centre proficiency training one. English for Specific Business Purposes (ESBP) courses in phone speaking and listening in a call centre context have been developed by commercial publishers (e.g., Lockwood & McCarthy, 2010) and these have high face validity in the market for potential applicants. However, the second market is for call centre account induction and on-the-job training and coaching support, where the industry requires highly tailored solutions to achieve high communications performance within the account. Commercial publishers have little interest in this kind of specialist ESP materials development due to limited target markets. There appears therefore to be a continuum of ESP for call centre work that ranges from general proficiency development on the one end to high performance development on the other. A systematic framework for ESP curriculum development in the Asian business context has been the subject of a recent article (Lockwood, 2013) and other studies (e.g., Belcher, Johns & Paltridge, 2011; Starfield & Paltridge, 2013) where fundamental differences in approach can be tracked along a continuum of specificity.

Early ESP studies (Hutchinson & Waters, 1987; Robinson, 1991; Swales, 1991; 2004; Dudley-Evans & St. John, 1998) have cited learner motivation, face validity and a desire to incorporate more of the 'target context' into English language teaching as reasons for tailoring materials. In order to become more focused, applied linguists perhaps need to take an interdisciplinary approach where context is central. Over two decades ago, White (1988) found the theoretical approaches to language curriculum design lacking. He says:

> Personal experience, as well as that of many others working in the field of language curriculum, confirm the importance of looking beyond the traditional concerns of the syllabus designer whose main influences are derived from applied linguistics. Although applied linguistics provides a basis for approach, design and procedure takes us right out of applied linguistics and straight into innovation management. This is because decisions about language curriculum rapidly cease to be decisions about ideas and become actions, which affect people. On such matters, applied linguistics is silent (White, 1988, p. 45).

In recent years, more theoretically grounded studies (Belcher, 2004; Belcher, Johns & Paltridge, 2011; Bhatia, 2009; Paltridge, 2009; Flowerdew & Wan, 2010; Hyland, 2012) have drawn on different frameworks for the discourse analyses of the different genres of workplaces and occupations. Such analyses show high-levels of specificity in the way certain texts are organised and in the ways certain lexico-grammatical features are further reflected and patterned in the texts. Whilst analyses of call centre exchange is situated within this genre-based approach (e.g., Forey & Lockwood, 2007; Hood, 2010; Hood & Forey, 2008; Forey & Lam, 2013), the important ethnographic studies of this complex context are highlighted where business stakeholder views on communication success are paramount.

Ways of approaching highly tailored ESP curriculum development increasingly rely on a detailed ethnographic study of different call centre accounts. Such analyses may include surveys of the account sites, authentic samples of spoken texts (e.g., the call exchanges which can be transcribed) and written texts (for example workplace appraisal and compliance documents). In addition, business/subject matter expert input into the content and outcomes for training ensure business impact, so this input is critical. It is notable, however, that in recent years, beyond workplace and professional genre text analyses and corpus studies, there is little in the educational training literature illuminating principled curriculum approaches for the ESBP practitioner (Friginal, 2007, 2008; Lockwood, 2012b).

A number of call centre studies have been carried out on inbound insurance and banking calls (e.g., Forey & Lockwood, 2007; Lockwood, Forey & Price, 2008) and it was found that CSRs found the interactional load of dealing with the pressures of customers who may be bereaved, angry, confused and even hard of hearing required very nuanced communication skills to navigate the call successfully. Further, it was found that explaining the insurance and banking products and processes demanded discoursal skills that were clear and logical and adapted to the needs of the customer, who may for example be a second language speaker. Similar studies in different accounts, for example a study on credit card collections accounts (Forey & Lam, 2013), showed that the interactional mode governing the selection of certain lexico-grammatical features (e.g., closed-question forms) dominated successful calls; 'success' being defined by the business as collections targets having been met. Demographic analyses of the customers, discourse analyses of the authentic exchanges, as well as a sound understanding of business expectations around what comprised a 'successful' call were found to be central in the ESP curriculum design process for these banking and insurance calls.

3.2 ESP assessment studies

Research into ESP performance assessment has similarly recognised the key role of understanding the context as a key contributor to assessment validity. As early as 1995, Brown (1995) reported the process of developing a tailored screening assessment for Japanese tour guides for Australia and concluded:

> Further research is required into the process of occupation-based performance test development, in particular the negotiation and development of the assessment procedures, and the extent to which these reflect the intuitive views of the people who are the ultimate critics, whether they be workmates, clients, employers or partners. (Brown, 1995, p. 14)

Related studies seek to answer the question increasingly posed by globalised workplaces as to why employees with good scores in spoken proficiency on such generic language tests as IELTS or even business English tests such as TOEIC/BEC often fail to perform well on the job. This has led to a number of ESP performance assessment experts (e.g., McNamara, 1989; Jacoby & McNamara, 1999; Elder et al., 2012) debating how, what have been coined 'indigenous criteria' (the judgments of occupational professionals themselves) can be successfully incorporated into ESP assessment tools and processes where they, as professionals, will be the end-users.

The importance of context and interaction in speaking performance assessment has been widely examined (e.g., Hamp-Lyons & Lumley, 2001). This represents a shift in focus from psychologically derived to socially constructed assessment tools and processes and has been explored by assessment experts (e.g., McNamara, 1989; Jacoby and McNamara 1999; Turner & Upshur, 2002; Fulcher & Davidson 2007; Fulcher, Davidson & Kemp, 2011; Elder et al., 2012) in an effort to improve the validity in language performance assessment. Occupational ESP assessment development, most notably the health professional and aviation tests being developed for job entry purposes, have considered how the context and experts in the field can contribute to the validity of these measures (e.g., Elder et al. 2012., Alderson, 2011).

Typically in the call centre industry, ESP spoken assessments have been developed internally by the business and/or have been sourced off the Internet, but without an applied linguistic understanding about what they should contain and how they should be administered; many have proven to be unreliable and invalid (Lockwood, 2012a; Friginal, 2013). This has resulted in a situation where the business has sought the advice of language assessment experts on how to enhance spoken communication measurement, making it more valid, reliable and practical. For the call centre industry, this had led to a highly tailored solution, the Business Performance Language Assessment System (BUPLAS). For a full discussion on the development of BUPLAS as an embedded system in the call centre business, see Lockwood (2012a).

4 Methodology

This research utilised a 'case study' approach to reveal problems of existing ESP curriculum and assessment practices used in a large third-party call centre in Manila. The data was collected as part of a 'language audit' consultancy at the case study site in Manila where I was hired as a consultant to make improvements. The needs analysis was carried out as a 'language audit' (e.g., Reeves, & Wright, 1996) where language needs were analysed as part of every job in the call centre site; employee language proficiency levels were measured and call centre accounts were evaluated for language difficulty. ESP language training and coaching were observed and the curricula evaluated, as were the ESP assessment solutions being used in recruitment, training and on-the-floor.

This chapter details the ESP curriculum and assessment recommendations and highlights issues pertinent in the subsequent development work carried out for this site.

5 Case study

In a 2005, a language audit consultancy was carried out for a major third-party provider in the Philippines, called for the purposes of this chapter, PeoplePower Asia (PPA). PPA had invested heavily in the development of an in-house PPA English language communications team to conduct pre-employment and on-the-job training, coaching and assessment, but were concerned that the team did not have the knowledge nor therefore the skills, in the words of their manager, 'to make a real difference' to the business. PPA specifically sought a consultant with applied linguistic curriculum and assessment expertise to carry out the audit, and this provided a unique opportunity for me to understand the specific needs and contexts of the PPA call centre accounts, make recommendations and be involved in subsequent ESP curriculum and assessment work with their team of communications trainers, recruitment and quality specialists.

The aim of the consultancy was ultimately to ascertain the veracity of its suite of ESP curriculum and assessment products and processes that were being used in-house. It was commissioned over a three-month period in order to provide a clear picture of existing needs and gaps in English language communication skills for recruitment, training and Quality Assurance (QA) processes on the job in the call centre. Specifically, the consultancy was to address the following agreed objectives:

- *Conduct* a language audit of the different job functions within the industry 'verticals' (retail, IT, telecommunications, banking and insurance) and assign English language proficiency levels required for those jobs. Such job functions included not only CSRs, but also recruitment personnel, team leads, account managers and quality assurance personnel;

- *Conduct* language assessments for a sample of key operational staff in selected accounts (e.g., recruitment personnel, team leads, account managers and quality assurance personnel);

- *Evaluate* the existing English language training, induction and support infrastructure in Training and Operations;

- *Review* quality assurance processes (curriculum and assessment) on the floor as they relate to improving English communication skills; and

- *Review* the recruitment processes (assessment) with a view to hiring the 'best' English language communicators for PPA, Manila. (2005 PeoplePower Asia Audit Report: 3)

As a result of the study, there were four key recommendations made to PPA relating to ESP curriculum and assessment development and these are described below. These recommendations are used to reveal and discuss the ESP curriculum and assessment needs in the Asian call centre context.

6 ESP curriculum recommendations for PPA

6.1 Recommendation 1: Develop a pre-hire course improving the level of spoken English language proficiency at recruitment

By 2005, companies in this rapidly developing industry were no longer able to source the good English language communicators for their call centres from top-tier universities in the Philippines. Recruiting from second- and third-tier universities and college graduates would now involve English language proficiency training prior to employment as this industry continued to demand high levels of spoken communication. At the time PPA had no spoken assessment tool to use for employment and training purposes, so the question of how long such a course should be became highly problematic for the business stakeholders, as did their many discussions about 'level' requirements of their employees for their accounts. The communications manager reported:

> The business thinks we can raise English language proficiency levels in a matter of days and we have great difficulty in persuading them that English skills development is different from product knowledge training … they think it is the same! And the issue of measuring gains in communication is highly problematic for us.
> (Communications Managers, mid-40s, European male)

6.2 Recommendation 2: Develop a series of on-the-job and account-specific English for Specific Purposes communications training packages for account induction and account coaching

Unlike the call centre pre-employment proficiency courses described above, this recommendation related to the development of highly tailored communications performance support courses for each account in PPA. These were to be used for both induction and coaching purposes. This ESP curriculum design process would require ethnographic studies of each account by linguistically analysing authentic calls for each, barging into live calls, talking to the account managers and working with the quality assurance personnel and coaches to get their input on what makes 'good' and 'bad' calls in their judgment. These findings could then be translated into ESP curriculum for use on the floor. At the time, the PPA communications team had difficulty, for strict privacy reasons, sourcing authentic calls from the accounts. One communications trainer complained:

> They [the account managers] on the one hand want us to develop induction and coaching specifically for their accounts, but won't let us hear the calls … without being able to listen and analyse these calls for communication breakdown, we can't tailor courses for them …
> (Communications Trainer, mid-30s, female Filipina)

Educating some of the key stakeholders on the time and resources for curriculum and assessment improvement form part of the discussion section at the end of this chapter.

6.3 Recommendation 3: Redesign the assessment tool for recruitment to ensure validity and reliability

Within the PPA call centre site in Manila, two floors of the building were dedicated to recruitment. Each day hundreds of hopeful CSR applicants would arrive to be assessed for their spoken communication skills and general suitability to work in the call centre. In 2005, the tools and processes used at recruitment reflected the business belief that grammar and pronunciation accuracy, using American native speaker norms, were the desirable language characteristics for this kind of work. Unfortunately, and perhaps unsurprisingly, the tasks they used (e.g., reading limericks with particular phonological difficulty for Filipinos) were excluding over 95% of applicants. This was a huge business problem where the businesses, at that time, were ramping up to meet the demands of newly arriving outsourced accounts.

In 2005, PPA as a third-party provider, had over 50 different industry accounts or what the industry calls 'verticals'. Each 'vertical' account had very different lines of business with each demanding diverse levels of English communication skills. For example, the banking and financial sector may have on the one hand a routine 'change of address' account but, on the other, a complex financial advising service for high-end investor clients. They obviously differed in their communications demands; however, PPA had not yet developed an assessment system that could benchmark such account differences to ensure a 'best fit' within its work pool. In fact, it was found that CSRs with low-levels of English were often sent to work in the more communicatively demanding accounts, whereas high-level speakers of English were getting bored in the more routine ones.

This finding had immediate implications for communications recruitment and placement assessment within PPA and it was recommended, as part of this audit consultancy, that all accounts should be 'tagged' for proficiency level. Tagging was carried out by listening and assigning a benchmark level to a sample of at least ten 'good' calls assigned by the business. Talking to the team leads, account managers and QA specialists attached to these accounts in this process was also important. The recruitment process subsequently became better able to assess and fit CSRs into accounts that matched their proficiency levels. Recruiting and tagging required the development of a tailored assessment tool that could be used internally by trained staff and this aspect is discussed later in this chapter.

One of the casually employed recruitment specialists reported:

> It seems very arbitrary to 'cull' CVs before applicants get invited for assessment; I have a daily cull target of 50%. But we don't know what the level required is for the accounts apart from being told they have to be 'high' … I look at the CV and if they went to a good school or university I ring them up … and then if they sound OK, especially I listen for accent, I bring them in for further assessment.
> (Female recruitment specialist, mid-20s Filipina).

Such a 'common sense' approach to the 50% cull, was resulting in many potential candidates who may be good communicators not getting jobs in the call centres. A standardised measure at this stage of recruitment was clearly needed.

6.4 Recommendation 4: Develop communications assessment scorecards and coaching packages for quality assurance personnel

The audit revealed that the team of QA specialists attached to these accounts had little knowledge of how best to diagnose English language problems evident on the phones, nor how to provide effective feedback and coaching. Few QA specialists had an understanding of Teaching English to Speakers of Other Languages (TESOL), but nonetheless claimed to have gained their skills by 'learning on the job'. To exacerbate this situation, there was strong evidence during the audit of 'negative washback', from a business management view, that communication failed because of pronunciation/accent and poor grammar. Coaching observed at the time consisted mostly of accent neutralisation workshops, pronunciation drilling and grammar accuracy workshops.

In 2005, the year of this audit, PPA were beginning to question the value of coaching because they saw little improvement on the phones as a result of their coaching investment. They were therefore open to a recommendation to strengthen the training of the coaches to diagnose and feedback on communication issues on the phones.

Whilst there were other recommendations in the language audit, I have only selected those that are relevant to this chapter. The unique context of this audit brought together business stakeholders, desperate for ESP curriculum and assessment solutions that would strengthen the business, and applied linguists. The subsequent ESP development work emerging from this audit and further implications are discussed below.
(Extracts taken from the Recommendations in PPA Audit. pp. 19–23)

7 Subsequent work with PPA on ESP call centre curriculum and assessment development

In the months after the audit recommendations were made and accepted, PPA embarked on two areas of major change resulting in curriculum and assessment development work to improve the communications performance of their accounts. These are described below.

7.1 ESP curriculum development for call centres

As explained in an earlier section of this chapter, ESP curricula can run along a continuum from general ESP to specific ESP. PPA had a requirement for both as reflected in the Recommendations 1 and 2. In the general proficiency development ESP call centre courses (called pre-hire courses), the outcome was to improve the overall level of speaking and listening in English. Such courses could be labelled as motivational for the participants and as having contextual 'face validity' because they are situated in a call centre. The listening skills development were based around telephone exchanges across many different accounts; authentic calls were not used for this kind of training but were scripted and recorded for low-level students. In contrast, developing the highly tailored programmes for the individual accounts required collaborative work with key account informants; the Subject Matter Experts (SMEs) and using authentic calls for analysis and programme development. For reasons of cost and privacy, it has been unusual for applied linguists to be invited to participate in these processes. However, in this case study, the applied linguist was also the consultant, and this afforded a unique opportunity to research the inside workings of this ESP curriculum planning process in PPA.

In-house communications trainers at PPA are typically assigned a load of about 4–6 client accounts, ideally from the same industry group. For example, one of these trainers reported:

I have four banking and credit card clients at the moment; two of them are collections accounts where we have to ring defaulting customers and chase up money. So I have to know the processes and targets the CSRs are working with and towards ... you'd think they would be identical, but in fact the 'culture' of each of these clients are so different. One of them sets high targets and is much more aggressive than the other ... and all this needs to be reflected in the training and coaching packages we produce. (PPA trainer, Filipino, mid-30s).

In order to get access to the individual account sites, careful negotiations took place with the managers and in some cases required the assistance of the Director of PPA who strongly supported the audit recommendations. Eventually trainers and the consultant were given access to calls, personnel and any documentation that assisted in course development.

7.2 ESP assessment development for call centres

There were two main challenges when working subsequently with PPA stakeholders on the ESP assessment tools and processes. The first related to establishing the validity of the assessments to be used at recruitment and quality assurance. This involved introducing the key stakeholders in recruitment, training and quality assurance personnel to an assessment tool that reflected a sociolinguistic framework for language assessment that probed criteria beyond 'accent and pronunciation' and 'grammar accuracy'. At the time of the audit consultancy different parts of the business were using a mixture of assessment tools; some of these tools were developed in-house, some poached from other call centres and some downloaded from the internet. Apart from the questionable validity of some of these measures, one of the main problems was that the multiple tool use was causing fragmentation across the worksite; there was no shared metalanguage on what internal stakeholders meant by 'good communication' ability across PPA.

The second challenge in this consultancy development work that followed the audit related to the issue of ensuring reliability of PPA assessments and reliability of the in-house communications assessors. The business model and business expectation of the communications assessment tool had to take into account that outsourced TESOL-trained assessors would not be used for assessment work within PPA. This meant designing assessment training workshops and regular calibration sessions to ensure that non-TESOL background raters in-house could be trained to use assessments both formatively and summatively for a range of call centre workplace needs.

Unique to this workplace is the requirement for the assessments to be both owned by, and embedded into, the call centre worksite itself. This has meant that internal employees such as recruiters, communications trainers and quality assurance personnel carry out the CSR assessments themselves. Of interest is how educational and testing providers have responded to this new context as the conventional business model of large testing agencies such as Cambridge ESOL and the Educational Testing Services (ETS) is a cost per head model where candidates will normally attend an off-site test with expected turnaround time for results being anywhere from a few days to weeks. This model is of little interest to the call centre business that needs to assess hundreds and sometimes thousands of potential employees on a daily basis, needs immediate results and needs to contain costs. Given the low recruitment rate as described earlier in this chapter, a per head cost is not attractive to this industry. As a result of this audit consultancy the following characteristics were recommended for an ESP assessment system for the call centre industry. This industry, in contrast to what was currently on offer by the large testing agencies at the time, required assessment tools and processes that:

- Were able to be uploaded to the typical call centre dashboard that tracks communication success and failure over time;

- Were able to provide an end-to-end assessment solution from recruitment to quality assurance with the facility to assign different weightings and criteria as required by the account;

- Were able to provide benchmarks for the different call centre account difficulty;

- Were able to provide immediate results as jobs are typically offered immediately for this fast growing industry;

- Were owned by the business so that costs could be contained; typically in recruitment 10–15% of those assessed are employed; and

- Were to be operationalised by a range of internal employers familiar with recruitment processes and on the job appraisal and coaching processes.

The Business Performance Assessment System (BUPLAS), using a sociolinguistic framework and building on research around that time as to the causes of communication breakdown, was ultimately tailored to this specific industry need (see www.BUPLAS.com). This framework appeared to be ideally suited to the call centre industry where 'communicative competence' involving interactional and discoursal skills were found to be challenging for CSRs in their calls. BUPLAS draws in particular on the work of those linguists who first define communicative competence for teaching and assessment purposes (e.g., Canale & Swain, 1980). As well, Systemic Functional Linguistics (SFL) (Halliday, 1985) has been useful in that its tripartite macro-functional definitions of the ideational, interpersonal and textual have informed the criteria and weighting of the BUPLAS domains.

In summary, BUPLAS is a five-level assessment ranging from *elementary spoken level* (1) to *expert spoken level* (5) and comprises the following criteria:

- **Pronunciation, stress and intonation [25%]:** This criterion poses the questions as to whether the agent is globally comprehensible and is using the prosodic features to make meaning appropriately.

- **Lexico-grammatical range and accuracy [25%]:** This criterion poses the questions as to whether the choice in the grammar and vocabulary is sufficient for the communication task at hand and also whether errors in grammar are systematic and pose a threat to communication.

- **Discourse capability [25%]:** This criterion poses the questions as to whether the CSR keeps control of the call and is able to explain information clearly and logically to the customer.

- **Interactive and strategic capability [25%]:** This criterion poses the questions as to whether the CSR is able to build a relationship and interact effectively according to the customer need.

A further criterion measuring specific product and process competency, called 'business solutioning' has recently been added to the on-the-job BUPLAS scale. An early version of BUPLAS was introduced to PPA as a result of the audit.

8 Discussion and conclusion

This worksite has provided a unique opportunity, where the consultant as researcher in this case, has become involved in these ESP curriculum and assessment design processes. In doing so, however, it has raised a number of questions for further discussion and research.

The first relates to research access; gaining access to the call centre workplace is difficult. Strict privacy regulations, where third parties [customers] are involved, will normally prevent outside researchers from doing ethnographic surveys and collecting authentic phone exchange data, so important in the process of ESP curriculum and assessment needs analyses. This means that the researcher ideally should have some other legitimate and primary function within the worksite; in the PPA case study, the researcher was a hired consultant. This entailed signing the Non-Disclosure Agreement (NDA) at the time and ultimately asking permission to use the scrubbed data and survey documentation, and ensuring anonymity of workplace and participants, for any future publications. Other call centre researchers have been employed as call centre employees (e.g., Houlihan, 2003; Duchene, 2009; Woydack, 2013). These different roles are in themselves areas for research as it could be said that each will provide a different and unique 'ethnographic gaze' on what is being observed, not to mention different ethical considerations that each role may require.

Arising out of this first point, is the key role of the business stakeholders, and in particular the SMEs on the ground, in the development of the ESP curriculum and assessment solutions. Current ESP studies talk about the intertextuality of written and spoken communication at work (Bhatia, 2009) and the need therefore to closely observe and understand the nature of the different texts being produced in any given worksite. This requires close collaboration with SMEs about the nature of communication and in particular, from the business standpoint, what makes for example, a successful call. This leads inevitably to the question of whether an applied linguist carrying out discourse analyses on the authentic exchanges is able to label the call successful without knowing what, from a business point of view, is a good call. These two judgments are interwoven and it is of interest to know more about how they are related ultimately in what both deem successful. This integration of business product/process knowledge in the calls with communication skills is key for the business and, therefore, needs to feature prominently in the more tailored ESP materials and assessments. However, the business does not only require close collaboration with their own SMEs in the forging of curriculum and assessment solutions, it also requires evidence that these solutions positively affect the bottom line. As applied linguists, we are used to basing English language curriculum and assessment development on a thorough understanding of the target language situation; however, becoming accountable ultimately for its success or otherwise to the business by demonstrating impact, opens up other research opportunities and collaborative workplace relationships.

Key to understanding the curriculum and assessment development and evaluation processes in the call centres is the business requirement to 'own' the product. This does not always mean owning the copyright of the intellectual property developed, but it does mean handing over the curriculum and assessment products for their own internal and unlimited use. For educational providers and testing agencies in particular, this means working with new business models and involves training up internal call centre staff (e.g., recruiters, trainers and quality assurance personnel) to use the curriculum and assessment tools and processes effectively. The business client is therefore the consumer and user of the ESP products, not the educational provider nor the consultant. This complete knowledge and skills transfer into the business challenges current ESP assessment beliefs about how we establish the validity of our assessment tools and how we maintain reliability in the assessment processes. I will first deal with the issue of validity.

Current studies in occupational assessment have highlighted the need to look beyond the issue of establishing the validity for only the test (e.g., construct and content validity), but also to look at the context and consequences of that assessment use (i.e., predictive and consequential validity). Extending the scope of validity beyond the traditional unitary construct of test development, has been the subject of other recently developed ESP tests (e.g., Knoch & Elder, 2013; Alderson, 2011). If the occupational stakeholders do not think the test works, then its validity is seriously called into question.

In terms of reliability of the assessment in the off-shored call centres, ownership means that L2 speakers of English who are not language teachers need to be trained as language assessors at different points in the business. For example, recruitment specialists need to screen and place CSRs in the right accounts; communications trainers need to measure the success of their CSRs after pre-employment training, and quality assurance personnel (including account managers and team leads) need to be able to appraise communication performance on the phones and diagnose failures in their feedback and coaching support. This leads to the important research question *'Can L2 speakers of English, who are also not language teachers, be trained to use ESP spoken performance tools and processes reliably?'* Whilst there is a substantial literature on L2 background rater bias/variability in assessing English (e.g., Zhang & Elder, 2011; Winke, Gass & Myford, 2013), there are fewer studies looking at the impact of rater experience (e.g., Lim, 2011) and of rater background (e.g., Brown, 1995) to assessment reliability. Further studies investigating these issues are highly relevant for ESP assessment in the Asian call centre context.

This and other LSP studies, particularly in the area of language assessment in occupational contexts, have opened up interdisciplinary and collaborative processes to ensure the relevance and value of what we do is not only understood by the groups of professionals that we work with, but ultimately is owned and used by them to assess and support English communication. Brumfit (2010) and Taylor (2011) have in recent years talked about the topic of 'assessment literacy'; Brumfit (2010, p. 3) described it as a trend where 'recent changes in global economics, politics and language use have placed the issue of interpreting multiple linguistic identities in the centre of our concerns'.

Increasingly businesses and professional/occupational groups require the array of applied linguistic literacies now domiciled in educational institutions and testing agencies. Our challenge, particularly in ESP curriculum and assessment development, is to open up the knowledge and skills contained in these 'literacies' and transfer them to where they are most needed.

References

Alderson, C. (2011). The Politics of Aviation English Testing. *Language Assessment Quarterly, 8,* 386–403.

Audit Report (2005). Confidential consultancy report.

Belcher, D. (2004). Trends in teaching English for specific purposes. *Annual review of Applied Linguistics, 24,* 165–186.

Belcher, D. Johns, A., & Paltridge, B. (Eds.) (2011). *New Directions in English for Specific Purpose Research.* Ann Research. Ann Arbor. The University of Michigan Press.

Bhatia, V. (2009). 'Intertextual patterns in English legal discourse'. In D. Belcher (Ed.), *English for specific purposes in theory and practice.* Ann Arbor: University of Michigan Press.

BPAP (2006). English is not the problem! Communication problem! Communication skills in the BPO industry. *BPAP Annual report* http//www.bpab.org/bpap/bpaprese.arch.asp. Retrieved August 28, 2006.

Brown, A. (1995). The effect of rater variables in the development of an occupation-specific language performance test, *12*(1), 1–14.

Brumfit, C. (2010) Literacy or literacies? Academic literacies? Academic identities in a language-sharing world. In G. Blue (Ed.), *Developing academic literacy.* Bern, Switzerland: Peter Lang.

Business Processing Association of the Philippines (BPAP) Annual Report (2006). Retrieved February 7, 2009, from www.bpab.org.ph.

Canale, M., & Swain, M. (1980). Theoretical bases of communicative approaches to second language teaching and testing. *Applied Linguistics, 1,* 1–47.

Duchene, A. (2009). Marketing, management and performance: Multilingualism as commodity in a tourism call centre. *Language Policy,* 8:27–50.

Dudley-Evans, T., & St. John, M. (1998). *Developments in English for Special Purposes: a multidisciplinary approach*. Cambridge: Cambridge University Press.

Elder, C., Pill, J., Woodward-Kron, R., McNamara, T., Mania, E., Webb, G., & McColl, G. (2012). Health Professionals' Views of Communication: Implications for assessing Performance on a Health-Specific English Language Test. *TESOL Quarterly. Vol. 146 (2)* 409–419.

Flowerdew, J., & Wan, J. (2010) The linguistic and contextual in applied genre analysis: The case of the company audit report. *English for Specific Purposes, 29,* 78–93.

Forey, G., & Lockwood, J, (2007). 'I'd love to put someone in jail for this': An initial investigation of English needs in the Business Processing Outsourcing (BPO) industry. *English for Specific Purposes, 26,* 308–326.

Forey, G., & Lam, M. (2013). Applying systemic functional linguistics: understanding the choices of quality in the workplace. *Journal of Applied Linguistics and Professional Practice. Vol. 9(2).*

Friedman, T. L. (2005). *The World of Flat.* New York: Farrar Straus and Giroux.

Friginal, E. (2007). Outsourced call centres and English in the Philippines. *World Englishes 26(3),* 331–345.

Friginal, E. (2008). Linguistic variation in the discourse of outsourced call centers *Discourse Studies 10,* 715–736.

Friginal, E. (2009). Threats to the sustainability of the outsourced call centre industry in the Philippines: implications for language policy. *Language Policy, 8,* 51–68.

Friginal, E. (2013). Evaluation of oral performance in outsourced call centres: An exploratory case study. *English for Specific Purposes, 32,* 25–35.

Fulcher, G., & Davidson, F. (2007). *Language testing and assessment: An advanced resource book.* London and New York: Routledge.

Fulcher, G., Davidson, F., & Kemp, J. (2011). Effective rating scale development for speaking tests: performance decision trees. *Language Testing, 25(5),* 5–27.

Halliday, M. A. K. (1985). *An Introduction to Functional Grammar.* London: Edward Arnold.

Hamp-Lyons, L., & Lumley, T. (2001). Assessing language for specific purposes. *Language Testing, 18,* 127–132.

Hood, S. (2010). 'Naming and negotiating relationships in call centre talk'. In Forey, G. & J. Lockwood, (Eds.) *Globalization, communication and the workplace: Talking across the world.* London: Continuum International Publishing Group.

Hood, S., & Forey, G. (2008). The interpersonal dynamics of call centre interactions: co-constructing the rise and fall of emotion. In *Discourse and Communication. 2(4)*, 389–409.

Houlihan, M. (2003). Making sense of call centres; working centres; working and managing the front line. Unpublished PhD thesis. University of Lancaster.

Hutchinson, T., & Waters, A., (1987) *English for Specific Purposes; A learning-centred approach*. Cambridge: Cambridge University Press.

Hyland, K. (2012). *Disciplinary identities: Individuality and community in academic discourse*. Cambridge: Cambridge University Press.

Jacoby, S., & McNamara, T. (1999). Locating competence. *English for Specific Purposes, 18*, 213–241.

Knoch, U., and Elder, C. (2013). A framework for validating post-entry language assessments (PELAs). *Papers in Language Testing and Assessment, 2(2)* 48–66.

Lim, G. (2011). The development and maintenance of rating quality in performance: A longitudinal study of new and experienced raters. *Language Testing, 28(4)* 543–560.

Lockwood, J. (2008a). What does the Business Processing Outsourcing (BPO) industry want from English language assessment? *Prospect, 23(2)*, 67–78.

Lockwood, J. (2012a). Are We Getting the Right People for the Job? A Study of English Language Recruitment Assessment practices in the Business Processing Outsourcing (BPO) Sector: India and the Philippines. *Journal of Business Communication. Vol 49*, Issue 2, 107–127.

Lockwood, J. (2012b). Developing an English for Specific Purpose Curriculum for Asian Call Centres: How the theory can inform practice. *English for Specific Purposes.*

Lockwood, J. (2013). English for (very) Specific Business Purposes – A pedagogical framework. *AESPJ Special Issue. Vol 9*. No. 2.

Lockwood, J., Forey, G., & Price, H. (2008b). Englishes in the Philippines Business Processing Outsourcing Industry: Issues, opportunities and research. In Bautista, M. L. and Bolton, K. (Eds.) *Philippines English: Linguistic and literary perspectives* (pp. 157–172) Hong Kong: Hong Kong University Press.

Lockwood, J., Forey, G., & Elias, N., (2009). 'Call centre communication: Measurement processes in non-English speaking contexts'. In Belcher. (Ed), *English for Specific Purposes in theory and practice* (pp. 289–296). Ann Arbor: University of Michigan Press.

Lockwood, J., & McCarthy, H. (2010). *Contact US!: Call center English skills*. Cambridge: Cambridge University Press.

McNamara, T. F. (1989). ESP testing: general and particular. In C. N. Candlin & T. F. McNamara (Eds.) *Language, Learning and Community. (pp. 125–142)* North Ryde, NSW National Centre for English Language Teaching and Research.

Nickerson, C. (2010). 'English as a Key Resource to Business and Development'. In Forey, G. and Lockwood, J., (Eds.) *Globalization, Communication and the Workplace*. London: Continuum.

Paltridge, B. (2009). 'Afterword: Where have we come from and where are we now?' In Belcher, D. *English for Specific Purposes in theory and practiced*. (pp. 289–296). Ann Arbor. University of Michigan.

Reeves, N., & Wright, C. (1996). *Linguistic Auditing: A Guide to Identifying Foreign Language Communication needs in Corporations*. Clevedon, UK: Multilingual Matters Ltd.

Robinson, P. (1991). *ESP Today: a Practitioner's Guide*. New York: Prentice Hall.

Starfield, S., & Paltridge, B. (2013). (Eds.) *The Handbook of English for Specific Purposes*. Oxford: Wiley-Blackwell.

Swales, J. (1991). ESP developments worldwide. In Luzares et al., (Eds.) *Proceedings of the ESP State of the Art Conference*. Manila: De la sale University. 11–19.

Swales, J. (2004). *Research genres: Explorations and applications*. Cambridge: Cambridge University Press.

Taylor, L. (2013). Communicating the theory, practice and principles of language testing to test stakeholders: Some reflections. *Language Testing, 30*(3) 403–412.

Taylor, P., & Bain, P. (1999) An assembly line in the head: work and employee relations in the call centre. *Industrial relations Journal, 30*(2), 101–117.

The New York Times, Manila Bulletin December 10th, 2011, Philippines is the new call center centre, – Neha Thirania.

Turner, C., & Upshur, J. (2002). Rating scales derived from student samples: Effects of the scale marker and the student sample on the scale content and student scores. *TESOL Quarterly, 36*(1) 49–70.

White, R. (1988). *The ELT Curriculum: Design, Innovation and Management*. Oxford: Blackwell.

Winke, P., Gass, S., & Myford, C. (2013). Raters' L2 background as a potential source of bias in rating oral performance. *Language Testing, 30*(2) 231–252.

Woydack, J. (2013). Standardisation and script trajectories in a London call centre: An ethnography of a multilingual outbound call centre. Unpublished PhD thesis. King's College, London.

Zhang, Z., & Elder, C. (2011). Judgments of oral proficiency by non-native and native English speaking teacher ratings: Competing and complementary constructs? *Language testing, 28*(1), 31–50.

The EAP course design quagmire: Juggling the stakeholders' perceived needs

Saba Bahareen Mansur: Department of Humanities, COMSATS Institute of Information Technology, Islamabad, Pakistan
Prithvi N. Shrestha: Department of Languages, The Open University, UK
Email: sbahareen@comsats.edu.pk and Prithvi.Shrestha@open.ac.uk

1 Introduction

This chapter explores the views of the three main stakeholders of an ESP programme: administrators, English for Specific Purposes teachers and MBA students at a premier Pakistani University, regarding MBA students' English language needs. The COMSATS Institute of Information Technology (CIIT), Islamabad Campus, is the milieu of this study. These MBA students come from all around the country, especially from comparatively underprivileged areas. Students may not have had access to good schooling and may have had very limited exposure to the English language. A sizeable number of students have even obtained their bachelor's degrees through distance learning programmes.

While teaching Business Communication (a wide-angled English for Occupational Purposes course) to MBA students at CIIT for around a decade, the first author encountered challenges such as diverse educational backgrounds and English language proficiencies, therefore, she conducted a needs analysis study of the English Language needs of MBA students (Mansur, 2010a). This research highlighted the need for an English for Academic Purposes (EAP) course with a special focus on basic language skills. The results of which were then communicated to the administrative personnel at COMSATS. However, the proposed EAP course was not made part of the scheme of MBA studies. The administration had showed an unwillingness to consider the inclusion of such a course in the scheme of studies of the MBA programme. Administrative 'red tape-ism' including lengthy Board of Studies and Board of Governors' approvals and a lack of experts to explain the need for the curriculum changes were cited as reasons for not incorporating the EAP course in the four-year scheme of studies of the MBA programme.

A few informal, small-scale efforts were made to initiate an English language support system for students with limited English by the first author and like-minded teaching staff. These endeavours could not be sustained because of the lack of administrative support as well as the intense workload of the faculty members involved. Now a fresh effort in the same line is underway to establish an English language support system with the support of some of the administrators; it is hoped that these efforts will endure the test of time.

This research explores the perspectives of COMSATS administrators, ESP teachers and MBA students on the English language needs of MBA students. It further tries to explore the strife caused by the administrative differences of opinion and outlook on the university's system that restrain it from bringing much needed change to the curriculum. In doing so the chapter also looks for a way forward, that is, a way to meet the English language needs of MBA students despite the disparity in the three respective standpoints. It also offers implications of this study to other global EAP contexts.

2 Literature review

The use of English as a medium of instruction for education (especially in higher education) has been on the rise in non-native English-speaking (NNS) countries particularly in Asia and Europe (see Gill & Kirkpatrick, 2012). This trend has made researchers and practitioners look into ways of facilitating NNS students' learning by providing English language support to students in the best possible way (see for example Hutchison & Waters, 1987; Dudley-Evans & St. John, 1998; Flowerdew & Peacock, 2001; Hyland, 2006). According to Hutchinson and Waters (1987, p. 19) 'ESP should be seen as an approach to language teaching which is directed by specific and apparent reasons for learning'. Therefore 'all decisions of content and method are based on the learner's reason for learning' (ibid).

If this is done in the context of Pakistani higher education many problems being faced by students, faculty and administrators can be solved. Pakistan is 'a classic' cultural society (Mansoor, 2005). Students with different mother tongues have to study at higher education in English, the country's official language. For many such students, English is a fourth or fifth or a foreign language (Shamim, 2008).

Despite the heavy doses of English in the undergraduate courses 'the results are abysmally low' in English as a subject (Abbass, 1998). Malik (1996) endorses the same view and expounds on it further by saying that the weak proficiency in the language has lowered the standard of performance at graduate and postgraduate levels where the medium of instruction and examination is English.

In Pakistan, although the awareness is gradually growing in many circles, English language teaching is, for the most part still 'a handmaiden of literary studies' and in the process of moving towards the notion that the teaching of language can with advantage be deliberately matched to the specific needs and purposes of the learner (Strevens, 1977, p. 89).

Researchers like Abbass (1993) and Haque (1993) have long called for the introduction and use of communicative language teaching and curricula to help the learner meet their communicative needs. In the words of Tribble and Shamim (2006, p. 32) the problem is:

> … the huge demand for English in the employment market and the relatively low levels of proficiency of graduates from public sector institutions of higher education in Pakistan.

In the mid-1990s a paradigm shift started to take place in ELT at university level. ESP wide-angled courses attempting to work on all four skills under the head of communications skills have been introduced in place of English literature. ESP as a discipline, therefore, is still in its infancy in Pakistan. The demand for high levels of English language and communication skills is not an isolated event in this part of the world. The skills and English language proficiency required for both academics and professionals have become more complex over the past decades (see Locker, 2003; Guffey, 2004; Stevens, 2004 & 2005; Flowerdew, 2008; Uzuner, 2008). More than ever before, the high demand of 'employability skills' (NCIHE, 1997) and the inclusion of visual and audio literacy into traditional literacies of discourse communities has complicated the demands on education for graduates.

These complex needs in the Pakistani context have not been explored at the higher education level. Hence, the 'awareness' of the reasons and needs of the students central to English for Specific Purposes course design has no research-based evidence although 'Needs Analysis' research has become a tool that is used and found to be very helpful in designing and meeting needs of students (West, 1994; Dudley-Evans & St. John, 1998; Zhu, 2004).

Needs analysis, according to Lytle (1988), is an important part of any instructional programme design from the individual learner's perspective and can benefit teachers as well as students. Researchers argue (see Hutchinson & Waters, 1987; Robinson, 1991; Dudley-Evans, 1998; Savignon & Wang, 2003) that a learner-centred approach to language learning, especially in ESP/EAP, is based on the premise that language teaching and learning programmes should be responsive to learners' needs.

Needs analysis instigates and steers EAP course design and development; it involves surveying students to collect data on their background and goals, wants, needs, linguistic and behavioural demands, and preferred learning/teaching strategies (Jasso-Aguilar, 1999). Students' needs assessment remains fundamental to EAP (Allison et al., 1994; Dudley-Evans, 1998; Dudley-Evans & St John, 1998; Jordan, 1997). It is the homogenising part of any EAP course as it helps in defining the objectives and content of each course according to learners' needs in the target language and how learners are expected to perform in conforming to the norms and conventions of their academic disciplines.

The needs assessment should be considered as an ongoing process designed to gather and analyse information about the target language needs of learners and whether these requirements are being achieved. It also helps with planning learners' and the EAP programme's future directions and making informed decisions (Purpura & King, 2003; Santopietro & Peyton, 1991).

The most significant question in relation to needs analysis research is conceptualisation of the term 'need'. Brindley (1989, p. 65) sees a distinction between various concepts of needs, such as between needs and wants and the ways in which the difference between these two is determined as a major source of ambiguity in the concept of language needs. Conversely, 'needs' can be seen as a measurable gap between the existing conditions and the desired future state (Berwick, 1989). Benesch (1996) posits that 'needs' may be seen critically, that is, questioned and understood to provide room for reform rather than accepting the status quo.

According to Pratt (1980, p. 79) 'needs assessment refers to an array of procedures for identifying and validating needs, and establishing priorities among them.' Zhu (2004) states that by analysing the views of content teachers on the English language needs of students, much can be found out about the instruction and literacies required by the students to cope with their studies. According to Richards (2001, p. 54 as cited in Hyland 2003, p. 59):

> In reality, needs reflect judgments and values and as a result are likely to be defined differently by different stakeholders with school administrators, government departments, parents, employers, teachers and learners themselves having different views.

Richards (2001) and Holmes and Celani (2006) suggest that needs be seen as unique characteristics of the educational context in which the studies are to take place. As students' needs vary in different contexts, only needs analysis and courses designed on the basis of this needs analysis can help students most effectively (Deutch, 2003). Brown (1995, p. 52) posits that '... multiple sources of information should be used in a needs analysis – although the specific combination appropriate for a given situation must be decided on the site by the needs analysts themselves.'

The studies using multiple methods to find out the needs of business graduates around the world are quite few. As can be seen by a cursory scan of the journals *Business Communication Quarterly* and the *Journal of Business Communication*, dealing with the interdisciplinary subject of business communication over of the past two decades reveal that the focus of research has been on the following strains:

(i) The perceptions of teachers and students' of students' communication needs in terms of students' strengths and weaknesses in writing in comparison with real-life business tasks (e.g., Bacha & Bahous, 2008; Epstein, 1999; Plutsky, 1996; Reinsch & Shelby, 1997);

(ii) Quality and standard maintenance in business communication instruction in MBA programmes (e.g., Bogert & Butt, 1996; Knight, 1999);

(iii) Comparison and contrast between teachers and professionals' perceptions of different aspects of student writing (e.g., Laster & Russ, 2010; Alred, 2006; Zhu, 2004; Leonard & Gilsdorf, 1990; Seshadri & Theye, 2000); and

(iv) Impact of different types of instructional techniques (e.g., team-teaching) on learning (e.g., Hotchradel, Long & Johnson, 2010; Grinols & Waller, 2010).

In addition, other studies have tried to look into English language needs of MBA students from angles different perceptions from the stakeholders of the courses (see e.g., Bacha, 2001; Zhu, 2004; Loudermilk, 2007). Most of these studies have focused on writing skills. Zhu (2004) looks at the target needs of MBA students by analysing writing tasks given to students at university. Loudermilk (2007) tries to show the highly complex nature of MBA essays whereas Bacha (2001) debates the pros and cons of different rating scales and ways of evaluating writing in EFL academic environments where English is used as the medium of instruction. Northcott (2001) uses an ethnographic approach to find out ways of making MBA lectures more interactive and effective. Basturkmen (1999) looks into the actual use of language in MBA seminars and the commonly used material in MBA EAP courses.

From the discussion above, it is evident that a number of studies have delved into the perspectives of the students, subject teachers and faculty about the English language needs of the students. However, few researchers have given even cursory mention of the administrative involvement and impact on ESP course design and implementation. In this connection, Tajino, James & Kijima (2005) call for meaningful collaboration between ESP teachers, content teachers as well as institutional administrators using the comprehensive systems methodology to design effective EAP courses. Evans and Green (2007) mention the concern and changing perception of administration and teachers towards English literacy in Cantonese-speaking countries including Hong Kong. In contexts like these the change in the medium of instruction at secondary and tertiary levels has resulted in the proliferation of EAP courses.

Researchers like Helmer (2013) calls for a 'rights analysis' rather than 'needs analysis', taking on a pragmatic approach to EAP in line with views of Pennycook (1994, 1997), Belcher (2006) and Benesch (2001a, 2001b). Helmer asserts the need for sensitivity towards the sociopolitical, linguistic and cultural needs of the contexts (Benesh 2001a; Pennycook 2010; Norton & Toohey, 2004).

Despite a wide recognition of the dire need of students with limited English at higher education there have been almost no published needs auditing studies on Pakistani students. The recommendation to train teachers to conduct English language needs analysis is part of the report submitted to the Higher Education Commission in 2006 entitled 'Case Studies of Organization of Teaching of English in Public Sector Universities in Pakistan' (Shamim et al., 2006). According to the same report, as well as research by others (Zafar, 2003 & 2009; Mansur 2010b) most teachers teaching ESP subjects are not trained to do so. Therefore, encouraging professional development of teachers teaching ESP can provide skills like conducting needs analysis research and aligning courses and material accordingly will help them.

The current study is exploratory in nature. In this chapter, we specifically examine the perceptions of university administration, ESP teachers and Pakistani MBA students regarding the students' English language proficiency at the reputable University of Pakistan. It also attempts to find a way to cater for the identified needs. More specifically, the study addresses the following research questions:

1. What do the administrators think are the English language needs of the MBA students?

2. How do the administrators feel the 'English language needs' can be fulfilled?

3. What do the ESP teachers think about the English language needs of the students?

4. How do the ESP teachers think these needs can be met?

5. What are the students' views about their English language needs?

6. How do these views of the stakeholders help in finding a way to address the English language needs of MBA students?

3 Problematisation of context

3.1 National

Pakistan is a post-colonial state which has a complex relationship (Mansoor, 2005; Mehboob, 2002) with English language. English is the official language of the country as well as the medium of instruction in higher education. The students that become part of the higher education, however, come from 'apartheid education systems' (see e.g., Shamim 2008; Siddiqui 2012): one stream has English as its medium of instruction while the other has Urdu or a regional language. Most prestigious jobs require high levels of proficiency in English language (Abbass 1993; Haque 1993; Shamim 2008; Mehboob 2009). This poses significant challenges to those students coming from Urdu or other language-medium education.

English language curricula at school and college level is based on literature, and the teaching methodologies are confined to grammar translation and lectures (Malik 1996; Mansoor 2005; Siddiqui 2012). Most teachers teaching ESP subjects such as Business Communication, Communication Skills and Functional English at higher education level hold Masters Degrees in English literature and are unaware of what ESP is (Shamim, 2006; Zafar 2003 & 2009; Mansur, 2010b).

3.2 Institutional

COMSATS Institute of Information Technology (CIIT) Islamabad is rather new (established in 1999 and receiving its charter in 2001) and yet is a prestigious higher education institute in Pakistan with seven fully functional campuses across the country. It offers degree programmes in 32 subject areas. The Department of Management Sciences is one of the oldest and most lucrative departments of CIIT. The Department of Humanities was established in 2010 although earlier it worked as a subsidiary of the Management Sciences Department.

4 Methodology

This study has used a mixed methods approach to find the perspectives of three different stakeholders regarding the English language needs of MBA students. The methods used are as follows:

1. Questionnaires: The first perspective takes into account the views of the MBA students using questionnaires.

2. Semi-structured interviews: The second perspective looks at the views of Administrators and ESP teachers teaching MBA students through interviews.

3. Reflective paper/auto-ethnography: The first author wrote an auto-ethnography recounting her experience in accordance with the research questions.

4.1 Quantitative method

Questionnaires

The MBA students of the first semester (sample of convenience) were taken as the sample group for this study. A questionnaire especially designed to learn about the English language needs was distributed among the students in their classes to be filled in.

The questionnaire mainly used Likert-scale questions as its basis and was piloted initially with 50 students. As a result of the piloting, some questions were modified to increase comprehensibility and align the questions with the aims of the study. An open-ended question was added to the questionnaire to give students freedom to say what they wanted on the issue.

The refined questionnaire was given to a total of 137 students to complete. The data that the usable questionnaires yielded was inserted into SPSS (the Statistical Package for the Social Sciences) software for analysis. Thirty-eight of these questionnaires were discarded as they were either not filled-in completely or the same option (e.g., option 'c') was chosen in all Likert-scale questions.

Questions 1–5 of the questionnaire were about general bio-data of the students (i.e., mainly general demographics). Questions 6–12 were regarding the educational histories of students. Questions were asked about the stream of schooling used (public or private); medium of instruction used in the schools/colleges previously attended. The next questions all pertained to language skills used at university level. The level of language-skill usage was enquired about in questions 13–17. Questions 18–21 dealt with problems students might have with individual language skills and their sub-skill sets. Question 22 was regarding the mode of instruction preferred by students. Questions 23–24 were regarding the use of a dictionary. Question 25 was an open-ended question asking for further comments from students.

4.2 Qualitative method

Semi-structured interviews conducted with administrative personnel and ESP teachers

The interview schedules for the administrative personnel and ESP teachers were developed in line with the research questions and the background of the research questions as well as the administrative constraints in initiating an EAP course in 2010.

In total, twelve administrative personnel and teaching staff were contacted for interviews. Seven out of the twelve contacted people consented to give the interviews. Three of the interviewees were working as part of the administration as well as teaching staff of the Management Sciences Department. The other four were members of the Humanities Department. One of the interviewees is the current administrative head of the Department, while two others were former administrative heads. The last remaining interviewee was an ESP teacher.

Auto-ethnography/reflective paper

The first author wrote a reflective paper, also known as auto-ethnography, sharing her own experience as an ESP teacher.

All interviews were audio recorded and later transcribed. After transcription, the process of data analysis began by taking printouts of the transcriptions, as well as of the reflective paper, then making surface generalisations of the kind of data available (Kitwood, 1977). Then data reduction was carried out by making 'marginal remarks' (Miles & Huberman, 1994) to decide the relevance of the data to the research questions and interview schedule. The next step was 'categorisation of content' (Kitwood, 1977) based on the research questions. These themes were then traced in all the interviews by marking chunks of relevant sentences. These themes were then placed under broader categories or headings to make the data manageable. This data condensation (Tesch, 1990 in Miles & Huberman, 1994) helped conclusions to be drawn. The open-ended question of the student questionnaire was analysed in a similar fashion.

5 Results and discussion

This section deals with the results of the analysis of the data along with discussion of their implications.

5.1 Views of stakeholders on MBA students' English-language needs

Firstly, the views of all stakeholders on the English language needs are presented to set the foundation of the results and subsequent discussions.

The first is the view of the MBA students about their English language needs and proficiency levels on the major four language skills. Table 1 presents the responses of students about skills which they feel are most needed for themselves at the university level:

Table 1: Students' evaluation of most important language skill at university

Most important skills	Percentage
Writing skills	56.6%
Speaking skills	77.8%
Reading skills	42.4%
Listening	45.2%
Grammar	53.3%
Any other	0.0%

As shown by the table above, students considered speaking, writing and grammar skills to be the most needed, followed by listening and reading skills. It is interesting that reading is rated as the least important skill despite the demand that higher education places on students in terms of reading academic material. This statistic may indicate that these students feel confident of their reading skills in the English language.

The responses of the students evaluating their level of proficiency at different language skills and specifically writing yielded interesting results. Around 50% students felt that they had a good command over writing skills, followed by a 32.3% who believed that they had a satisfactory level of competence in writing in English (see Table 2).

Table 2: Students' self-evaluation of their writing skills

Students' perception of their writing skills level	Percentage
Excellent	8.1%
Good	48.5%
Satisfactory	32.3%
Poor	7.1%
Uncertain	4.0%

Coming to speaking skills (see Table 3), a little over half the (51.5%) students believed they possessed satisfactory speaking skills. This was again completely in contrast to the teachers' views about the students' speaking abilities in English.

Table 3: Students' self-evaluation of their speaking skills

Students' perception of their speaking skills level	Percentage
Excellent	4.0%
Good	22.2%
Satisfactory	51.5%
Poor	19.2%
Uncertain	3.0%

A total of 56.6% students believed that they were good readers while 14.1% thought they were excellent readers.

Table 4: Students' self-evaluation of their reading skills

Students' perception of their reading skills level	Percentage
Excellent	14.1%
Good	56.6%
Satisfactory	18.2%
Poor	11.2%
Uncertain	0.0%

Students again seemed to have highly optimistic views about their listening skills as can be gauged from the following (Table 5).

Table 5: Students' self-evaluation of their listening skills

Students' perception of their listening skills level	Percentage
Excellent	12.1%
Good	40.4%
Satisfactory	34.3%
Poor	10.1%
Uncertain	2.0%

41.4% students felt they had a satisfactory grip over the grammar of the English language as reflected in the following table.

Table 6: Students' perceptions of their grammar skills

Students' perception of their grammar level	Percentage
Excellent	6.1%
Good	23.2%
Satisfactory	41.4%
Poor	23.2%
Uncertain	6.0%

According to all administrative personnel as well as the ESP teachers, the English language proficiency of MBA students 'is not up to mark' as is expected from Masters level students. Two of the three administrators interviewed from the Management Sciences Department and three of the five participants from the Humanities Department related their experiences with MBA students not even having enough English language proficiency to comprehend the lecture. As in the words of a former administrator and teaching staff member from the Department of Management:

> ... in general case at comprehension is such a serious issue that I can never forget that particular example of a spelling when someone wrote cigarette as s-i-g-e-r-i-t.

According to a former administrator of the Department of Humanities, the students' command of 'English language skills to express their ideas fluently and accurately ..., are terribly lacking.' All ESP teachers highlighted the fact that most students have very weak basic English language structure which is evident from their writing.

Two other participants from the Humanities Department shared their experiences of repeated requests from students to deliver the lecture or instructions in Urdu rather than English. This may indicate not only low English language proficiency but also poor listening skills.

Spoken English and presentation skills are one of the weakest areas which are also considered important by the students surveyed. Lack of proficiency in these skills is compounded by lack of confidence and no prior experience of or exposure to speaking English with others – let alone presenting in front of a class full of students. This suggests that ESP teachers have to help students not only in the area of English language but also with soft and transferrable skills.

The above discussion illustrates the point that the views of administrative staff and ESP teachers regarding students' English language proficiency are very different from those of their students. This clash in perceptions can have repercussions on motivation for students as well as teachers while learning and teaching.

5.2 Reasons for weak proficiency of students in English language

Most of the interviewees suggested that the poor quality of English language teaching at college level in Pakistan is the basic reason for students having such low language skills. A former administrator of the Department of Management Sciences stated:

> I think they are bringing a lot of baggage with them, they clearly have not had proper English teaching. And the distinction between this can be easily understood if you see the performance of students who have done A-levels and O-levels as compared to those who have come from the other channel of language because in A- or O-level whether they are hard working or not, at least comprehending the course is not an issue.

This view is verified by research conducted by Malik (1996), Rehman (2004), Mansoor (2005), Shamim (2006 & 2008) and Siddiqui (2012).

The current administrator of the Humanities Department expounds further on the same point by saying:

> ... for the most part, education (in Pakistan) is given at a superficial level with the end result that students that have a strong background tend to do well. Those who don't, don't get much support and they are disadvantaged over and over again.

This view is elaborated upon by Siddiqui (2012) where he critically examines the Pakistani education system. According to Siddiqui the Pakistani education system, instead of providing 'equal opportunity' and empowering the poor, is doing the exact opposite and thus needs a complete overhaul.

5.3 Is the Business Communication course fulfilling all language needs of MBA students?

Again, all seven interviewees, also recorded in the first author's auto-ethnography, believe that the maiden MBA English Language Business Communication course is insufficient to cater for the coaching needs of MBA student. This is mainly because of time constraints and the course not being fully relevant to the students' needs.

5.4 How can the English language needs of MBA students be fulfilled?

All three administrators from the Management Department believed that inclusion of another English language course in the MBA programme was not the right way to fulfil the needs of the students. In the view of one of the administrators, additional courses (non-credit bearing but compulsory) need to be designed and organised for MBA students:

> ... these courses can be conducted in the summer time or when the students are selected to be part of the programme. They can be oriented with an extra – zero semester to groom them. Special workshops/courses need to be designed for students that are nearing graduation, that is students in the 7th or 8th semesters so that when they go into the job market they know how to communicate and present themselves.

Another former administrator of the Management Sciences Department and teaching staff member even goes a step further suggesting that:

> If you really want a student to feel proficient in the language you need to have tests like TOEFL and [work out] who needs to be given special assistance in the language and for those students it should start from zero semester or zero-1 or zero-2 depending upon the kind of attention that students need ... because just like when you go to Germany or France you have to spend a year or a year and a half to understand the language before they put you in to their professional course.

This view of the administrator echoes the models where students are assessed once they are admitted to university and provided with instruction to enhance their English language proficiency, according to the assessment in the system as described by Read (2008). The idea of using an assessment rather than a high-stake test seems more appropriate to expound on the positive nature of the assessment.

In the views of two of the interviewees, making the Business Communication course more practical with indigenous case studies 'coming from the experience or projects of the students' could improve the course enormously by making it context sensitive. Developing indigenous case studies, material and research may lead to criticality and possibly transformative pragmatic English for academic skills practices (Morgan 2009; Benesch 2001a & 2001b).

5.5 How do these views of the stakeholders help in finding a way to address the English-language needs of MBA students?

According to the views of the interviewees, the most practicable way forward is to develop English language courses that start with a diagnostic test when students enter the university. This diagnostic test then needs to be used to make an estimate of how much extra coaching through pre-sessional courses would benefit the students with limited English and help them to gain a level of proficiency in English language and meet the minimum criteria to be able to cope with their academic needs.

In addition, students that are about to graduate from university need their skills English-language to be 'brushed up' with CV clinics and interview skills and presentation skills workshops. These, according to the Management Sciences Department administrators, are possible ways forward.

The ESP teachers and administrative personnel from the Humanities Department suggested that the course outlines standardised in 2005 need to be 'revisited'. This course, as identified by the interviewees, lacks focus on grammar, basic sentence structure and spoken skills.

Given the different perspectives of three stakeholders, an EAP/ESP practitioner is faced with challenges despite a positive note from an administrator from Humanities:

> I seriously and really believe that there is always a way to what you want. You just have to find the right path and you do that by analysing the situation and the people you are working with.

One of the major challenges in bringing about changes at grass-roots level in bureaucratic systems is that the administration may often not understand why the teaching faculty are suggesting recommendations as they, as an administrator said, are 'not on the ground, they are not even interacting with the students, they don't know them and they don't understand them'.

A way forward towards receiving support from administrators may be as noted by another former administrator: 'I think they should visit the classroom and see for themselves where do we need to improve ...'

5.6 What to include in extra courses?

According to the data, based on both the student survey and the interviews, the following areas have been identified as essential elements of an ESP/ EAP course for the MBA programme:

1. Basic English for comprehension of lectures

2. Listening skills

3. Basic English construction (clear, grammatically correct sentences)

4. Spoken skills

5. Negotiation skills

6. Presentation skills

Writing in clear, understandable and grammatically correct language is another area that is seen to be a basic need. All but one (negotiation skills) areas identified in this research as needing extra attention for MBA students were also highlighted as problem areas in the needs analysis conducted in 2010 (Mansur, 2010a).

6 Conclusion and global implications

Despite the deadlock experienced after the needs analysis in 2010, this research indicates that there is some possibility of getting some institutional support for developing a more responsive EAP course for MBA students' emerging needs. This study shows that EAP practitioners encounter formidable challenges if they are not careful enough to include all stakeholders involved in the needs analysis process. Inclusion of administrators in this process has emerged as one of the most important factors so that EAP practitioners are not met with hostility when implementing the course. It is especially important to find ways to engage (Fowler & Gilfillan, 2003; Yarrow, Robson & Owen, 2004; Moore, Asay, & Curry, 2006) all stakeholders in 'negotiating' (Salas, Mercado, Ouedraogo & Musetti, 2013) the process of curricula development and implementation (AASHE, 2010). Higher education in contexts like Pakistan, where power relations are delicately balanced, may have serious implications for both students and EAP professionals.

At the time of writing this chapter, the new EAP/ESP course based on the findings had not been designed and thus, following this exploratory study we propose the following which may be applicable to other similar EAP/ESP contexts in the world where English is the medium of higher education despite the language being a foreign language or lingua franca:

> A diagnostic assessment of student needs should be carried out when students first enter university. Similar recommendations, e.g., an English language proficiency test like IELTS have been made by Mansoor (2005, p. 361). This will help to identify those students who may be at risk of failing their studies due to limited English language skills early on. This assessment needs to be the basis of earmarking students for extra coaching in the various English language skills. The focus of skills should be driven by students' needs identified by the diagnostic assessment.

The university can offer a pre-sessional English language course to those students who come from non-English-medium education colleges/schools prior to their first semester. Such an offering could be credit-bearing as well. In addition, it is important to provide in-semester English language support mechanisms that may be non-credited but compulsory for students to start their degree programmes. This support could be available to all students as academic disciplines have their own academic practices and these may be new to even those students who come from English-medium education. In fact, a similar recommendation was made by Mansoor (2005, p. 361). By doing so, the institution may be able to improve its retention and attainment figures given the fact that language is a key barrier to students' success.

Additionally, if resources allow, extra and specialised courses for graduating students need to be conducted to brush up their skills. Such extra courses need to focus on employability skills (e.g., interview skills, negotiation skills, etc.) that involve the use of English language. If necessary, such courses can integrate local or national languages too, thus promoting multilingual education in higher education and in students' professional development.

References

AASHE. (2010). *Sustainability Curriculum in Higher Education – A Call for Action.* Denver: Association for the Advancement of Sustainability in Higher Education.

Abbass, S. (1993). The power of English in Pakistan. *World Englishes. 12*(2), 147–156.

Abbass, S. (1998). Sociopolitical Dimensions in Language: English in Context in Pakistan. *Applied Language Studies, 23,* 42.

Adzami, N. A., Bidin, S., Ibrahim, S. & K. Jusoff (2009). The Academic English Language Needs of Industrial Design Students in UiTM Kedah, Malaysia. *English Language Teaching, 2,* 171–178.

Allison, D., Corcos, R., & Lam, A. (1994). Laying down the law? Reflecting on course design in progress. *Hong Kong Papers in Linguistics and Language Teaching, 17,* 1–11.

Alred, G. J (2006). Bridging Cultures: The Academy and the Workplace. *Journal of Business Communication, 43,* 79–88.

Anderson, R. S., & Speck, B. W. (1998). 'Oh what a difference a team makes': Why team teaching makes a difference. *Teaching and Teacher Education, 14,* 671–686.

Bacha, N. (2001) Writing evaluation: what can analytic versus holistic essay scoring tell us? *System, 29,* 371–383.

Bacha, N., N., & Bahous, R. (2008). Contrasting views of business students' writing needs in an EFL environment *English for Specific Purposes, 27,* 74–93.

Basturkmen, H. (1999). Discourse in MBA seminars: Towards a description of pedagogical purposes *English for Specific Purposes, 18*(1), 63–80.

Belcher, D. (2006). English for Specific Purposes: Teaching to perceived needs and imagined futures in worlds of work, study and everyday life. *English for specific purposes, 40*(1), 133–156.

Benesch, S. (1996). Needs Analysis and curriculum development in EAP: An Example of a critical approach, *TESOL Quarterly, 30*(4), 723–738.

Benesch, S. (2001a). *Critical English for academic purposes – theory, politics and practices.* New Jersey: Lawrence Erlbaum Associates.

Benesch, S. (2001b). 'Critical pragmatism: A politics of L2 composition'. In T. Silva & P. K. Matsuda (Eds.), *On second language writing* (pp. 161–172). Mahwah, NJ: Lawrence Erlbaum.

Berwick, R. (1989). Needs assessment in language programming: from theory to practice. In Johnson, R. K. (Ed.), *The second language curriculum* (pp.48–62). Cambridge: Cambridge University Press.

Bogert, J., & Butt, D. (1996). Communication instruction in MBA programs: a survey of syllabi. *Business Communication Quarterly, 59,* 20–44.

Brindley, G. (1989). The role of needs analysis in adult ESL program design. In Johnson, R. K. (Ed.), *The second language curriculum* (pp. 63–78). Cambridge: Cambridge University Press.

Brown, J. D. (1995). *The elements of language curriculum: A systematic approach to program development.* Boston: Heinle & Heinle Publishers.

Chambers, F. (1980). A re-evaluation of Needs Analysis in ESP. *The ESP Journal, 1*, 25–33.

Cohen, L., Manion, L. & Morrison, K. (2000). *Research methods in education.* 5th ed. London: Routledge Falmer.

The Dearing Report: Higher Education in the Learning Society, Report of the National Committee of Inquiry into Higher Education, chaired by Sir Ron (now Lord) Dearing, July 23, 1997, House of Lords Papers, 1997–98 (The Stationery Office: Aug. 1997) (collection of reports and recommendations; the central report is 460 pages in print) http://www.leeds.ac.uk/educol/ncihe/

Deutch, Y. (2003). Needs analysis for academic legal English courses in Israel: A model of setting priorities. *Journal of English for Academic Purposes, 2*, 125–146.

Dudley-Evans, T. (1998). An overview of ESP in the 1990s. (EDRS: ED424775).

Dudley-Evans, T., & St. John, M. J. (1998). *Developments in English for Specific Purposes.* Cambridge: Cambridge University Press.

Edwards, N. (2000). Language for business: effective needs assessment, syllabus design and materials preparation in a practical ESP case study. *English for Specific Purposes, 19*, 291–296.

Epstein, M. H. (1999). Teaching field-specific writing: Results of a WAC survey. *Business Communication Quarterly, 62* (1), 29–40.

Eslami, Z. R. (2010). Teachers' Voice vs. Students' Voice: A Needs Analysis Approach to English for Academic Purposes (EAP) in Iran. *English language Teaching, 3*, 3–11.

Evans, S., & Green, C. (2007). Why EAP is necessary: A survey of Hong Kong tertiary students. *Journal of English for Academic Purposes, 6*, 3–17.

Ferris, D., & Tagg T., (1996). Academic Oral Communication Needs of EAP learners: What subject matter instructors actually need. *TESOL Quarterly, 30*(1), 31–58.

Flowerdew, J., & Peacock, M. (Eds.) (2001). *Research perspectives on English for Academic Purposes.* Cambridge: Cambridge University Press.

Flowerdew, J., (2008). Scholarly writers who use English as an Additional Language: What can Goffman's "Stigma" tell us? *Journal of English for Academic Purposes, 7*, 77–86.

Fowler, A., & Gilfillan, M. (2003). A Framework for Stakeholder Integration in Higher Education Information Systems Projects. *Technology Analysis & Strategic Management, 15*(4), 466–488.

Geertz, C. (1973). Thick description: toward an interpretative theory of culture. In C. Geertz *The interpretation of cultures* (pp. 2–32). New York: Basic Books.

Gill, S. K., & Kirkpatrick, A. (2012). English in Asian and European higher education. In C. A. Chapelle (Ed.), *The Encyclopedia of Applied Linguistics*. Oxford: Blackwell Publishing Ltd.

Goby, P. V. (1999). All business students need to know the same thing! The non-culture-specific nature of communication needs. *Journal of Business and Technical Communication, 13*(2), 179–189.

Grinols, A. B., & Waller, R. (2010). Team Teaching: Old Chefs Come Up With New Recipe. *Business Communication Quarterly, 73*, 101–105.

Guffey, M. E. (2004). *Essentials of Business Communication*. 6th ed. USA: Thomson-South Western.

Hamp-Lyons, L. (2001). Fourth generation writing assessment. In T. Silva & P. K. Matsuda (Eds.), *On Second Language Writing* (pp. 117–128). Mahwah, New Jersey: Lawrence Erlbaum Associates.

Haque, A. R. (1993). 'The position and status of English in Pakistan'. In R. Baumgardner (Ed.), *The English language in Pakistan*, (pp. 13–18). Pakistan: Oxford University Press.

Heigham, J., & Crocker, R. A. (Eds.) (2009). *Qualitative research in Applied Linguistics: A practical introduction*. New York & Hampshire: Palgrave Macmillan.

Helmer, A. H. (2013). Critical English for Academic Purposes: Building on learner, Teacher and program strengths. *Journal of English for Academic Purposes, 12*(4), 273–287.

Hochradel, R., Long, J., & C. Johnson. (2010). Team-Teaching: Communication Is the Key When Integrating Graduate Coursework. Business Communication Quarterly *73*, 196–200.

Holmes, R. & Chalauisaeng, B. (2006). The learner as needs analyst: The use of participatory appraisal in the EAP reading classroom. *English for Specific Purposes, 25*, 403–419.

Houghton, D. (1991). Mr Chong: A case study of a dependent learner of English for Academic purposes,. *System, 19*(2), 75–90.

Huerta, T., Ibanez, I., & Kaulen, A. (1986). Balancing Institutional and Motivational Factors in ESP Syllabus Design. *English for Specific Purposes, 5*(2), 189–195.

Hujala, E. (2009). English as a Lingua franca in workplace: one-size-fits-all? – in search of deeper understanding of Finnish speakers of EFL, Unpublished masters thesis, University of Jyväskylä, Department of Languages, Finland.

Hutchinson, T. & Waters, A. (1987). *English for Specific Purposes – A learner-centered approach*. Cambridge: Cambridge University Press.

Hyland, K. (2003). *Second Language Writing*. Cambridge: Cambridge University Press.

Hyland, K. (2007). Genre pedagogy: Language, literacy and L2 writing instruction. *Journal of Second Language Writing, 16*, 148–164.

Jasso-Aquilar, R. (1999). Sources, methods and triangulation in needs analysis: A critical perspective in a case study of Waikiki Hotel Maids. *English for specific purposes*, *19*(1), 27–46.

Jordan, R. R. (1997). *English for academic purposes: a guide and resource book for teachers*. Cambridge, UK and New York, NY: Cambridge University Press.

Kikuchi, K. (2005). Students and teachers perceptions of learning needs: A cross analysis, *Shiken: JALT Testing and evaluation SIG newsletter*, 9, 8–21. Retrieved from http://jalt.org/test/kik_1.htm

Kitwood, T. M. (1977). *Values in adolescent life: towards a critical description*, unpublished PhD dissertation, School of Education, University of Bradford.

Knight, M. (1999). Writing and other communication standards in undergraduate business education: a study of current program requirements, practices and trends. *Business Communication Quarterly, 62*, 10–28.

Laster, N. M., & Russ, T. L. (2010). Looking across the divide: Analyzing cross disciplinary approaches to teaching business communication. *Business and Professional Communication Quarterly, 63*, 248–264.

Leonard, D., & Gilsdorf, J. (1990). Language in change: academics' and executives' perceptions of usage errors. *The Journal of Business Communication, 2*(7), 137–158.

Locker, K. O. (2003). *Business and Administrative Communication* (intl. ed.). USA: McGraw Hill Higher Education.

Long, M. H. (1999). 'Methodological issues in learner needs analysis'. In Long M. H. *Second language needs analysis* (pp. 19–76). Cambridge, England: Cambridge University Press.

Loudermilk, B. C. (2007). Occluded academic genres: An analysis of the MBA Thought Essay. *Journal of English for Academic Purposes, 6*(3), 190–205.

Lytle, S. L. (1988). From the inside out: Reinventing assessment. *"Focus on Basics," 2*(1), 1–4. (EDRS No. ED 300 638).

Malik, F. J. (1996). *The Teaching of English in Pakistan: A Study in Teacher Education*. Lahore: Vanguard Books.

Mansoor, S. (2004). The Medium of Instruction Dilemma: Implications for Language Planning in Higher Education. In S. Mansoor, S. Meraj & A. Tahir (Eds.), *Language Policy, Planning, & Practice – A South Asian Perspective* (pp. 53–78). Oxford: Oxford University Press.

Mansoor, S. (2005). *Language policy and planning at Higher Education level in Pakistan*. Oxford: Oxford University Press.

Mansoor, S. (2009). 'Regional languages of Pakistan: Issues, Concerns for Language Planning in Higher Education'. In S. Mansoor, A. Sikandar, N. Hussain & N. M. Ahsan (Eds.) *Emerging Issues in TEFL – Challenges for Asia* (pp. 31–58). Oxford: Oxford University Press.

Mansur, S. B. (2008). How can 'Needs Analysis' research be used as a means of solving issues in teaching and designing an effective ESP course for MBA students in Pakistan? Unpublished report, School of Education, University of Leeds.

Mansur, S. B. (2010a). Analyzing students' voices: English Language Needs of MBA Students in a Pakistani University, Unpublished research paper.

Mansur, S. B. (2010b). Pakistani University English Teachers: reluctant settlers in ESP-land. *Journal of IATEFL ESP SIG, 36,* 18–36.

Mehboob, A. (2002). "No English, No Future" Language Policy in Pakistan. In S. Obeng, G. & B. Hartford, (Eds.) *Political Independence with Linguistic Servitude: The Politics about Languages in the Developing World* (pp. 15–39). New York: Nova Science Publishers.

Merriam, S. B. (1998). *Qualitative Research and Case Study Applications in Education.* San Francisco: Jossey-Bass.

Miles, M. B., & Huberman, A. M. (1994). *Qualitative Data Analysis.* London: Sage Publishers.

Moore, T., Asay, S. and Curry, B. (2006). Listening to the stakeholders: exploring possibilities for family and community science education in the US. *Journal of Vocational Education & Training, 58*(2), 191–204.

Morgan, B. (2009). Fostering Transformative practitioners for critical EAP: Possibilities and Challenges. *Journal of English for Academic Purposes, 8, 86–99.*

Nishihori, Y. (1994). An investigation of English language education at university level: Questionnaire survey given to 300 senior students of 12 universities. *Language and culture: A publication of Hokkaido University, 25,* 97–137.

Northcott, J. (2001). Towards an ethnography of the MBA classroom: a consideration of the role of interactive lecturing styles within the context of one MBA programme. *English for Specific Purposes, 20*(1), 15–37.

Norton, B., & Toohey, K. (Eds.) (2004). *Critical Pedagogies and Language Learning.* Cambridge: Cambridge University Press.

Ostler, S. E. (1980). A survey of Academic needs for Advanced ESL. *TESOL Quarterly, 14*(4), 489–502.

Pennycook, A. (1994). *The cultural Politics of English as an international language.* London: Longman.

Pennycook, A. (1997). 'Cultural alternatives and autonomy'. In P. Benson & P. Voller. *Autonomy and Independence in Language Learning* (pp. 35–53). Harlow: Longman.

Pennycook, A. (2010). Critical and alternative directions in Applied Linguistics. *Australian Review of Applied Linguistics, 33*(2), 16.1–16.16.

Pilbeam, A. (1979). The language audit. *Language Training, 1,* 4–5.

Plutsky, S. (1996). Faculty perceptions of students' business communication needs. *Business Communication Quarterly, 59*, 69–76.

Pratt, D. (1980). *Curriculum design and development.* New York: Harcourt Brace Jovanovich.

Purpura, J. and Graziano–King, J. (2003). Investigating the Foreign Language Needs of Professional School Students in International Affairs. *Working Papers in TESOL & Applied Linguistics, 4*(1), 1–33.

Read, J. (2008). Identifying academic language needs through diagnostic assessment, *Journal of English for Academic Purposes, 7*, 180–190.

Rehman, T. (2004). English Language Teaching Institutions in Pakistan. In S. Mansoor, S. Meraj & A. Tahir (Eds.), *Language Policy, Planning, & Practice – A South Asian Perspective* (pp. 27–52). Oxford: Oxford University Press.

Rehman, T. (2009). 'Language Policy, Language Death and Vitality in Pakistan'. In S. Mansoor, A. Sikandar, N. Hussain & N. M. Ahsan (Eds.), *Emerging Issues in TEFL – Challenges for Asia* (pp. 3–30). Oxford: Oxford University Press.

Reinsch, N., & Shelby, A. (1997). What communication abilities do practitioners need? Evidence from MBA students. *Business Communication Quarterly, 60*, 7–29.

Richards, J. (2001). Curriculum Development in language teaching. Cambridge: Cambridge University Press.

Robinson, P. (1991). *ESP Today: A practitioner's guide.* UK: Prentice Hall international.

Salas, S., Mercado, L. A., Ouedraogo, L. H., & Musetti, B. (2013). English for Specific Purposes: Negotiating Needs, Possibilities and Promises. *English Teaching Forum, 51*(4), 12–19.

Santopietro, K. & Peyton, J. K. (1991). Assessing the literacy needs of adult learners of ESL. ERIC Digest (ERIC Identifier: ED34871) Retrieved from: http://files.eric.ed.gov/fulltext/ED334871.pdf

Savingson, S. J. & Wang, C. (2003). Communicative Language Teaching in EFL Contexts: Learner attitudes and perceptions. International Review of Applied Linguistics in Language Teaching, *41*(3), 223–249.

Seshadri, S., & Theye, L. (2000). Professionals and professors: substance or style? *Business Communication Quarterly, 63*, 9–23.

Shamim, F. (2006). English as a language for development in Pakistan: Issues, challenges and possible solutions. In H. Coleman (Eds.), *Proceedings of the International Language and Development Conference, Language and Development: Africa and Beyond* (pp. 76–90). Ethiopia: The British Council.

Shamim, F. (2008). Trends, Issues and Challenges language education in Pakistan. *Asia Pacific Education Journal, 28*(3), 235–249.

Shamim, F., & Tribble, C. (2005). *Current Provisions for English Language Teaching in Higher Education in Pakistan.* Report Submitted to National Committee on English, Higher Education Commission, Islamabad, Pakistan.

Shamim, F., Khurram, B., Shahabuddin, F., & Usmani, W. (2006). *Case Studies of Organization of Teaching of English in Public Sector Universities in Pakistan.* Report submitted to National Committee on English, Higher Education Commission: Islamabad, Pakistan.

Siddiqui, S. (2012). Education, Inequalities and Freedom – a Sociopolitical Critique. Pakistan & USA: Narrative Publications.

Stevens, B. (2004). How satisfied are employers with graduate's business communication skills? A survey of Silicon Valley employers. Retrieved from http://www.westga.edu/~bquest/2004/graduates.htm

Stevens, B. (2005). What communication skills do employers want? Silicon Valley recruiters respond. *Journal of Employment Counseling, 42*(1), 2–9.

Strevens, P. (1977). *New orientations in the teaching of English.* Oxford: Oxford University Press.

Swales, J. M., Barks, D., Ostermann, A. C., & Simpson, R. C. (2001). Between critique and accommodation: reflections on an EAP course of Masters of Architecture students. *English for Specific Purposes, 20,* 439–458.

Tajino, A., James, R., & Kijima, K. (2005). Beyond needs analysis: soft systems methodology for meaningful collaboration in EAP course design. *Journal of English for Academic Purposes, 4,* 27–42.

Uzuner, S. (2008). Multilingual scholars' participation in core/global academic communities: A literature review. *Journal of English for Academic Purposes, 7,* 250–263.

West, R. (1994). Needs analysis in language teaching. *Language Teaching, 27*(1), 1–19.

Yarrow, D. & Robson, A. (2004), Organizational excellence: Do your stakeholders agree?, *Total Quality Management and Business Excellence, 15*(5–6), 869–878. ISSN 1478–3363

Zafar, M. (2003). The Management of teacher change in ESP programmes in Pakistan. Centre of English Language Teacher Education, Warwick University. Unpublished Masters dissertation.

Zafar, M. (2009). 'English language teaching at tertiary level in Pakistan: A case for English for specific purposes'. In N. Hussain, A. Ahmed & M. Zafar. (Eds.)., *English and empowerment in the developing world* (pp. 151–164). Cambridge: Cambridge Scholars Publishing.

Zhu, W. (2004). Faculty views on the importance of writing, the nature of academic writing and teaching and responding to writing in the disciplines. *Journal of Second Language Writing, 13,* 29–48.

Report of the National Committee of Inquiry into the Higher Education 1997.

The needs of new EAP learners: Content and language integrated learning (CLIL) teachers

María Ángeles Martín del Pozo, Universidad de Valladolid, Spain
Email: maryange@dlyl.uva.es

1 Introduction

In non-English-speaking countries like Spain, ESP and EAP have thus far mainly targeted preparation to study abroad or for international research activities. Current trends such as the internationalisation of universities and the subsequent practice of English Medium Instruction (EMI) are creating new circumstances for ESP/EAP. EMI demands new competences in higher education staff, who, in most cases of this unprecedented scenario in non-English-speaking countries, are themselves non-native speakers of English.

Due to the lack of double focus of language and content, the term EMI is preferred at higher education, while CLIL (Content and Language Integrated Learning) is used regardless of the educational level. All through this chapter EMI will be used only for tertiary education and CLIL for the other levels of education or for general comments on this approach. The divergence between CLIL and EMI regarding language focus is thus summarised:

> There is an area where CLIL and EMI diverge from each other; this is the attention that each of them pays to language learning. While CLIL is a dual focused process, aiming to overtly develop both language and content knowledge, EMI focuses mainly on subject learning and exploits the language of instruction as a mere neutral tool to perform that goal. (Francomacaro, 2011, p.34)

So far the linguistic competence of EMI lecturers has been described in terms of the Common European Framework of Reference (CEFR), a scale which has proven to serve for homogeneity in the description of general language competences in Europe. This chapter suggests that, in the specific context of EMI, the debate would be more productive if attention focused on the type of language required for successful EMI rather than concentrating on language qualifications. The analysis of the data tries to shed light on two questions: the role of ESP/EAP in EMI contexts and the contribution of ESP and EAP to make EMI practices more effective and efficient.

In addition, as Hyland warns 'many EAP courses still lack a theoretical or research rationale and textbooks too often continue to depend on the writer's experience and intuition rather than on systematic research' (2006, p. 5). The study reported here attempts to contribute to research-based identification of the linguistic needs. Consequently, there will be a contribution to the training of EMI/CLIL teachers. The innovation lies in approaching the EMI lecturers as a new type of EAP learners.

2 Literature review

2.1 Content and language integrated learning and English-medium instruction at university

The use of a foreign language as a medium of instruction at European universities dates from the Middle Ages with Latin as a lingua franca for teaching and publishing. Coleman (2006) identifies two new elements in this practice at the end of the 20th century: English as the chosen language and the reasons and forces that drive universities into the use of this language. These reasons can be classified into seven categories: CLIL, internationalisation, student exchange, research and teaching materials, staff mobility, graduate employability and the market of international students. In addition, the adaptation to the *European Space of Higher Education* (ESHE) (Bologna Declaration, 1999) has accelerated the expansion and turned EMI from an added value to a must at third-level institutions in countries where English is not the first language. Nevertheless 'foreign language learning in itself is NOT the reason why institutions adopt English medium teaching' (Coleman, 2006, p. 4). This emphasis has important implications. The main one is that language objectives are not explicit, either at corporate level or at individual level. Institutional documentation does not specify what English language has to or can be learnt in the English medium taught subjects, nor do the syllabi of the different subjects make reference to expected linguistic gains. In spite of this, the common belief and expectation that some English language will be learnt along with the specialised contents of the subjects is spread among those involved (lecturers and students). This is the case for the contexts investigated in other studies and for most of the EMI environments (Marsh & Laitinanen, 2005; Dalton-Puffer, 2007; Dafouz, 2011, Francomacaro, 2011; Doiz, Lasagabaster & Sierra, 2012).

However, with the exception of some studies in the Canadian context (Lyster, 2007) far too little attention has been paid to what variables can contribute to compensate for the lack of explicit language learning objectives and counteract the drawbacks of naturalistic learning conditions. As Dalton-Puffer (2007) had emphasised, the CLIL classroom has potential for learning the academic language, a language domain which is unlikely to be found and as a result learnt in other contexts. Therefore an important variable to contribute to the successful learning of academic language is the quantity and quality of academic language spoken in the classrooms. In the case of lectures, a prominently monologic event (Young, 1994), the language comes from the lecturer's discourse. Any contribution to make this discourse more academic means enriching the input to which students are exposed to and consequently increasing the potential of (incidentally) learning academic language. The objectives of my research are to determine what ESP/EAP issues can be addressed in training lecturers for EMI.

In the middle of these new bilingual scenarios, CLIL teacher training is a significant issue which concerns both CLIL theorists and practitioners and remains unsolved. Abundant evidence of this need can be found in the literature (Dafouz, 2008; Lasagabaster & Ruiz de Zarobe, 2010; Doiz et al., 2012; Ball & Lindsay, 2012 and Martín del Pozo, 2013 *inter alia*).

Additionally official documentation has pointed at this need from the beginning of this practice in Europe (CLIL Cascade Network Think Tank Report, 2010; Eurydice Report 2006, 2012) as well as other less official sources (websites, expert forums, special interest research groups). This issue is also considered a key factor for CLIL implementation and success. As Coyle, Hood and Marsh state 'the key to future capacity building and sustainability is teacher education' (2010, p. 161). Debate continues about the required competences for CLIL teachers. There is agreement in two main dimensions of education needed to teach in and through a second language: linguistic education and methodological education. As regards the first dimension, one of the most significant current discussions is language competence level for CLIL/EMI practitioners (Dafouz, 2008; Lasagabaster & Ruiz de Zarobe, 2010; Doiz et al., 2012; Ball & Lindsay, 2012; Martín del Pozo, 2013). As language is a key aspect of CLIL/EMI, the next section reflects on the different types of language converging in the CLIL event. The consideration of these language types could, in my view, be more productive than discussing the competence level as CEFR does.

2.2 ESP/EAP in CLIL/EMI language models

A growing interest and attention to the use of language in CLIL has generated several theoretical models which endeavour to define the role of language in CLIL. This section discusses three of these models by virtue of the prominent position of ESP and EAP in them. These models are: the Language Triptych (Coyle et al., 2010); the Languages for CLIL (L4Cs) model (Gierlinger, 2013) and the distinction between Basic Interpersonal Communicative Skills (BICS) and Cognitive Academic Language Proficiency (CALP) (Cummins, 1984).

The presence of ESP/ EAP in these models is specified in the table below.

Table 1: ESP/EAP in CLIL language models

Language Triptych	Language OF learning	ESP
	Language FOR learning	EAP
Languages for CLIL	Domain-specific language	ESP
	Classroom language	BICS
	Academic language	EAP
	General language	BICS

Model 1: The Language Triptych (Coyle et al., 2010)

This model comes from an educational framework and aims to provide teachers with 1) a means to analyse the linguistic needs in CLIL contexts and 2) a tool to differentiate the linguistic demands in CLIL. The model offers three perspectives of language (Coyle et al. 2010, pp. 34–37):

1. *Language of learning*: language needed to access the basic concepts and skills of a topic. There is a growing interest in researching genres from a systemic functional grammar point of view. This has important pedagogical implications, as the teacher has to turn from a linguistic progression based on grammatical structures to one based on functional and notional aspects.

2. *Language for learning*: language required to operate in an academic context that will enable students to learn in a second language. Academic functions (describe, explain, contrast, define etc) are language for learning because they provide speech acts related to content. According to Coyle *et al.* (2010), this type of language is the most crucial.

3. *Language through learning*: there cannot be effective learning if there is not an active relation between language and thought. It is the use of language to refer to new acquired meanings.

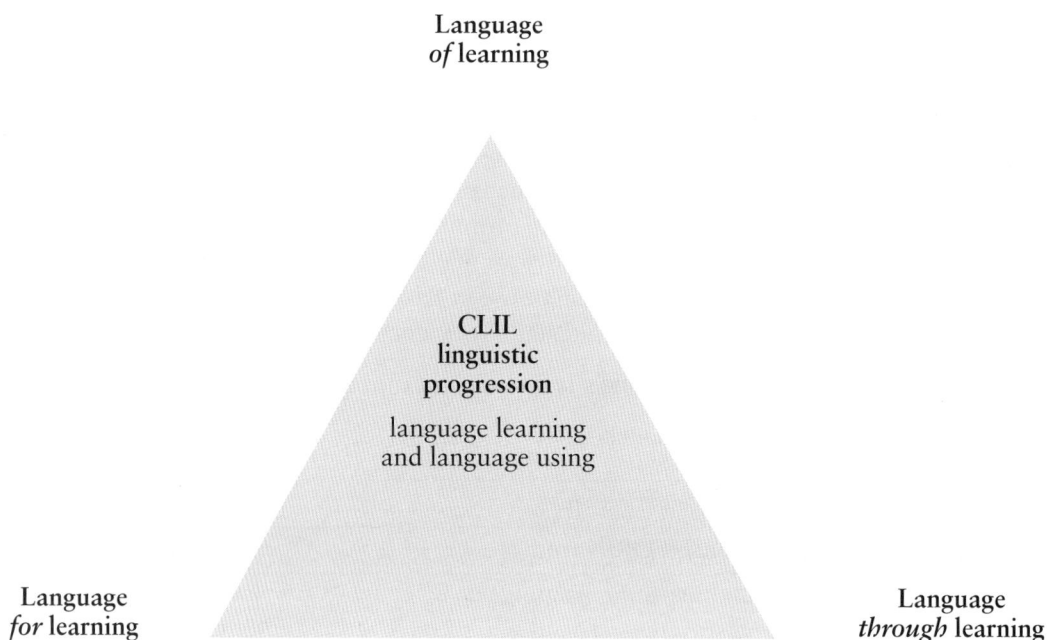

Language
of learning

CLIL
linguistic
progression

language learning
and language using

Language
for learning

Language
through learning

Figure 1: The Language Triptych (Coyle *et al.*, 2010, p. 34)

Model 2: Languages for CLIL (L4Cs) model (Gierlinger, 2013).

Competences indicated by CEFR are not useful to categorise the types of language that CLIL teachers should master. This model fills this gap. Languages for CLIL (Gierlinger, 2013) aims to aid teachers to identify their linguistic training needs.

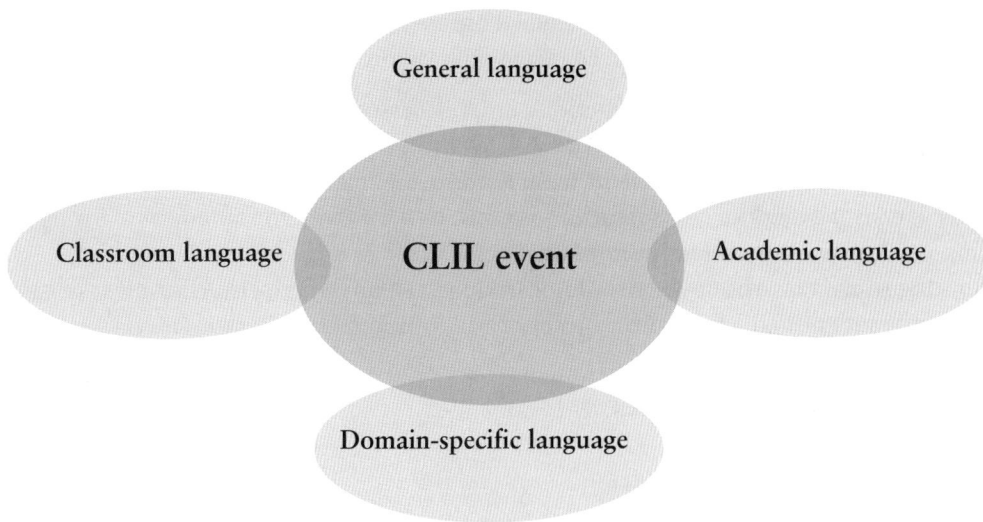

Figure 2: The Languages for CLIL model (Gierlinger, 2013)

Model 3: Basic Interpersonal Communicative Skills (BICS) and Cognitive Academic Language Proficiency (CALP) (Cummins, 1984).

More than a model of languages in CLIL, the distinction BICS/CALP refers to the linguistic competences that have to be developed for successful teaching/learning in bilingual contexts. This dichotomy is considered one of the most valuable legacies of research results in Canadian immersion programmes (Cummins, 1984). The pedagogical implications of differentiating between language use in academic context and language used in conversational contexts has shed light on what language competences should be targeted by language teaching.

A third important concept in this model is Common Underlying Proficiency (CUP). It explains how first language supports the learning of a second or third language. I highlight the relevance of this concept when differentiating the teaching of ESP/EAP to undergraduate students and to lecturers or researchers. The already developed CALP of the latter in their native language will support the development of CALP in English.

CALP, the competence required for successful achievement of academic goals, includes knowledge and skills from ESP and EAP. The next section discusses relations between CALP development and ESP/EAP.

2.3 Need for reorientation of CLIL/EMI along ESP/EAP principles

In her groundbreaking study, Dalton-Puffer (2007) analysed 40 CLIL lessons in Austrian secondary schools. Regarding the use of academic language in these lessons, findings revealed the following about definitions, explanations and hypothesis expression:

1. Very low number of occurrences of these functions in both teacher and student discourses.

2. Poor or mediocre form and linguistic signalling of these functions.

Dalton-Puffer concludes: 'the CLIL classrooms studied cannot be said to represent an environment that is conducive to the learning of academic language skills of this kind.' (2007, p. 170)

This first systematic study of academic functions in CLIL lessons highlighted the need for a 'reorientation of CLIL along the principles of EAP' (Dalton-Puffer, 2007, p. 296). That is to say that CLIL/EMI pedagogy would benefit from a more explicit attention to EAP. By this Dalton-Puffer means leaving the consideration of CLIL as a panacea for language learning and situating it in the position it really should have: CLIL as an approach to learn the language specific to the classroom which cannot be acquired anywhere else. The most urgent linguistic objectives identified are (Dalton-Puffer, 2007, pp. 297–299):

- Identify skills and academic functions needed

- Implement them systematically

- Develop discipline specific vocabulary

- Develop academic general vocabulary

Her suggestion is to orientate these objectives towards what is specific in the classroom and, as her findings reveal, is not being fully exploited: *academic language skills necessary for knowledge acquisition*. This proposition has the potential to join cognition and language and connects with the previous idea of Swales (1990) *Writing across the curriculum* for native speakers and EAP as the equivalent for non-native speakers.

The research to date has tended to focus on the product in CLIL/EMI instruction (language learning gains) rather than in the process of teaching and learning. Considering the elements in the process could provide valuable insights for the objectives listed above. The empirical study reported on in the rest of this chapter endeavours to identify the linguistic requirements related to the first objective of identifying skills and academic functions needed.

3 Context description

'Spain is rapidly becoming one of the European leaders in CLIL practice and research.' (Lasagabaster & Ruiz de Zarobe, 2010, p. ix). Regional education authorities are endorsing plurilingual policies mainly at secondary level. In contrast, Spanish universities follow the trends and present the features gathered in the ENLU (European Network for Language Learning Amongst Undergraduates) Report about English as the medium of instruction in European Higher Education (Marsh & Laitinanen, 2005). The reasons for this implementation are those already listed at the beginning of this chapter and identified by Coleman (2006): internationalisation, student exchange, research and teaching materials, staff mobility, graduate employability and the market of international students.

The data for my study were collected at Escuela Universitaria de Informática (Universidad de Valladolid, Campus Segovia, Spain) where teaching through English has been an optional practice since 2006. In this context 'The shift towards L2 medium education in English does not correlate with the introduction of CLIL' (Marsh & Laitinanen, 2005, p. 2). This means, as already said, there are not explicit language objectives neither at institutional nor at individual level at the university. Nonetheless, it is expected that students' linguistic competence will benefit from the bilingual programme *Ingeniero técnico de informática de gestión*.

The researcher's connection with the Escuela Universitaria de Informática dates from 2003, when she taught English for computing for one academic year. In 2006, when the institution was about to start this programme, she was asked for some advice due to her research interest in ESP and EAP. During the first two years of the programme, she provided some training to the lecturers involved, mainly conversation and academic English lessons. This teaching was based on experience and intuition. The systematic approach to the lecturers' discourses reported in this chapter means that future teaching could be based on empirical research evidence.

The subjects taught through English at Escuela de Informática range from Economics, Operating Systems, Software Engineering, Maths, Physics, Information Systems, Programming and other related knowledge areas. The attitudes and perceptions of students and lecturers for the first two years of the experience were reported in Martin del Pozo (2008) along with some narratives of lecturers' difficulties, strategies and achievements.

4 Data collection and methodologies employed

To ensure the validity of the sample, the subjects were selected on the basis of gender, subject and more than two years' experience of teaching through English. Six lecturers were videotaped during the delivery of a sample lecture. The transcriptions of the verbal language formed the corpus. Relevant features of this corpus are specified in the table:

Table 2: Corpus description

Lecturer	Topic	Recording time (minutes)	Number of words	EMI experience (years)
Lecturer 1	Processes in operating system	31	2,580	2
Lecturer 2	Information representation in quantum arithmetic	27	2,140	5
Lecturer 3	Consumer preferences	40	3,300	3
Lecturer 4	Graph theory	51	2,650	5
Lecturer 5	Basic concepts of mathematics	22	2,273	4
Lecturer 6	Gauss's Theorem and applications	36	3,470	4
Total	Number of lectures: 6	207 minutes	16,413 words	

These data could be approached from different perspectives and used to investigate numerous research questions. The present focus of this chapter is on how the six lecturers used the academic functions of definition, explanation and expression of hypotheses. This observation is expected to provide insights about their linguistic strengths and weaknesses in an academic environment. That is to say this will provide an approximation of their CALP by considering the quantity and quality of these academic language functions in their discourse. To accomplish this aim, three specific research questions will be answered individually for each one of the three mentioned academic language functions (following Dalton-Puffer's questions for the secondary context):

1. How many occurrences of these academic functions are there in the corpus?

2. What is the linguistic form of these academic functions?

3. Is there any signalling language or metalanguage around them?

Therefore, this research combines quantitative and qualitative modes. To answer the first question, the opening move in the research process was to identify what constitutes a definition, an explanation and an expression of hypothesis. Once these functions were identified, the analysis of each one of them was undertaken following different taxonomies. The reasons why the taxonomies were adopted are given in the following paragraphs and Table 3 illustrates the categories of the taxonomies with samples from the corpus.

Flowerdew's (1992) classification was chosen for the study of the definitions, because it comprehends and expands Trimble's (1985) solid taxonomy (formal, semi-formal, non-formal definitions). Flowerdew (1992) considers that in spite of the specific features of orality (false starts, doubts, repetition and reparations) oral definitions could reach the level of precision of the written ones, described in Trimble's (1985) previously proposed taxonomy.

It was decided that the best taxonomy to adopt for the function of explanation was one also coming from a functional perspective rather than based on semantic relationships. Brown (2006) classifies the explanations used in dyadic situations (communicative situations with two main interlocutors such as in education and health science) in three categories according to their intention:

1. Interpretative explanations respond to the question 'What?' and are very close to definitions.

2. Descriptive explanations respond to the question 'How?' and centre on processes, structures and procedure.

3. Reason giving explanations respond to the question 'Why?' and provide reasons and causes.

For the expression of hypothesis, the chosen taxonomy was the traditional classification of conditionals according to the criteria of reality and possibility of the 'if'-clause: real, possible and impossible. The main reason for this option was the difference in the complexity of the syntactic structures required for each of the three different types. The analysis grid developed from these taxonomies and some examples found in the corpus are summarized in Table 3.

Table 3: Taxonomies and examples

Academic function of definition			
Type	Example	Metalanguage/form	Total
Formal	The heap is the memory segment of a process which allocates dynamic variables.		
Semi-formal	The process scheduling us how the operating system organize the execution of different processes in the system The data structure which represents this abstract data type is <u>known as</u> Process Control Block	*known as*	
Non-formal	The <u>basic definition</u> of a process is only a program in execution, There are several <u>terms</u> to <u>refer to</u> Processes for example, in Batch systems the programs are <u>named as</u> jobs.	basic definition *terms* *refer to* *named as*	
Ostensive			

Semi-formal definitions are characterised by the absence of a hyperonym, because it is either obvious or irrelevant in the context. Some samples from the corpus include:

3. The set of indifference curve is called indifference map. (L3 m38)

4. Graphs informally are sets of nodes also called vertexes and lines joining this nodes, usually called edges. (L4 m2)

5. we can say that an indifference curve is a … represents the locus of points representing various combinations of commodities that provide a consumer with the same level of satisfaction (L3 m19)

Flowerdew (1992) refers to non-formal definitions as substitution (synonym, paraphrasing). The boundary between this type and explanations is fuzzy and some of the examples could fit in both categories. As can be seen from Graph 3, the non-formal category varies the most across lecturers, as this mechanism recurs in some lectures abundantly while others opt for the other types of definition. An example of substitution:

6. The number of **nodes** is called the number of **vertices.** We write it like that #, the number of vertices is called, order of the graph.

In contrast to Dalton-Puffer's (2007) findings, valuable metalanguage accompanying definitions and linguistic signalling can be found in my corpus: *called, (basic) notion, known as, named as, we can say, means we talk about defined* and *definition*:

7. **By definition** the absolute value of a number is the number itself if the number is positive or zero. And in case the number is negative its absolute value is minus the number. (L5 m16)

8. The **basic definition** of a process is only a programme in execution, OK? (L1 m16)

5.2 Academic function of explanation

The academic function of explanation was the most difficult to identify as it lacks the structural and functional regularity of the other two functions investigated: 'explanation is pervasive rather than identifiable at particular points in the interaction' (Dalton-Puffer, 2007, p. 152). The distribution of this function and the different subcategories (Graph 4) suggest that the frequency and the type of explanations could be very much dependent on discipline or/and topic of the lectures. For example, the topic chosen by Lecturer 4, consumer behaviour, demanded reason-giving explanations. On the contrary, the Operating Systems lecture (L1) focused on interpretative explanations. Both Mathematics lecturers (4 and 5) present a very similar frequency of the three types of explanations.

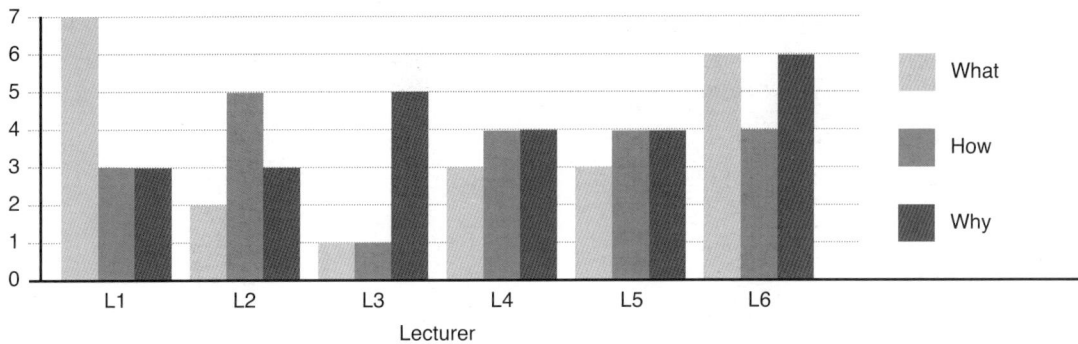

Graph 4: Frequency and the type of explanations

Explanations that provide information complement definitions. Therefore they are physically close to definitions:

9. DEFINITION The flux being the amount of water getting through this whole in a particular amount of time. 'WHAT' EXPLANATION So the flux also depends on sometime of angle. It is not the same if it falls perpendicularly to the surface or not (L6 m4)

'What' explanations are functionally very close to descriptions. Hence, any explicit work on any of these two functions may benefit linguistic competence for both.

'How' explanations refer mainly to processes and procedures. In the specialised language of Mathematics this may include the presentation of formulas and theorems:

10. Euler's theorem … there is a <u>method</u> that consists of the following. <u>Initially</u> we take a point, a vertex, V1 and <u>then</u> you have G and you have to construct C as ??? a how to try C you start with a point and then you consider. You start from H and then while H has edges you have to find a cycle in H incident in a vertex of C (L4 m44)

11. to multiply, to, to multiply two powers with the same base, **you** keep the base and **you** just add the exponents. To divide them **you** keep the base and **you** subtract the exponents and this way (L5 m4)

The two previous examples (10 and 11) show some of the most relevant linguistic features of explanations found in the current data. Firstly, inclusive personal pronouns (*we, our*) or pronouns to address the receptor (*you, your*) are widely used while impersonal forms are scarce. For example, there are only two occurrences of passive structures in the corpus.

A second frequent feature of explanations is the presence of elements to establish an order such as sequencers and elements referring to the different parts of a process. The use of *then* is recurrent and repetitive, as well as the noun *way* to refer to methods, routines, procedures and techniques. This will be reconsidered under pedagogical implications.

An example of good practice is example (12). The lecturer enriches the process explanation with sequencers and verbs indicating sequence such as *start, continue, terminate* and *end*

12. You **start** writing 1 and then 1 and 1 on the second line and the third line you have 1 at the beginning, 1 at the end and in the middle you have the sum of these two numbers. And you **continue** in this way. (p.5 m11)

'Why' explanations were easily identified due to the repetitive use of *because* as the main conjunction to express causal relationships presented in the discourse of the six lecturers investigated.

13. Not possible, **because** if I take 4 I must give you 4. If I take 2 is impossible that I must give you 10. (L3 m17)

14. **Because** these numbers are very easy to see, **because** you just focus on a particular vertex. You can sum all edges, 8+ 10+ 18 and then the sum of the degrees is the double of the number of vertices, there should be 18 vertices. (L4 m22)

This high frequency is due to its simplicity and its repetitive presence in non-formal registers. Orality favours the production of this nexus although lecturers could have other linguistic options in their passive vocabulary which they would probably choose in written communication.

The expression of consequences, a type of explanation directly connected to causality, show some occurrences in my corpus, introduced by *as a consequence of* and combined with process explanations:

15. As consequence of the execution of a process, a process comes before and input/output operation for example, ok? Then until this operation will be performed the process has not continue its execution and then pass to this state, the waiting state. (L1 m9)

Performative lexemes such as *explanation* and *explain* are also found (samples 16 and 17). The benefits of this metalanguage for student comprehension are again highlighted.

16. We are now trying **to explain** the central part of the subject, of this Euler Circuits. So let's start with some history. Graph theory began in history when Euler was asked to solve the so called Konigsberg Seven bridge Problem. (L4 m24)

17. And as you have heard we have mentioned another concept the we need to **explain** first. (L6 m2)

5.3 Academic function of hypothesis expression

Graph 5 illustrates the distribution of occurrences of hypothesis expression. In spite of its scarcity, it outpaces the frequency found in Dalton-Puffer's (2007) data, in which the arithmetic media was below one hypothesis per class and in this study it is above five per class. Nonetheless, this function is concentrated mainly in the third lecture and a further analysis of the linguistic form of this formulation reveals repetition, lack of stylistic variety and of syntactic complexity. *Suppose*, *imagine* and *if* + real conditional are the most widely and repetitively used forms in the data. Semantically, many of these sentences could be considered just conditionals and not hypotheses in the sense of leaving reality to suggest possibility or impossibility. In fact, only two unreal conditionals and none of the impossible are found (see Table 3 for examples). Both types demand complex syntactic structures and cognitive abstraction.

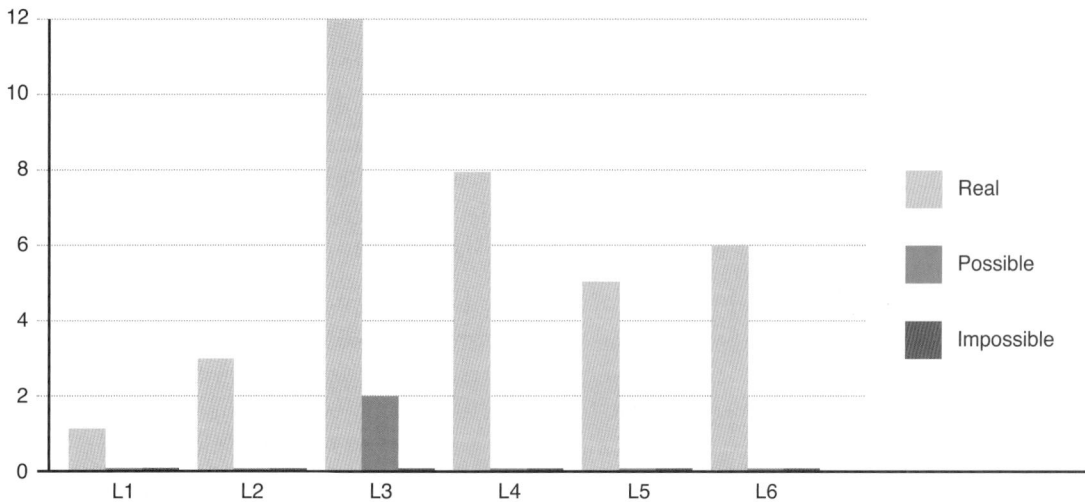

Graph 5: Distribution of hypothesis expression

This study supports Dalton-Puffer's (2007) conclusion about the causes behind this low frequency: not only the demand of complex language for the formal expression of these functions but mainly the fact that the investigated lectures seem to focus on information transmission and not in reasons, opinions or beliefs, cognitive activities which may have required the use of hypothetical expressions. This absence could indicate that facts (present or past) are at the centre of the class to the detriment of other cognitive activities.

Stylistically, the forms found for the real hypothesis mainly recur in the use of lexemes which express reality within a lesser possibility such as *suppose, imagine*:

18. **Imagine that** I am a soldier. I have to do a tour and then I have to survey all the bridges. (L4 m 26) **Let us suppose** that a consumer is able of ordering bundles of commodities according to the value this consumer gets from them. And **let's suppose** we have two market baskets. (L3 m4)

5.4 Answers to research questions

Together these results provide important insights into the features of Spanish lecturers using English to teach content subjects. In addition, the findings answer the research questions. Regarding the first one, the frequency of academic functions in the corpus, the discourse of the investigated lecturers shows a more favorable number of occurrences than Dalton-Puffer's (2007) data. This finding supports the recommendation of 'reconsidering the value of teacher monologue (in well-considered dosage), both in the interest of presenting coherent conceptual networks of topic content and in the interest of providing sustained, syntactically complex oral input' (Dalton-Puffer, 2007, p. 296). This higher frequency in a lesser amount of data maybe attributed to the monologic structure of these lectures in contrast to the Initiation–Response–Follow structure of the Austrian lessons. Samples of these academic functions were also found in the written materials (PowerPoint, notes) used by these lecturers. This means greater potential contact of students with the academic functions, another deficiency of sessions and materials observed by Dalton-Puffer (2007).

This researcher condemned the scarcity of the academic functions in the bilingual class because this entails a loss of learning opportunities. In our context, chances for learning may be reduced due to the lack of language awareness by lecturers. It is suggested that increasing the awareness of content lecturers would improve their discursive skills and facilitate students' comprehension and learning.

The second question, the linguistic form of these academic functions, reveals another feature of them in my corpus: a repetitive minimal use of formal complexity or variety. This was predominantly observed in the expression of hypothesis. Regarding the third research question, linguistic signalling of academic functions, a selection of metalanguage was found (such as *define*, *explain*). This quantity is significant when contrasted to Dalton-Puffer (2007), but it is far from reaching the amount of what could be considered a valuable catalyst for communication and learning.

In summary, the lecturers' teaching experience and discipline expertise give them self-assurance and this may be how they transfer all their linguistic strategies from Spanish to lecturing in English, that is to say transfer, their CALP from L1 to L2. The problem seems to be related to the ability to use a minor linguistic variety of academic English. Repetitions, calques (that is, word for word translations) and lesser precision are some of the consequences of this lack of stylistic choice. These observations of the present study match those found in previous investigations which contrasted lecturers in Spanish and English (Dafouz, 2006; Dafouz & Núñez, 2010; Dafouz, 2011).

The frequency and form of the academic functions could be affected by two groups of factors:

1. The topic and discipline of the investigated lecture, as Bhatia (2002) forewarned about disciplinary variation for academic genres in general.

2. The personal distinctive use of language and teaching style of each one of the lecturers.

The presentation of results is concluded by recalling one of the main advantages of corpus-based research: 'We can claim with some confidence that showing what does not occur, negative evidence if you wish, is one of the great benefits of a corpora approach, especially when we consider the pedagogical implications of these dispreferences' (Swales & Malczewski, 2001: 161). Having pointed out that 'what does not occur' provides dimensions of EMI lecturers' language competence which require reinforcement, the next section deals in depth with this issue.

6 Pedagogical implications

The pedagogical implications derived from the findings could be grouped into two categories:

1. linguistic needs regarding the particular investigated elements, that is the academic functions,

2. a more general category which comprehends linguistic needs derived from global features of lecturer discourse.

6.1 Linguistic needs regarding academic functions

The examination of the academic function of definition in the corpus denotes the need to train lecturers in the formulation of the different types and to provide linguistic resources to enable them. By teaching lecturers *to define*, their awareness of the importance of this function will increase. This can potentially benefit the production of well-formed definitions by their students. A further aim is to avoid the loss of linguistic and cognitive opportunities that occurs when, as Dalton-Puffer (2007) lamented, teachers use translations, synonyms or paraphrasing which prevents students from gaining exposure to canonical definition or from producing definitions themselves. In agreement with Dalton-Puffer I defend that 'thinking explicitly about definitions would deepen students' understanding and enrich the semantic representation of central concepts of the subjects they are studying, thus making an important contribution to subject matter learning' (2007, p. 138).

Explanations point towards the convenience of including impersonal forms to achieve formal register. This aspect will be further commented on in the conclusion. The data show a repetitive and exclusive use of *because* in giving reasons for explanations. Therefore, another need is to enhance stylistic variety to express causality. The same applies to conjunctions in process explanations. In this case, *then* and the signalling noun *way* were the most repeated options.

Finally, hypothesis expression could considerably improve if lecturers exploited more complex syntactic structures. Awareness of the importance of this function is another factor that would affect its frequency and usage.

The presentation of results and the discussion of pedagogical implications highlights the need for explicit teaching of these academic functions not only as second language tools but as tools to reorganise the process of teaching and learning (language for learning in the Language Triptych model). This knowledge would facilitate the production of academic functions and would have a positive effect on lecturers' first language CALP.

6.2 General linguistic needs

In the data analysed, the prevalence of personal forms (that is the use of pronouns *we* and *you*) over the impersonal ones (such as passives) on the one hand, and the use of inclusive forms (*we, us, our*) and pronouns to address the receiver (*you, your*) on the other, give the lecturers an interactional style. Therefore, it could be concluded that the lack of linguistic tools (impersonal structures, for example) has a positive consequence: a movement towards the receiver. In spite of this positive achievement, in the highly specialised academic context of lectures, the use of impersonal forms could be essential for reaching a formal register. The pedagogical implication is obvious. Lecturers need the language required for that formal register. Very possibly, lecturers have knowledge of these impersonal structures such as passive forms and are able to understand them in both written and oral communication. The pedagogical intervention should target the transfer of this skill from the lecturers' passive knowledge to active knowledge and raise lecturers' awareness about their prominent role in the attainment of formal and academic register.

It can be argued that teaching content lecturers the language needed for EMI could have a very positive effect on their first language CALP. One of the specific benefits would be awareness of the elements that create a formal register. Thus EMI could improve one's own teaching practice in first language. This can also be sustained from the theoretical model of Common Underlying Proficiency for two languages (Cummins, 1984) already explained.

The next table summarises the findings and their pedagogical implications. The discursive features found in the data are presented in the first column. The implications derived from them are listed in the second.

Table 4: Summary of findings and their pedagogical implications

Features of the six Spanish EMI lecturers investigated	Linguistic needs/pedagogical implication
Abundance of inclusive forms (*we, our,* very low frequency of impersonal forms)	1. Reinforce the production of impersonal structures
Examples of good discursive teaching and communicative practices	2. Awareness of good practices, linguistic tools to strengthen them
Academic function of definition	3. Awareness of the different types 4. Awareness of the facilitator role of metalanguage and of hyperonyms 5. Stylistic variety
Academic function of explanation	6. Awareness of the facilitator role of metalanguage 7. Stylistics variety of nexus and signalling roles
Academic functions of hypothesis expression	8. Awareness of importance 9. Complex structures

7 Conclusion

The internationalisation of universities in non-English-speaking countries has created a need to attract foreign students. This can only be achieved if a lingua franca is used for communication. European universities are thus moving towards EMI. This practice is content based though all involved have the expectation that some English will be learnt along with the content. For this reason, EMI lecturers' discourse needs to be enriched. The study reported in this chapter has tried to shed light on two questions: the role of ESP/EAP in CLIL/EMI contexts and the contribution of ESP and EAP to make CLIL/EMI practices more effective and efficient.

The learning needs and the pedagogical implications derived from the discussion of the results could be summarised in two main points:

1. The new type of EAP learners (the CLIL/EMI lecturers) possess CALP in their native language, as expected in a content expert. This competence could and should be further exploited for lecturing in English, a practice that demands CALP in that language. The Common Underlying Proficiency model sustains this possibility. In addition, the results of this research support the idea that the development of CALP in English using the already developed CALP in the native language could potentially benefit lecturers more than attention to general language skills.

2. These EAP learners can autonomously enhance their competence if provided with two instruments: awareness of academic functions and linguistic tools for the expression of these functions in English. Providing autonomy to the lecturers entails not only the linguistic tools for successful communication in certain situations, but mainly the competence to transfer this knowledge and develop new skills.

As noted previously, some of the important decisions related to EAP programme design are often based on experience rather than on any systematic research. This needs analysis was based on research questions. The pedagogical implications presented here emanate from a very specific context but match those found in other similar ones (Dafouz, 2006; 2008; 2011; Dalton-Puffer, 2007; Dafouz & Nuñez 2010).

The findings indicate ESP/EAP elements that should be included in a training course for prospective or in-service EMI lecturers. One of them is the descriptive work of academic language functions. Hence, analysis of the teaching and learning process has served to identify a dimension of teachers' language competence which requires reinforcement. Studies of the EMI process provide insights and new research questions. One question that needs to be asked, however, is whether the teaching of these academic functions to EMI lecturers should be cross disciplinary or discipline based. 'This tension between disciplinary overlap and variation underpins the tension between pedagogic convenience and pedagogic effectiveness, which has been at the very heart of EAP and ESP' (Bhatia, 2002, p. 25). The new scenario of CLIL/EMI practice can widely benefit from the sister disciplines of ESP and EAP and also contribute to them. Contributions may derive from local innovations (EMI) which, if approached with solid theoretical and research frameworks (ESP/EAP) as this study attempted to, could provide valuable global perspectives.

Acknowledgement

I thank lecturers at Escuela Universitaria de Informática de Segovia for allowing me to film the sample lectures which constitute the main data for this research.

References

Ball, P. & Lindsay, D. (2012). 'Language demands and support for English Medium Instruction in tertiary education'. In A. Doiz, D. Lasagabaster, & J. M. Sierra (Eds.), *English-Medium Instruction at Universities: Global Challenges* (pp. 44–64). Bristol: Multilingual Matters.

Bhatia, V. K. (2002). 'A generic view of academic discourse'. In J. Flowerdew (Ed.), *Academic discourse* (pp. 21–39). London: Longman, Pearson Education.

Bologna Declaration (1999). *The European Higher Education Area.* Joint Declaration of the European Ministers of Education Convened in Bologna at the 19th of June 1999.

Brown, G. (2006). Explaining. In O. Hargie (Ed.), *The Handbook of Communication Skills* (pp. 204–224) London: Routledge.

Brown, G. & Atkins, M. (1998). *Effective Teaching in Higher education.* London: Routledge.

Clil Cascade Network (2010). *Talking the Future: Languages in Education 2010–2020.* CCN Foresight Think Tank Report: University of Jyväskylä.

Coleman, J. (2006). English-Medium Teaching in European Higher Education. *Language Teaching* 39, 1–14.

Council of Europe. (2001) *Common European Framework of Reference for Languages: Learning, Teaching, Assessment.* Cambridge: Cambridge University Press.

Coyle, D., Hood, P., & Marsh, D. (2010). *Content and Language Integrated Learning.* Cambridge: Cambridge University Press.

Cummins, J. (1984). *Bilingualism and special education: Issues in assessment and pedagogy.* Clevedon, England: Multilingual Matters.

Dafouz, E. (2006). Solidarity strategies in CLIL university lectures: teachers' use of pronouns and modal verbs. *VIEWZ: Vienna English Working Papers*, *15*(3), 9–15.

Dafouz, E. (2008). La Universidad y el reto bilingüe. ¿Está preparada la educación superior para el learning en una lengua extranjera? *AULA de Innovación Educativa*, *168*, 45–49.

Dafouz, E. (2011). English as the medium of instruction in Spanish contexts: A look at teacher discourse. In Y. Ruiz de Zarobe, J. M. Sierra, y F. Gallardo del Puerto, (Eds.), *Content and Foreign Language Integrated Learning: Contributions to Multilingualism in European Contexts* (pp. 89–110). Bern: Peter Lang.

Dafouz, E. & Núñez, B. (2009). CLIL in higher education: devising a new learning landscape. In E. Dafouz & M. Guerrini (Eds.), *CLIL across education levels* (pp. 101–112). Madrid: Richmond Publishing.

Dafouz, E. & Núñez B. (2010). 'Metadiscursive devices in university lectures: A contrastive analysis of L1 and L2 performance'. In C. Dalton-Puffer, T. Nikula, & U. Smit (Eds.), *Language use and language learning in CLIL classrooms* (pp. 213–231). Amsterdam & Philadelphia: John Benjamins.

Dalton-Puffer, C. (2007). *Discourse in Content and Language Integrated Learning (CLIL)*. Amsterdam: John Benjamins Publishing.

Doiz, A., Lasagabaster, D. & Sierra, J. M. (2012) (Eds.). *English-Medium Instruction at Universities: Global Challenges*. Bristol: Multilingual Matters.

Eurydice Network. (2006). *Content and language integrated learning (CLIL) at school in Europe*. Brussels, Belgium: Eurydice.

Eurydice Network. (2012). *Key Data on Teaching Languages at School in Europe 2012*. Brussels, Belgium: Eurydice.

Flowerdew, J. (1992). Definitions in science lectures. *Applied Linguistics, 13*, 202–219.

Francomacaro, M. R. (2011). *English as a Medium of Instruction at an Italian Engineering Faculty: an Investigation of Structural Features and Pragmatic Functions*. (Doctoral Thesis) University of Naples, Italy.

Gierlinger, E. (2013). *The languages for CLIL Model*, Retrieved February 11, 2014, from http://clilingmesoftly.wordpress.com/clil-teachers-tl-competence/

Hyland, K. (2006). *English for Academic purposes: An advanced resource book*. London: Routledge.

Lasagabaster, D, & Ruiz de Zarobe, Y. (Eds.) (2010). *CLIL in Spain: Implementation, Results and Teacher Training*, Cambridge Scholars Library: Newcastle.

Lyster, R. (2007). *Learning and teaching languages through content: A counterbalanced approach*. Amsterdam & Philadelphia: John Benjamins.

Marsh, D. & J. Laitinen (2005). *Medium of instruction in European higher education: Summary of research outcomes of European Network for Language Learning Amongst Undergraduates (ENLU)* Task Group 4. Jyväskylä: UniCOM, University of Jyväskylä.

Martín del Pozo, M. A. (2008). La enseñanza de contenidos en inglés: estudio de caso de una ingeniería técnica en la Universidad de Valladolid. *Actas del I Congreso Internacional de Interacción comunicativa y enseñanza de lenguas* (pp. 381–388). Valencia: Universitat de Valencia.

Martín del Pozo, M. A. (2013). Formación lingüística del profesorado universitario para la docencia en inglés. *Revista de Docencia Universitaria. REDU, 11*(3), 197–218.

Swales, J. (1990). *Genre analysis: English in academic and research settings*. Cambridge: Cambridge. University Press.

Swales, J. M., & Malcewski, B. (2001). Discourse management and new episode flags in MICASE. In R. C. Simpson & J. M. Swales (Eds.), *Corpus Linguistics in North America: Selections from the 1999 symposium* (pp. 145–64). Ann Arbor: University of Michigan Press.

Trimble, L. (1985). *English for science and technology: A discourse approach*. Cambridge: Cambridge University Press.

Young, L. (1994). University lectures macro-structures and micro-features. In J. Flowerdew (Ed.), *Academic listening: research perspective (*pp. 159–179), Cambridge: Cambridge University Press.

Developing a research-informed academic writing curriculum using a textbank of student writing

Neil Matheson and Helen Basturkmen,
University of Auckland, New Zealand
Email: nj.matheson@auckland.ac.nz and h.basturkmen@auckland.ac.nz

1 Introduction

Despite the popularity of generic English for Academic Purposes (EAP) writing courses at the tertiary level, criticism is often levelled at the overly generalised and decontextualised view of academic writing they may present. The concern is that such courses will not adequately prepare students for the challenges of disciplinary writing. English for Specific Purposes (ESP) research reinforces this concern by documenting genre and style variation in academic writing, while Academic Literacies theorists argue that discourses cannot be divorced from disciplinary practices and beliefs, leading to calls for writing support to be embedded within disciplinary practice. As there are often practical reasons why discipline-specific writing courses are not adopted by universities, generic EAP courses are likely to remain the default form of writing support. However, we argue that it is possible to avoid some of the risk of over-generalisation and decontextualisation in such writing courses. This chapter describes research conducted into undergraduate student writing in the Faculty of Arts at the University of Auckland. Findings from this study are being used to inform the ongoing development of an EAP writing course catering to students from a range of Arts disciplines, incorporating Humanities and Social Science subjects. The genre-focused elements of the course focusing on specific text types are being revised to incorporate instruction that focuses on both shared and discipline-specific qualities of academic writing and text types.

The methodologies employed in the research may also be of interest. Three research strategies were employed: the creation of a textbank of proficient undergraduate writing in Arts disciplines, interviews with academics from these disciplines and the collection of a range of supplementary materials. An analysis of a data subset, examining three Arts disciplines – English, History and Sociology – illustrates how the integrated use of these research strategies has allowed us to explore the topic more extensively than previously achieved. In particular, the analysis of textbank texts during interviews enriched findings and deepened our understanding of disciplinary expectations for undergraduate writing. While results of this study are discipline-specific, this integration of research strategies is an innovation that could be applied by researchers, developers of academic writing curricula and EAP practitioners in other contexts.

2 Context of study

English Writing 101 is a Faculty of Arts-based course designed primarily for those with English as a first language. It focuses on academic text types and writing conventions as a practical way to assist students with the challenges of academic writing. Demand for the course is increasing, with enrolments tripling in the last five years to 400 mainly first-year students per year, approximately 10% of first year enrolments in Arts subjects. Offering 2 hours of lectures as a whole class and 1 hour of practice in tutorials of 25 students weekly for 12 weeks, the course combines process writing with a Systemic Functional Linguistics-inspired approach focusing on common academic text types, such as argument, definition and classification, comparison and contrast, critique, literature review, report and case study. This genre-focused component is the focus of this study; other aspects, such as process writing and critical thinking skills, were not included at this stage.

Increasing course enrolments has meant greater diversity in student backgrounds, and a greater range of subject major choices among those students. This prompted the course director, one of the authors of this chapter, to question the usefulness of the existing curriculum for students faced with the demands of writing in diverse disciplines. The concern was that the course may be presenting an overly generalised and decontextualised view of academic writing, with the models and text types introduced being less representative of texts expected in specific disciplines and more along the lines of tasks Wardle (2009, p. 774) studied in a US university writing centre course, described by her research assistant as 'mutt genres'.

ESP research reinforces such concern by documenting genre and style variation in academic writing (Basturkmen, 2009, 2012; Hyland, 2000, 2009; Kusel, 1992; Lea & Street 1998, 2006; Monroe 2003; Nesi & Gardner, 2006, 2012; Paltridge, 1997; Parry, 1998; Samraj, 2004, 2008; Swales, 1990; Tardy, 2011). Vocabulary, linguistic features and style, along with broader structures and content cannot easily be divorced from the social and disciplinary contexts in which they are embedded. Although genres may be labelled in similar ways (such as 'essay' or 'report'), in practice they are often discipline-specific.

Academic Literacies theorists such as Lea and Street (1998, 2006) also argue that discourses cannot be divorced from disciplinary practices and beliefs. They believe that alongside the critical study of such discourses, the institution must adapt to greater diversity among the student body and provide disciplinary-centred writing support throughout the curriculum (Ganobcsik-Williams, 2006; Ivanic & Lea, 2006). For all these reasons, there have been calls (Arkoudis, Baik & Richardson, 2012; Beaufort, 2007; Catt & Gregory, 2006; Etherington, 2008) for writing support to be embedded within disciplinary practice, instead of being taught in more generic writing courses.

Embedding writing practice within disciplinary contexts may make pedagogical sense; however, this may not always be possible. Time, teaching resources or pedagogical know-how among disciplinary specialists (Beaufort, 2007) may be lacking. Similarly, EAP teachers may lack required subject knowledge to teach effectively within an academic discipline.

Attitudes can also interfere: subject specialists may feel their role is to teach subject content, not how to express ideas. Hyland (2009, 2013) suggests some academics believe that because they learned to write the hard way, so should students, as part of becoming acculturated into the discipline. Academics might know implicitly what they want, but it may be left to students to find out exactly what that is. Lillis describes the essay as 'an enactment of the institutional practice of mystery' (2001, p. 58). Tacit, unspoken assumptions of those involved in a discipline mean that for novice academic writers, even when instructions are given, it can be like 'negotiating a sea of unfamiliar objects and practices' (Macbeth, 2006, p. 196).

Realistically then, generic EAP courses such as *English Writing 101* are likely to continue to be the practical default mechanism assisting students with the demands of academic writing. The study reported in this chapter is designed to ensure *English Writing 101* fulfils this role while avoiding the pitfalls of an overly generalised, decontextualised course. It aims to enhance the genre-focused component of the course by providing a sound, research-informed curriculum focusing on qualities of writing shared across academic disciplines, acknowledging disciplinary variation where necessary, and introducing appropriate text types illustrated with relevant samples. With this aim, two questions guided the research:

1. To what extent are qualities desired in student writing similar across Arts disciplines at this university?

2. Which text types are commonly required of students in Arts disciplines at this university?

3 Literature review

Existing research in academic writing genres has usually focused on published academic or graduate level writing. Published work is more accessible and more prestigious than under-graduate writing (Johns, 2008; Wingate, 2012), which is often read only by a tutor. Undergraduate writing is also harder to define (Dudley-Evans & St. John, 1998; Dudley-Evans, 2002), compared to published reports for example, with their Introduction, Methods, Results, Discussion structure. Existing undergraduate writing studies are mainly small-scale projects analysing errors, or identification of text types through question prompt analysis or questionnaires (Gardner & Nesi, 2012), which Bruce (2010) suggests can only predict what is actually produced. Actual text analysis is less common.

A more recent approach, however, has been the development of corpora of student writing, allowing texts to be systematically explored. The Michigan Corpus of Upper Level Student Papers (MICUSP) (Romer & O'Donnell, 2011) and British Academic Written English (BAWE) corpus (Nesi & Gardner, 2012) are two examples, with the latter made up of predominantly undergraduate texts representing four disciplinary groups at four British universities. Comprising nearly 3000 texts, BAWE's aim is 'to capture the broad scope of assessed proficient university student writing' (2012, p. 8) in the United Kingdom.

Writing teachers are increasingly drawing on such corpora in teaching materials, and combining these with genre-based approaches (Flowerdew, 2000, 2012; Gardner, 2012; Hyland, 2000, 2011; Samraj, 2004, 2008). Texts can be seen as representing 'wider rhetorical practices' (Hyland, 2011, p. 174), so as well as shedding light on commonly required text types in a specific setting, text analysis can help describe the disciplinary communities that use them. A textbank of student writing can also act as a source of example texts useful for illustration in a writing course. Texts produced by students are often better suited for teaching purposes (Catt & Gregory, 2006) as they provide an attainable model of writing (Flowerdew, 2000) in accessible language. The use of texts from courses students may take themselves also means the content is likely to be relevant.

Interviews with subject specialists are now also widely recommended for the insights they can provide (Dudley-Evans, 2002; Etherington, 2008; Hyland, 2000, 2011; Tardy, 2011). Martin and Rose (2003) suggest using the expertise of core members of a field to identify quality textual examples when conducting genre analysis. Hyland recommends interviews to identify purposes of texts, ways ideas are expressed and retrieved, and reader responses in order 'to interpret textual data as socially situated practice' (2000, p. 136). Tardy (2011) suggests interviews as a promising future direction as they can create more complex understandings of academic genres. Studies have used interviews to inform researcher analysis of text structures (e.g., Gardner, 2012) or to comment on graduate-level writing (Samraj, 2004), but the analysis of undergraduate texts during interviews with subject specialists is an under-researched area that deserves further attention.

A third approach recommended for building a richer description of the academic context for student writing is the collection of relevant supplementary materials (Dudley-Evans, 2002; Nesi & Gardner, 2012; Prior, 1998). Martin and Rose (2003, p. 273) suggest finding ways to develop 'insider knowledge' of a discipline. Materials such as subject writing guides, course descriptions, assignment questions, readings and marking guides can help build this richer view of a discipline.

4 Methodology

Based on the findings of the literature review, three research strategies were employed to address the research questions. A textbank of proficient undergraduate Arts student texts was developed first. Interviews with academics from Arts disciplines followed. Supplementary materials were collected alongside the textbank and interview stages (see Table 1). The implementation of each strategy is explained below.

Table 1: Methods, data analysis and brief subset findings for each research question

Methods employed (subset size)	Data analysis	Subset findings
Interviews (2 per discipline)	Themes and sub-themes identified in interview and supplementary data Themes include course content, discipline, expression, miscellaneous, organisation, pedagogy, problems, qualities, support, text type Example of sub-theme: Theme: Support Sub-themes: evidence, examples, referencing, research, source use, theory	**Research Question 1: Desired qualities** **Shared qualities** clear, well-structured, on-topic, academic style; texts develop supported argument, employ critical analysis Discipline-specific qualities English: evidence of text analysis skills, effective expression History: use of multiple sources, evidential support Sociology: use of theory, development of critical perspective **Research Question 2: Text types** **Assessment types** English: critical summary and argument, essay, interview, literary experiment, personal narrative, response to text History: annotated bibliography, book review, essay, library assignment Sociology: academic blog, annotated bibliography, essay, socio-autobiography Essay most commonly required assessment – encompasses range of text types Essay descriptions commonly include need for development of position, supported by argumentation (similar to BAWE essay definition)
Supplementary Materials (relevant data from each discipline)		
Textbank (36 texts; 12 per discipline)	BAWE classification adopted: 13 genre families based on social purposes and staging	2 of 13 BAWE genres represented in 36 text subset: Essay (argument genre – demonstrate/develop ability to reason independently and construct a coherent argument) 35 texts Essay sub-genres: Expository essay (state claim or thesis in Introduction, support with evidence in Body) 26 texts Commentary essays (comment on a text rather than issue, focus on analysis more than argument) 6 texts Discussion essay (examine alternative positions before reaching position/reconciling view in Conclusion) 2 texts Factorial essay (focus on causes) 1 text Narrative recount (narrates fictional or real events) 1 text 3 moves employed in text Introductions: context (97%), thesis statement (92%), preview of body (83%)

4.1 Textbank development

As the textbank was to be used during interviews with academics, it was created first. With the study aimed at strengthening the curriculum of *English Writing 101*, the 20 most common subject majors of students in this course were identified. Arts subjects (which at University of Auckland include social and human sciences subjects such as Anthropology, Geography, Politics and Sociology, along with Humanities subjects) were most common as the course is based in that Faculty. From these 20 subjects, 94 courses were selected based on three criteria: courses compulsory in the first year of study, courses encompassing relevant, current or otherwise interesting topics (such as gender, art, the Pacific, pop culture and music, racism, ethics, media and sport, and criminology) and courses taught in that semester.

Ethics consent was received and course directors were approached for assistance in identifying students who had received A- (80–84%) or higher in recent writing tasks. Students were contacted, either directly via email, or by addressing the class during a lecture. Permission was requested to use their writing for teaching purposes. We stressed that any type of writing that had received similar marks would be helpful. Consent forms were worded so students retained copyright over their text while providing permission for use in teaching and publication. With consents collected, students emailed one or more texts. This process was repeated in the following semester. In total, 141 student participants (53% of those contacted) offered texts.

In a subsequent semester, the same students were asked for other writing which had received A- or higher in any subject. This time, texts from non-Arts subjects and also graduate level texts were also offered. This third round of text collection increased the number of courses represented in the textbank to 150 and doubled the number of texts to over 400. To date, 31 subjects from seven faculties or schools – mainly arts but also business, creative arts, education, law, medical and health sciences and science are represented. The word count for texts collected to date is approximately 750,000.

4.2 Interviews

Once the textbank was developed, interviews were conducted. Disciplinary heads were asked to suggest possible lecturers to interview, to avoid researcher selection bias. Interviews were in two parts (see Appendix 1), the first broadly based on interview questions conducted in the BAWE project (Nesi & Gardner, 2006, p. 116), the second focused on three textbank texts provided before the interview. Texts were from the interviewee's discipline, and when possible, from their own courses. We were interested in the degree to which the text met expectations for student writing in the discipline. We wanted a disciplinary insider's perspective to develop our own understanding of the text, the genre and the discipline it represented. Interviews, approximately 50 minutes in length, were recorded, transcribed and analysed for common themes.

4.3 Supplementary material collection

During both the textbank development and interview phases, supplementary materials were also collected. These were sourced from lecturers, students, directly from departments, subject information online and ourselves, and included department and discipline writing guides, course outlines, marking rubrics, assignment questions and readings, feedback on marked essays, tutorial writing tasks, class tests, textbank contributor email comments and researcher field notes.

5 Analysis of data subset

To illustrate how these three strategies can address the research questions, findings from a data subset are presented below. English, History and Sociology, identified as main disciplines by 35% of students in *English Writing 101*, were selected for analysis in this subset. Interviews with two lecturers from each subject, relevant supplementary material and 36 texts, 12 from each subject, formed the subset. Texts were selected from three levels of undergraduate study, incorporating as many courses, topics and authors as possible to increase the likelihood of a range of text types being represented.

Analysis of text types requires a way to distinguish between them, with various classification systems developed for this purpose. MICUSP corpus creators identify seven paper types, based on rhetorical purpose and defining features (Romer & O'Donnell, 2011), while the BAWE corpus distinguishes between 13 genre families, based on social purposes and key stages of texts (Nesi & Gardner, 2012, p. 26). As the BAWE corpus is based on a large data set and is composed predominantly of undergraduate level texts, we have adopted its classification system in our text analysis.

Analysis of interview and supplementary material was carried out by identifying themes and sub-themes in the data. Categories were developed throughout this process as newly collected data were analysed, requiring some re-categorising as new themes emerged or as previously similar concepts became distinct. Table 1 provides a brief overview of methods employed, the data analysis process and main findings for the two research questions.

Several opportunities for data triangulation existed in the data subset. Interview and supplementary data were used to examine qualities desired in student writing, while all three research strategies were drawn on to investigate text types. For example, interviewees explained types of writing required, supplementary data corroborated this by showing commonly asked for assignment types, and textbank analysis then supported this further by revealing the most common text types. The analysis of textbank texts during interviews was also a way of combining data sources to corroborate findings.

6 Findings

6.1 Qualities desired in student writing

There was broad agreement across the three disciplines on qualities desired in student writing. Clarity, logical structure and appropriate style in texts which directly address the question, the development of a well-supported argument and employment of critical analysis were commonly mentioned qualities. For example, one lecturer listed four criteria by which to judge an essay:

> The writing – is it clear, accurate, grammatically correct; the structure – is it answering the essay question with a thesis statement or argument, is it developing the argument over the body paragraphs, are the paragraphs structured properly with the topic sentence ... and then the content, which is the evidence that they are producing, ... and notes and bibliographies.

(History lecturer)

The second History lecturer listed similar requirements: 'rule number one answer the question ... secondly ... any essay must have an argument of some sort ... it should be well structured ... in a logical sequence ... and it should be written in proper, accurate, academic language ... in that order of priority too.' An English lecturer required evidence of close reading skills to show independent engagement with a text: 'analytical skills ... what kind of argument can I build, ... and just clear expression'. A Sociology lecturer required critical thinking about texts, questioning of argumentation and assumptions made, and articulation of this 'in these small essays ... to put together an argument ... offer examples, to be able to apply this knowledge'. Critical analysis was seen as central to Arts disciplines by the second Sociology lecturer: 'we assume that they are always going to critically analyse ... that's the implicit thing in Arts'. He emphasised the ability 'to write in a clear, coherent and sometimes persuasive style' and the need to structure a text sequentially and logically.

Interviewees also emphasised certain qualities commonly associated with their discipline. For example, one of the English lecturers commented on the way detailed text analysis can build argument: 'Close reading is actually always about argument ... because ... close reading is interpretation, and you need to justify your interpretation or at least ... work the evidence hard enough'. The other English lecturer compared his focus on expression to the fine tuning of an engine: "I often talk about torquing the final version ... so you get more work out of the energy you're actually putting in ... [for example] being able to manipulate clauses, dependent clauses to more effectively communicate their argument".

Both History lecturers, in comparison, referred to the need to use multiple sources to build and support a position. One stated the aim of assignments was to 'test students' ability to assess quite a large amount of information [and] ... bring their own critical ... reasoning processes into creating their own response ... based on their research'. The other lecturer emphasised the role of evidence in History: 'in History it's very evidence-based and they get that evidence from secondary resources, primary sources ... given the public sphere, where people can spew opinions ... with no evidence ... we are teaching if you have a point you're buttressing it with evidence'.

Sociology lecturers distinguished their discipline in the way it encouraged a particular critical perspective: 'the emphasis on the theory that we use will be different. I'd like to think that we're actually more questioning, more critical [than other disciplines]'. Desired outcomes from Sociology courses included the ability 'to apply social theory … to articulate different ideas, argumentations, understand limitations' and to develop 'a particular disciplinary expertise, a particular … disciplinary way of thinking'.

Possible variations in approach within or across disciplines were also acknowledged, though these were usually related to content, while qualities of writing were regarded as similar across disciplines. One English lecturer for example, compared writing in History with writing in English, and noted 'what I consider good writing seems to be good writing … wherever it is. There might be some differences in terms of the kinds of data that you use and the various ways you construct arguments'. History and Art History approaches were also compared:

> [There are] different forms of knowledge and how to write essays that students from each discipline bring with them … but … the standards are still very much the same across the two departments … you still need to have an argument that's expressed in accurate language and a well-structured essay.
>
> (History lecturer)

Supplementary materials were also examined to gain further information on qualities desired in student writing. These appeared to reinforce interviewee perspectives, although materials such as course outlines varied widely in the degree of explanation of such qualities within and across the three disciplines. History appeared to provide more specific directions and aims for assignments, and was the only discipline to provide a Coursework Writing Guide describing types of essays, the writing process and qualities of good assignments. There tended to be less specific explanation offered in Sociology and English, although at least one English course provided materials such as annotated sample answers. These differences may be due to more explicit requirements for written work in History or may simply be based on the different pedagogical approaches of individual course directors.

6.2 Text types

In both interviews and supplementary materials, essays were referred to as the most commonly required written assignment, with other forms less frequent. Course outlines for example called most assignments essays, although other names, such as personal narrative, annotated bibliography and academic blog also appeared – see Figure 1. Some of these other assignments were also referred to as essays in interviews and course materials:

> Written language as visual gets some really interesting results … so I have essays that are in fact CD ROMs which [is] the ultimate version.
>
> (English lecturer)

We're asking for an essay ... then the task may be different, you might be analysing a primary source, you might be doing a historiographical essay, you might be answering a basic historical question, whatever the task, doesn't matter, the form is going to come to us in an essay.

(History lecturer)

Assignment 1: A research-based socio-autobiography. This is an essay [in which] you relate at least three sociological concepts ... to your personal life.

(Sociology course outline)

Despite the fact that the term 'essay' appeared to encompass a range of tasks and text types, descriptions of essays across the three disciplines usually included the need for the development of a position on a topic, supported with argumentation. For example, 'critical, thesis-driven essays' were required in one English course. In a course with an essay as the main assessment, 'competence in argument and in expressing and connecting ideas' was a key aim. English lecturers referred to the need for a position and argument in essays: 'the argument is to have a thesis, right? To actually have a point of view. For a good number of students ... that's a real challenge.'

How do I use my close reading skills to build argument ... [and] to engage this concept ... Particularly because the essay question is so open, they have to establish the parameters ... what is the position I'm going to take.

(English lecturer)

A History course essay was 'designed to test a student's ability to successfully synthesise a substantial amount of information into a logically developed argument.' The History Department Coursework Guide equated argument directly with a position: 'All History essays require an argument, or a point of view. It is not enough simply to say what happened. You should express an opinion in response to the question.' The History lecturers expressed similar ideas. One wanted students to 'answer the essay question with a thesis statement or argument'. The other lecturer described a common problem when students simply reworded the essay question in their Introduction:

... "in this essay I will discuss whether witchcraft was an important factor in sixteenth century or not", which is just the essay question ... it's really important to actually set forth your opinion, you state your argument, state your conclusion in the introduction in other words, so that the reader then knows what to expect.

(History lecturer)

In descriptions of Sociology essays, argument was also central: 'there are some things you really can't avoid – typically critical theory, articulating arguments, having a debate within those essays'. The establishment of a clear approach was also valued:

I often tell students Introductions are good ways of signalling clearly to the marker how you interpret the question, and how you intend to attack it … the social world is very messy, it's complex … and typically, there won't be a single right answer. So introductions are … useful … to say for the purposes of this essay, I will focus on A, B and C; had time permitted, I may have looked at X, Y and Z.

(Sociology lecturer)

This focus in the interview and supplementary material on developing a point of view on a topic by building an argument closely resembles the BAWE corpus definition of the essay as an 'argument genre' which demonstrates or develops 'the ability to reason independently and construct a coherent argument' (Nesi & Gardner, 2012, p. 94). In addition, the emphasis on establishing this position early in the essay, with a thesis statement in the Introduction for example, resembles the definition of the 'Exposition essay', one of the six essay sub-genres BAWE creators adapted from Coffin (2004). The Exposition essay states a claim or thesis in the Introduction, and supports this with evidence in the Body.

These similarities were also seen in the subset texts. 35 (97%) of the 36 texts most closely fitted the BAWE definition of essay. The remaining text was classified as a Narrative Recount, a genre which narrates fictional or real events. Of the 35 essays, 26 (72% of the total) fitted the Exposition essay description, as they clearly established a position on the topic in the Introduction and supported this with evidence in the Body. Six essays (five from English) were Commentaries, essays which comment on a text rather than an issue, and focus more on analysis than argument. Two essays, from History and Sociology, were classified as Discussions, essays which examine alternative positions before reaching a position or reconciling the different views in the conclusion. One Sociology essay was what BAWE term a Factorial essay, focusing on causes.

The dominance of Exposition essays occurred despite considerable variation in assignment topics and questions across the three disciplines. Questions asked for analysis, argument, assessment, causes, comparison, discussion, explanation and evaluation among others, suggesting a range of possible structures in response. The high number of Exposition essays, despite this variation in question type, suggests textbank writers know a clear, well supported position is often expected in these disciplines, no matter how the topic is worded.

7 Implications for EAP course development

While it is beyond the scope of the chapter to discuss all the ways this study is informing the development of *English Writing 101*, two examples are provided below to illustrate the potential.

7.1 Provision of sample texts

In the second part of interviews, lecturers provided detailed analysis of the three sample textbank texts from their disciplines, explaining the degree to which each text met expectations. For example, they discussed contextual background for a topic and the depth of treatment of the subject. They commented on text Introduction and Conclusion structures and what they would ideally like to see in these sections. They remarked on source use, wording and overall coherence of a text, often relating such aspects to the aim of that assignment, to general course aims or to disciplinary values. Such comments helped us to decide which texts would be suitable for use as example texts in *English Writing 101*. The sample texts also provided the lecturers with an opportunity to illustrate the qualities described earlier in the interview. As well as confirming that the textbank provides a source of proficient example texts for use in *English Writing 101*, lecturer comments can be used directly to annotate the texts when used to illustrate such qualities in the course.

7.2 Teaching Introductions

Text Introductions are often problematic for novice academic writers, so to inform the teaching of this section, we also analysed subset text Introductions for moves, following the approach developed by Swales (1990). Three moves were identified: the provision of contextual information (in 97% of texts and always appearing first), the writer's overall position in the form of a thesis statement (in 92% of texts), and a preview of the essay Body (in 83%), broadly resembling findings in an analysis of 20 BAWE Sociology and English essays by Bruce (2010), who found context moves in 95% of Introductions and preview moves in 65%.

Some variation in move lengths was evident across disciplines. English and History texts tended to provide more contextual information than Sociology. The situation was reversed for the preview move, with the majority of English and History texts employing just one sentence or less as preview, while 83% of Sociology texts used two or more sentences as preview. A related difference was the use of endophoric markers, such as 'This essay will examine' and 'In this essay' in the preview move. While these were present in almost half of History and Sociology texts, only one English text employed such signals. Again, Bruce (2010) found a similar difference, with far less endophoric markers in BAWE English essays compared to Sociology essays.

Interview data appeared to confirm such disciplinary differences in Introductions. A History lecturer for example commented 'as a historian ... dates are important, the chronology is important ... I do like a fairly expansive introduction ... especially in History, setting the context generally [is useful]'. In Sociology, it appeared that while some context may be useful, the key moves are the thesis and preview:

> I appreciate they haven't got many words to play with ... I would not spend too much time there just quickly introduce your subject and get on with it ... and they need to clarify what the main points [are], I mean the same as we do with our writing of articles.
>
> (Sociology lecturer)

In English however, an overt preview move appeared less important, although clear expectations for Introductions were still apparent:

> I don't want an introduction that sets out and then I say this and then I say that, just … plot the summary of the entire thing, but it's like … what does a reader need to know to appreciate what I'm doing … just an over sight of the terrain … enough to orient themselves … and know what the purpose is … a very attractive looking itinerary that saves some of the key features for surprises along the way.

(English lecturer)

Explaining the three moves is therefore a logical choice when teaching Introduction structures in *English Writing 101* (to be reported at a later date), while acknowledging the slightly different emphases across the three disciplines. This example also illustrates the way the methodologies employed have provided a more comprehensive view of expectations for student writing than if we had for example, simply collected texts or conducted interviews. The comments above on Introductions were made when lecturers were discussing sample textbank texts, illustrating the way the strategies worked in conjunction with each other to provide concrete evidence of qualities and text types considered significant in disciplines. Supplementary materials informed our analysis of textbank texts, textbank texts guided questions asked in interviews, and interviews, grounded in textual analysis, furthered our understanding of sample texts and background supplementary materials.

7.3 Summary of findings

The chapter has reported findings from a subset of data in a broader, ongoing study of undergraduate writing, informing curriculum development for an Arts-based EAP writing course at the University of Auckland. In the disciplines of English, History and Sociology, broadly similar expectations for student writing were identified. Clear, well-structured, and stylistically appropriate writing which develops a well-supported, critically argued position on an assigned topic was desired across the disciplines. Certain qualities were linked with specific disciplines: evidence of detailed analysis of texts and carefully worked expression in English, multiple source use providing evidential support in History, and the development of a critical, questioning approach drawing on theoretical perspectives in Sociology.

Essays, defined in the BAWE corpus as texts which employ independent reasoning and coherent argumentation, were identified as the most commonly required text type in both interviews and supplementary materials, and this was mirrored in the textbank subset, in which 97% of texts were essays. 72% of subset texts were one kind of essay, the Exposition, which states a position in the Introduction and offers support in the Body. Interview data and a moves analysis of text Introduction sections confirmed this focus on a position, with thesis statements identified in 92% of texts. Contextual information was found in 97% of texts and preview moves in 83%, with some variation across disciplines in move lengths.

8 Global implications

This section outlines implications of this study for researchers, curriculum developers and EAP teachers who may be considering ways to ensure EAP writing courses are research-informed and relevant to learner needs.

Literature has tended to portray academic writing instruction as either generic or discipline-specific. Our experiences suggest it may be possible for an EAP course such as *English Writing 101* to accurately generalise about expectations for undergraduate writing and the text types required across a range of disciplines, while acknowledging disciplinary variation when significant. Nesi and Gardner (2012) point out undergraduates are required to perform across a wider range of disciplines than established academics in the United Kingdom and this may be even truer in countries such as New Zealand, where students do not specialise early in their degrees to the same extent as in the United Kingdom. Academics may therefore expect student writing, especially at lower undergraduate levels, to be of a more generic type. At the same time, making students aware of disciplinary-specific expectations where they do exist would be helpful, so they can begin to vary their writing across subjects as they specialise at higher levels (Etherington, 2008).

Wholesale implementation of findings into the curriculum of EAP writing courses requires further research. A larger data set, including a greater number of disciplines, interviews, supplementary material and texts may reduce the relative consistency in desired qualities and text types observed here. However, the methodology employed in this study could be adopted to develop academic writing course curricula in other contexts. The three research strategies of textbank development, interviews and supplementary material collection complemented each other by confirming and clarifying findings. Use of the textbank in interviews in particular provided deeper insights into disciplinary expectations for writing than if the strategies had been used independently of each other and is an important innovation of this study.

While the most fruitful approach may be one employing multiple research strategies, providing opportunities for data triangulation and understanding on a broader scale, EAP researchers and teachers could undertake a more compact version of this. Informal interviews with even a small number of academics are likely to enhance understanding of disciplinary expectations for writing, especially in subject areas the EAP practitioner is less familiar with. If interviews incorporate analysis of sample texts, the rewards are likely to be even greater. The perspectives of students nearing the end of their study may also be useful for teachers working with novice academic writers. The question prompts shown in Appendix 1 may be used as a starting point for those interested in conducting their own interviews.

Textbanks such as ours can be used by teachers and course developers in a number of ways. For example, they can act as a source of good quality sample texts for illustration when teaching writing, and when used in conjunction with interviews, can be annotated with the perspective of those who teach, research and write in that discipline. Students could evaluate texts using an assignment marking rubric to help them understand why they were graded highly, and then compare to drafts of their own texts to identify areas for improvement. With online access, texts can be used as self-reference tools by students who want to understand more about writing in a certain discipline or for those developing teaching materials.

Annotated texts would be a particularly helpful form of support for students with English as a second language, as it would help unpack texts, showing why they are structured and expressed in certain ways, and how they are received. Such information may help reduce the wholesale borrowing from a model that can occur when learners are faced with the challenge of writing in a second language.

This chapter has shown how student writing research is being used to improve the genre-focused component of an EAP writing course catering to students from a range of disciplines. We are ensuring the course incorporates a focus on shared qualities of academic writing and text types, as well as those required in particular disciplines, thus making instruction more relevant to student needs. The findings, approach and methodologies we have described in this chapter will hopefully be of interest to EAP teachers and researchers in both first and second language contexts.

Acknowledgements

The authors wish to thank interviewees for their kind assistance and expert knowledge, textbank authors, transcribers, reviewers, departmental colleagues for encouragement and advice and the University of Auckland's Faculty of Arts for research support.

References

Arkoudis, S., Baik, C., & Richardson, S. (2012). *English language standards in higher education: From entry to exit*. Camberwell: ACER.

Basturkmen, H. (2009). Commenting on results in published research articles and masters dissertations in language teaching. *Journal of English for Academic Purposes, 8*, 241–251.

Basturkmen, H. (2012). A genre-based investigation of discussion sections in research articles in dentistry and disciplinary variation. *Journal of English for Academic Purposes, 11*(2), 134–144.

Beaufort, A. (2007). *College writing and beyond: A new framework for university writing instruction*. Logan, Utah: Utah State UP.

Bruce, I. (2010). Textual and discoursal resources used in the essay genre in Sociology and English. *Journal of English for Academic Purposes, 9*(3), 153–166.

Catt, R. & Gregory, G. (2006). 'The point of writing: Is student writing in higher education developed or merely assessed?' In L. Ganobcsik-Williams (Ed.), *Teaching academic writing in UK higher education: Theories, practices and models* (pp. 16–29). Basingstoke: Palgrave Macmillian.

Coffin, C. (2004). Learning to write history: The role of causality. *Written Communication*, *21*, 261–289.

Dudley-Evans, T. (2002). The teaching of the academic essay: Is a genre approach possible? In A. Johns (Ed.), *Genre in the classroom* (pp. 225–235). Mahwah, NJ: Lawrence Erlbaum.

Dudley-Evans, T. & St John, M. J. (1998). *Developments in English for Specific Purposes: A multi-disciplinary approach*. Cambridge: Cambridge University Press.

Etherington, S. (2008). 'Academic writing and the disciplines'. In P. Friedrich (Ed.), *Teaching academic writing*. (pp. 26–58). London: Continuum.

Flowerdew, L. (2000). Using a genre-based framework to teach organisational structure in academic writing. *ELT Journal, 54*(4), 369–378.

Flowerdew, L. (2012). *Corpora and language education*. Basingstoke: Palgrave Macmillan.

Ganobcsik-Williams, L. (2006). *Teaching academic writing in UK higher education: Theories, practices and models*. Basingstoke: Palgrave Macmillian.

Gardner, S. (2012). Genres and registers of student report writing: An SFL perspective on texts and practices. *Journal of English for Academic Purposes, 11*, 52–63.

Gardner, S., & Nesi, H. (2012). A classification of genre families in university student writing. *Applied Linguistics 2012*, 1–29. doi: 10.1093/applin/ams-24

Hyland, K. (2000). *Disciplinary discourses: social interactions in academic writing*. London: Pearson.

Hyland, K. (2009). *Academic discourse*. London: Continuum.

Hyland, K. (2011). 'Academic discourse'. In K. Hyland, and B. Paltridge (Eds.), *The Continuum companion to discourse analysis* (pp. 171–184). London: Continuum.

Hyland, K. (2013). Faculty feedback: Perceptions and practices in L2 disciplinary writing. *Journal of Second Language Writing, 22*(3), 240–253.

Ivanic, R. & Lea, M. R. (2006). New contexts, new challenges: the teaching of writing in UK higher education. In L. Ganobcsik-Williams. (Ed). *Teaching academic writing in UK higher education: Theories, practices and models* (pp. 6–15). Basingstoke: Palgrave Macmillian.

Johns, A. (2008). Genre Awareness for the novice academic student: An ongoing quest. *Language Teaching 41*(2), 237–252. doi: 10.1017/0261444807004892

Kusel, P. (1992). Rhetorical approaches to the study and composition of academic essays. *System, 20*(4), 457–469.

Lea, M. R., & Street, B. (1998). Student writing in higher education: an academic literacies approach. *Studies in Higher Education, 23*, 157–172.

Lea, M. R., & Street, B. (2006). The "Academic Literacies" model: theory and applications. *Theory to Practice, 45*(4), 368–377.

Lillis, T. (2001). *Student writing: Access, regulation, desire.* London: Routledge.

Macbeth, K. P. (2006). Diverse, unforeseen, and quaint difficulties: The sensible responses of novices learning to follow instructions in academic writing. *Research in the Teaching of English, 41*(2), 180–207.

Martin, J. R., & Rose, D. (2003). *Working with discourse: Meaning beyond the clause.* London: Continuum.

Monroe, J. (2003). *Local knowledges, local practices: Writing in the disciplines at Cornell. Pittsburgh series in composition, literacy, and culture.* Pittsburgh, PA: University of Pittsburgh Press.

Nesi, H., & Gardner, S. (2006). Variation in disciplinary culture: university tutors' views on assessed writing tasks. In R. Kiely, G. Clibbon, P. Rea-Dickins, & H. Woodfield (Eds.), *Language, culture and identity in applied linguistics* (pp. 99–117). London: Equinox Publishing.

Nesi, H., & Gardner, S. (2012). *Genres across the disciplines: Student writing in higher education.* Cambridge: Cambridge University Press.

Paltridge, B. (1997). *Genre, frames and writing in research settings.* Amsterdam: John Benjamins.

Parry, S. (1998). Disciplinary discourse in doctoral theses. *Higher Education 36*, 273–299.

Prior, P. (1998). *Writing / disciplinarity: A sociohistoric account of literate activity in the academy.* Mahwah, NJ: Lawrence Erlbaum.

Römer, Ute & O'Donnell, M. B. (2011). From student hard drive to web corpus (Part 1): The design, compilation and genre classification of the Michigan Corpus of Upper-level Student Papers (MICUSP). *Corpora, 6*, 159–177.

Samraj, B. (2004). Discourse features of student-produced academic papers: Variations across disciplinary courses. *Journal of English for Academic Purposes, 3*, 5–22.

Samraj, B. (2008). A discourse analysis of master's theses across disciplines with a focus on introductions. *Journal of English for Academic Purposes, 7*, 55–67.

Swales, J. M. (1990). *Genre analysis: English in academic and research settings.* Cambridge: Cambridge University Press.

Tardy, C. M. (2011). Genre analysis. In K. Hyland, and B. Paltridge (Eds.), *The Continuum companion to discourse analysis* (pp. 54–68). London: Continuum.

Wardle, E. (2009). 'Mutt Genres' and the goal of FYC: Can we help students write the genres of the university? *College Composition and Communication, 60*(4), 765–789.

Wingate, U. (2012). 'Argument!' helping students understand what essay writing is about. *Journal of English for Academic Purposes, 11*, 145–154.

Appendix 1 Interview Questions

1. What is the aim of written assignments in your department?

2. What kinds of assignment do students write in [discipline name]?

3. What are the main ways written assignments differ?

4. What qualities are desired in writing by students in [discipline name]?

5. What sort of things do you dislike finding in students' written work?

6. How do expectations change as students progress from year to year?

7. How do expectations of writing vary within [discipline name]?

8. Do you know of any differences in expectations between writing in [discipline name] and writing in other disciplines?

Questions on sample texts

9. If the text is from your course, what was the aim of this assignment?

10. To what extent does this text meet those aims?

11. Could you comment on the content, organisation, expression, source use, style of this text?

12. To what extent does this text illustrate the qualities desired in writing in [discipline name]?

13. What grade would you give this text? Why?

Innovative use of mobile technologies in EAP oral assessment: A pilot study from The Open University

Prithvi N. Shrestha, Jo Fayram and Valérie Demouy,
Department of Languages, The Open University, UK
Email: prithvi.shrestha@open.ac.uk

1 Introduction

In this chapter, we explore the use of mobile technologies in English for Academic Purposes (EAP), which is an emerging field both in language teaching and EAP. The value of mobile technologies in language learning and teaching is widely recognised (e.g., Demouy & Kukulska-Hulme, 2010; Kukulska-Hulme, 2009; Shrestha, 2012). However, the research on mobile technologies within EAP is extremely sparse, particularly as opportunities for practising English academic speaking skills in open and distance learning (ODL) are often limited, unlike in a face-to-face context. By the same token, assessing oral skills in ODL academic contexts is further complicated and demanding administratively and pedagogically. Therefore, the current practices in ODL are limited to assessing less or non-interactive oral skills such as oral presentations.

In response to this problem, computers have been used recently to assess oral language skills, particularly in commercial tests (e.g., Xi, 2010). Yet, there are issues around human versus machine rating. This chapter reports on an innovative application of mobile technologies in teaching and assessing academic English-speaking skills in ODL. A pilot study was conducted with a group of English for Academic Purposes students once they completed their existing course between October and December 2010. A series of activities were designed and delivered through Talkback®, a voice response system powered by Learnosity (www.learnosity.com). Talkback® allowed students to use mobile phones including smartphones, landlines, Skype or OU Voice (iTunes app) for practice and doing assignments. These students' experience of using this system was investigated through weekly online survey questionnaires and telephone interviews. The chapter reports on the results from the study.

We first critically review the relevant literature in the field of mobile technology use in EAP briefly. Then, the context of the study is described. This is followed by a description of the project reported here. Next, we explain the methodology employed in the study and the type of data collected, which is followed by the results. The results are discussed in light of the research questions given in the literature review section. Finally, we conclude the chapter by presenting a number of pedagogical implications of the use of Talkback® for EAP oral assessment and speaking practice in the light of the results which may be applicable to other EAP contexts.

2 Brief review of the use of mobile technologies in EAP assessment

A recent surge in the use of ICTs is having an impact on how English and other languages are taught and learned (e.g., Beatty, 2010; Motteram, 2013; Stockwell, 2007). The value of ICTs for language learning is widely accepted, albeit in some cases with caution (Warschauer & Ware, 2008). Mobile technologies for English language teaching and learning are still an emerging field. However, studies in developing and developed countries do offer evidence of mobile technologies' impact across various global contexts in regards to the aforementioned fields (e.g., Kukulska-Hulme, 2012; Motteram, 2013; Shrestha, 2012).

Unlike tethered technologies, mobile technologies offer learners more flexibility and mobility with regard to accessing language learning resources. For example, the learner does not have to be in one particular place. More importantly, mobile technologies break the barrier of distance between the teacher and the learner (Beckmann, 2010). Given the rapid growth of users of mobile devices such as mobile phones and tablets globally (for global mobile phone subscribers, see ITU, 2013), the prospect of mobile technologies for language learning has increased over the last ten years. However, despite the increasing trend in using mobile technologies for English language teaching and learning, they are under-used in the field of English for Specific or Academic purposes (ESP/EAP). For example, it is recognised that they are useful tools for both ESP and EAP and yet there appears to be no specific study measuring the use of mobile technologies in these fields (Gilbert, 2013; Kern, 2013). With regard to English language assessment, the use of technologies such as computers and specific softwares (e.g., speech recognition software) has been investigated (Chapelle & Chung, 2010; Chapelle & Douglas, 2006; Xi, 2010). Such technologies, nevertheless, do not appear to be examined in the context of EAP assessment (i.e., assessing the use of English for academic studies). For example, when the articles in two key EAP and ESP journals, *Journal of English for Academic Purposes* and *English for Specific Purposes Journal* were searched, there were no articles that directly addressed assessment and technologies, let alone the use of mobile technologies in EAP assessment. This may be true because most EAP and ESP teachers are interested in practical solutions to their challenges and thus may not have examined their context from a research perspective for various reasons.

Based on the brief review of literature above, it is clear that there is more need for understanding what affordances mobile technologies offer to EAP assessment, particularly EAP oral assessment. It is not only about affordances of mobile technologies for EAP oral assessment but also about their impact on students and their learning contexts. Keeping these issues in mind, an exploratory study was conducted which addressed the following research questions:

- What affordances does Talkback® offer to EAP oral assessment?

- What is the student's experience of using Talkback® for EAP oral practice and assessment?

- What are pedagogical implications for EAP programmes?

3 Local context

The study reported here took place at The Open University, UK (OUUK), which offers higher education through an open and distance learning (ODL) mode. It is the largest university in Europe and is well-known for providing education on a large scale. Within the university, the Department of Languages offers a number of language modules in various languages (e.g., German, Spanish). EAP is one of the modules offered to students. Given the open and distance mode of teaching, EAP students (currently about 2,000) do not have any face-to-face contact with their tutors or fellow students. As a result, these students lack opportunities to practise oral skills in EAP unlike their counterparts in traditional universities. Similarly, they have limited resources for practising listening skills which may be a reflection of the general trend in higher education where the main mode of demonstrating student performance is through writing (Lea & Street, 1998; Lillis & Scott, 2007; Shrestha & Coffin, 2012). However, both listening and speaking skills are essential for academic and professional purposes (for a review of research, see Lynch, 2011). There was, therefore, a need to address this problem in a cost-effective way in an ODL context. Given the OUUK's pioneering role in using educational technologies, an immediate option was to explore any potential technologies for a solution. How this was done is explained in the next section.

4 Methodology

The OUUK offers a credit-bearing EAP module (30 points) to students. As noted above, students' oral practice in this module is extremely limited. This issue had emerged persistently in an annual end of the module student survey. Of course, this module includes some oral practice and assessment which is, however, not interactive. It concentrates on a non-interactive oral skill, namely presentations. This focus on oral presentations raised questions about the claim the module could make about students' oral skills in EAP. Additionally, these students who move on to study other subjects required interactive oral skills. Therefore, a pilot project called 'Interactive Oral Assessment' was developed to explore how mobile technologies could enable students to develop more interactive oral skills in EAP.

5 Interactive Oral Assessment project

5.1 Objectives

The main objective of this pilot project was to trial Learnosity's voice response system known as Talkback® for use in the formative and summative assessment of listening and speaking skills in French and EAP. However, this chapter will report on the EAP data only. The project ran for six weeks in the autumn of 2010.

5.2 Learnosity's Talkback®

Learnosity is a company which specialises in providing simple user-friendly ICT tools to educational institutions for the practice and assessment of languages. Talkback® is one of the tools they offer. It is a tool designed for the practice and assessment of listening and speaking skills.

Talkback® is an interactive voice response system that works through a simple phone call. It is akin to what is used in telephone banking and other services. A series of audio questions, which together make up an activity, prompts students to respond orally. There is no visual support nor are there any text prompts.

Answers to the questions for each activity are recorded and can be played back straightaway on the phone via the phone review. The phone review lets students listen to the series of questions, each followed by the student's answers themselves, followed by recorded sample answers where appropriate. Additionally, students can review their activities online via a dedicated website and access other related resources such as the transcription of prompts where given.

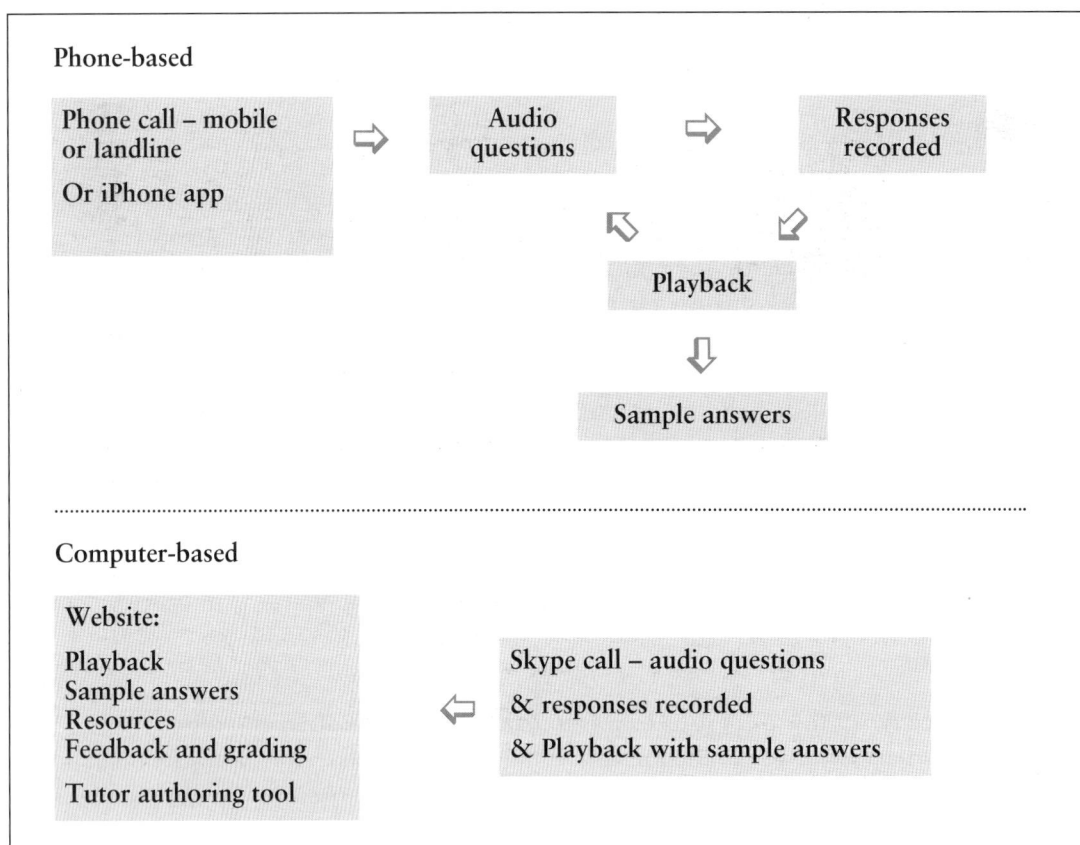

Figure 1: Using Talkback® on the phone and/or computer

However, Talkback® is not just a practice tool. It allows tutors to access their students' activities online via the same dedicated website so that they can comment and grade their students' work. Feedback is immediate and students can then access their results and teachers' comments via the same website.

Additionally, Talkback® has a simple authoring tool which allows teachers to create questions and activities. Teachers can record questions by using the tool's recording facility or if they prefer by uploading pre-recorded MP3 or WAV files.

On the IOA project, activities could be accessed in a variety of ways (see Figure 2):

- a landline or mobile phone through a lo-call (low cost) 0330 number

- Skype VOIP (through a contact name and so free of charge)

- 'OU Voice' the iPhone/ iPod Application designed by Learnosity and available in the iTunes shop free of charge

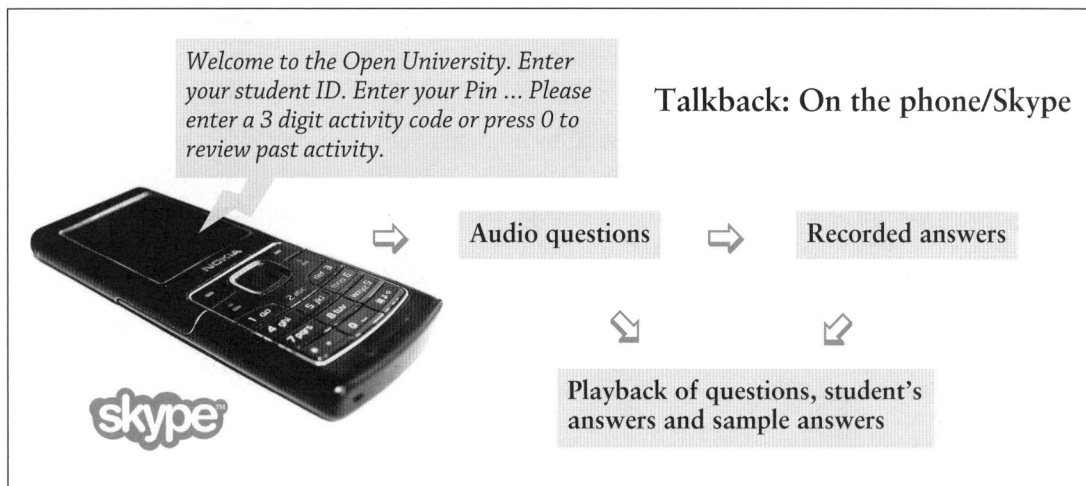

Talkback: On the phone/Skype

Welcome to the Open University. Enter your student ID. Enter your Pin ... Please enter a 3 digit activity code or press 0 to review past activity.

Audio questions ⇒ Recorded answers

Playback of questions, student's answers and sample answers

Figure 2: Different options for using Talkback®

Students were provided with a unique Student ID and password (PIN) to key in, in order to access activities on the phone or online. Once 'in', students had access to the activities by entering the relevant activity code to the activities created for them by the project team. Students could attempt the activities as many times as they wanted. Tutors on the project were given a unique username and password to access their students' activities online via the same dedicated website used by students.

A virtual learning environment (VLE) workspace (see Figure 3 below) was created hosting information resources for students such as the module guide, an overview document showing all activities per week on the pilot, overview documents for the assignments, other materials used in preparation for some activities and a link to the IOA Learnosity website (giving access to the activities online for teachers and students). A forum on the website allowed students to communicate with the project team and with each other.

Talkback: Online

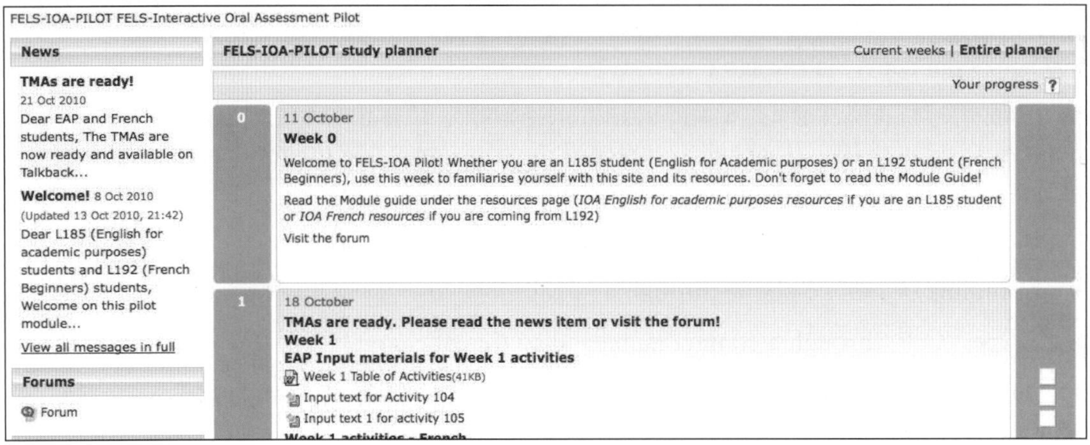

Figure 3: A screenshot of a VLE site

5.3 Design of EAP oral materials

The design of the EAP materials was informed by a language in context model developed within Systemic Functional Linguistics (e.g., Coffin, Donohue, & North, 2009). This model views language as a meaning-making resource for a social purpose in a sociocultural context. As such, in this project, key language features and functions in an academic context were considered. A wide range of activities were designed accordingly. These activities were developed to reflect the reality of academic study in higher education. Therefore, they focused on how language is used in university seminars and workshops. A particular focus was on a number of speech functions that are common in such seminars and workshops. They are listed below:

- describing one's cultural/educational/linguistic background;
- asking and answering questions;
- asking for clarification;
- explaining/giving reasons;
- agreeing;
- disagreeing;
- interrupting;
- giving opinions;
- introducing a presentation;
- summarising key points;
- persuading (through the main part of the presentation); and
- drawing conclusions in a presentation.

Each week, the activities concentrated on at least two of the functions listed above. In total, students were expected to spend up to four hours practising EAP listening and speaking skills. While the activities in the first three weeks allowed students to practise seminar and discussion skills, the last two weeks helped them to enhance their academic presentation skills.

Most of the activities had questions that required some preparation. For this purpose, a summary of the activities for each week was posted on the VLE workspace. Activities that needed preparation relied on various sources of information. These included reading texts, and accessing videos and audios provided on the workspace.

In addition to the practice activities, there were two assignments. Assignment 1 assessed the skills covered in Week 1 and 2 activities (e.g., asking for clarification, explaining/giving reasons). The maximum mark for this assignment was 40. Here is an example of a task given in Assignment 1:

In preparation for a seminar on online learning with children, your teacher asks:

"Maybe some of you have got children or have regular contact with children but even if you haven't, can you think of some opportunities and challenges for children when learning online?"

Respond to your tutor.

Assignment 2 tested skills practised in Weeks 3, 4 and 5 and the maximum mark was 60. The main purpose of Assignment 2 was to assess oral academic presentation skills. The marking criteria were different for each assignment given the nature of the response required for each. They are given in Tables 1 and 2 below.

Table 1: Marking criteria for mini oral responses (academic discussions)

Marks	Marking criteria
	Relevance of information/response as required by the question • Is the response relevant to the question? • Is the task requirement fulfilled?
	Cohesion and fluency • Are the ideas linked together well (e.g., use of linking words, conjunctions, etc.)? • Are the sentences sequenced logically? • Does the speaker speak at a normal rate of speech (i.e., no hesitation) continuously?
	Appropriate style • Does the speaker use a range of subject-related vocabulary? • Does the speaker show an appropriate relationship with the listener? • Does the speaker use any evaluative language (e.g., attitudes towards the listener, topic/issue)?
	Grammatical accuracy • Does the speaker use a range of recognised sentence patterns in English accurately? • Are the verb tenses formed correctly? • Is the communication impeded by any grammatical inaccuracies?
	Pronunciation • Is the pronunciation intelligible? • Is an appropriate tone used?

Table 2: Marking criteria for oral academic presentation

Marks	Marking criteria
	Relevance of information as required by the task • Are the content and issues in the presentation relevant to the task? • Are technical terms defined where necessary? • Are relevant sources used to support a point/claim?
	Cohesion, organisation and fluency • Are the ideas linked together well (e.g., use of linking words, conjunctions, etc.)? • Are there phases/stages of the presentation (i.e., beginning, middle and end) clearly indicated? • Are the sentences sequenced logically? • Does the speaker speak continuously at a normal rate of speech (i.e., no hesitation)?
	Appropriate style • Does the speaker use a range of subject-related vocabulary? • Does the speaker show an appropriate relationship with the listener? • Does the speaker use any evaluative language (e.g., speaker's view on the issue or topic)?
	Grammatical accuracy • Does the speaker use a range of recognised sentence patterns in English accurately? • Are the verb tenses formed correctly? • Is the communication impeded by any grammatical inaccuracies?
	Pronunciation • Is the pronunciation intelligible? • Is an appropriate tone used?

5.4 Participants, data collection and analysis methods

The participants for this project were recruited from an EAP module. These students were approached by following the university's standard ethical guidelines and process. The project was advertised on the EAP module website at the beginning of September 2010. The advertising message explained what the pilot consisted of and what was expected of participants. Students were invited to register their interest via an electronic registration form or by email by 30 September. In addition, the message stated that participants would be selected on a first come, first served basis. In total 20 students registered for participation however, 9 of them visited the workspace but never started the activities despite further reminders by emails and phone calls. This left 11 students participating in the project. While 11 students completed Phase 1 (i.e., Week 1), 10 students completed Phases 2, 3 and 5 and only 6 students finished Phase 4 (see Figure 4 below). It is not known why only 6 students completed Phase 4.

The graph below shows the number of the participants responding to the questionnaire in the five phases of the project.

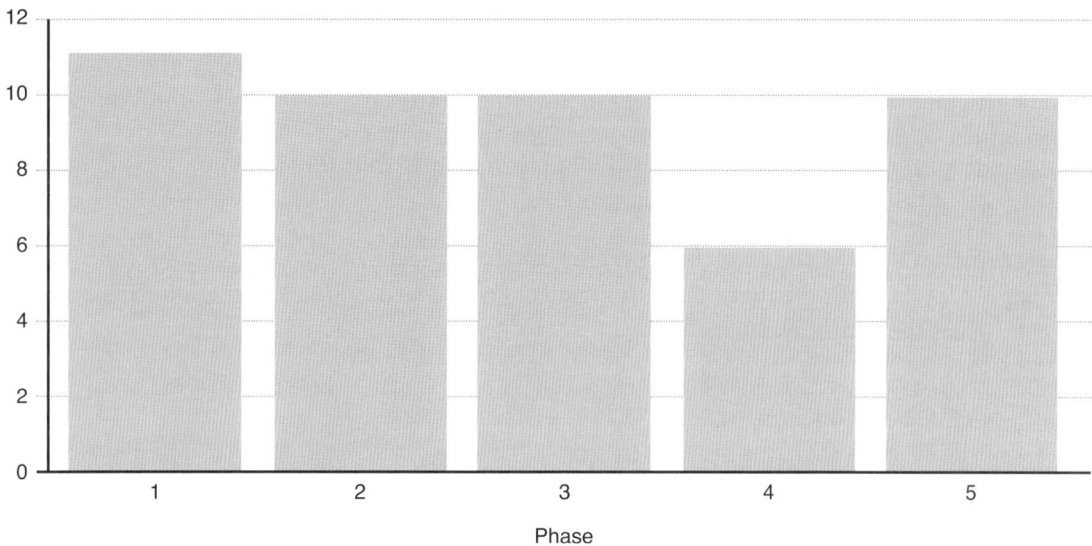

Figure 4: Bar chart showing the number of participants responding to the questionnaire for each phase of the project

The data were collected from the participants in four different ways. Firstly, a weekly online questionnaire for each phase/week of the project was sent to students. Questionnaires in Phase 1 included a section on 'getting started' with the module and the tool. Phases 3 and 5 included a section on the assignments and Phase 5 included a section on the overall experience of the project. Questions focused on the preferences of participants regarding the mode of access of the activities (Skype, landline, mobile etc.), the context, the workload and frequency of use as well as the functionality of the tool and the pedagogical aspect of working with such a tool for practice and assessment. Secondly, an interview with one participant after the pilot had finished and a preliminary analysis of the data collected by the online questionnaires had taken place. Thirdly, students were asked to record feedback on Talkback® after each activity was completed. Fourthly, the VLE forum on the workspace as well as the dedicated email address which provided additional feedback or gave participants the option to address queries and suggestions.

Once the data were collected, the survey data were statistically analysed. Given the small number of participants, the statistical data were manually analysed. In order to complement the statistical data, the open-ended comments and the interview data were examined.

6 Findings

In this section, we report the findings based on the various data sets. The findings are presented in the themes that emerged from the data collected.

6.1 Context and modes of access

All participants mentioned that they carried out the activities at home. Most of these participants reviewed the activities online on their home computer. During Phases 1, 2 and 4, only one participant reviewed the activities on a work computer. On the other hand, some participants did not review the activities online at all: three in Phase 1, 2 in Phases 2 and 5, and 1 in Phases 3 and 4. It is not clear why these students did not review the activities. The interview data (1 participant only) suggest that Talkback® allows students to do the activities 'anytime' but not 'anywhere'.

Figure 5 (below) shows the result for the preference of a technology for accessing the activities. Almost the same number of the students chose to use Skype and a landline phone, except during the second week.

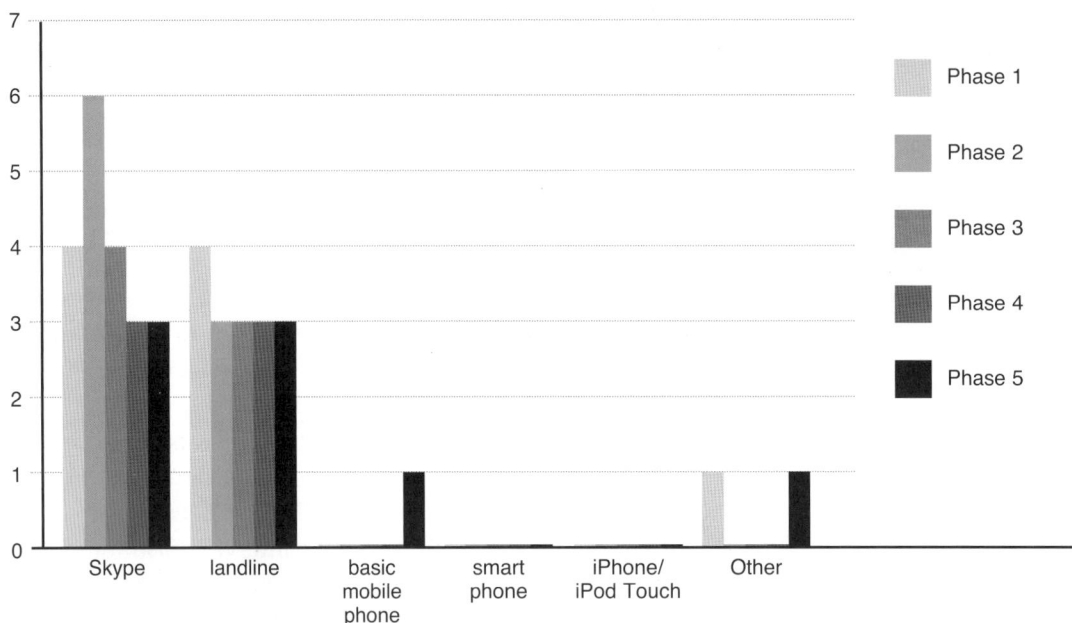

Figure 5: Bar chart showing which technology was used to access the activities. Note that participants could use more than one technology per phase (N=7–9)

6.2 Functionality and technical issues

Most participants found starting the first two activities either 'very easy' or 'easy'. Only two participants reported that they found this 'not easy at all'. Almost all participants reported that they had no problem accessing the activities via Talkback®. However, there was one participant in Phase 1 and two in Phase 5 who indicated that they had a difficulty. They did not provide further information as to why except that they found it hard to access some of the sample answers.

Considering the functional aspect of accessing Talkback® through various media, nearly all participants found it 'very easy' or 'easy'. Likewise, when reviewing the activities on the phone or online, all the participants reported it to be either 'very useful' or 'useful'. In Phase 5, however, one or two participants found it difficult. The participants stated that the option to attempt an activity more than once was an advantage. For example, a participant said: 'It is always good to repeat activities' and another said: 'You could listen to your answer. If you made mistakes, you could attempt it again'.

As mentioned earlier, most students did the activities via Skype and a landline. Most of the students reported that it was either 'very easy' or 'easy' to access the assignment results and feedback. Only one student indicated that it was 'difficult' for Assignment 1 while, for Assignment 2, one said it was 'not easy' and the other 'difficult'.

The participants mentioned that initially there were some technical issues (e.g., the use of Skype, recording, etc.) but it was mainly during Assignment 1. None of the students had any technical problems with Assignment 2.

6.3 Workload and frequency

The time spent per week carrying out the activities varied greatly depending on students' circumstances and whether there was an assignment or not. However, at least 5 students spent between 1 and 3 hours in Phases 1 and 2 while 4 students took 4 hours or more for Phase 3 which included Assignment 1. It appears that on average it may have taken up to 3 hours to complete the activities in each phase although the expectation was that it would take up to 4 hours for each phase. Likewise, the average time spent on any one session seems to be up to 30 minutes although it varied each week.

6.4 Activity types and preferences

The participants had access to a weekly planner which detailed the activity number and the type of activity. In addition, the planner indicated if the students needed to prepare for the activities in question. As mentioned earlier, the EAP oral activities were designed on the basis of the speech functions that students may encounter in an academic context in higher education. In order to reflect these speech functions, the following types of activities were designed:

- short dialogues;
- listen and respond to a situation (e.g., seminar);
- listen and respond to prompts;
- giving opinions;
- summarising information; and
- mini academic presentations.

The weekly questionnaire asked the students to state what they preferred from among the activities each week. On the basis of their responses, it appears that they like listening activities which integrate multimedia materials such as audio and video as source materials. Some students also liked the short academic presentation.

The students reported that they completed the activities in a chronological order. Nonetheless, the majority of them did not use the weekly planner to choose the activity. Those who utilised the planner explained that due to the new technology, they decided to use the planner.

6.5 Assignments (content, length and feedback)

The participants were asked to comment on the content and length of the assignments. When asked about the difficulty level of the assignments, most of the participants stated that they were at the appropriate level. Some of them mentioned a recording issue for the second assignment which was a presentation and required a relatively longer time than the first one did. They were also asked to indicate which part of the assignment was easy or difficult. Most of them reported that the beginning questions in each assignment were easier while the later ones were more challenging. This confirms the intention of the principle on which the assignments were designed. Likewise, most students thought that the length of the assignments was 'about right'. The table below summarises the result.

Table 4: Results of categorisation of participants' answers to:
'What is your opinion on the length of the assignment?' for Phase 3 and Phase 5

	Phase 3			Phase 5		
	Too short	About right	Too long	Too short	About right	Too long
No.	1	6	0	2	5	0
%	14%	86%	0%	29%	71%	0%

Additionally, the participants reported on the assignment feedback, marks and student performance. Figure 6 summarises their perception of the assignment feedback and marks regarding their layout and readability. As can be seen in the figure, most of the participants thought they were either 'very clear and easy to understand' or 'clear and fairly easy to understand'.

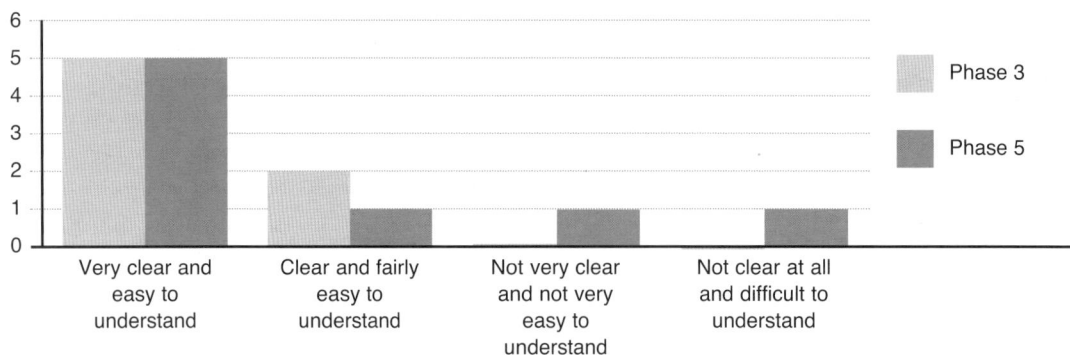

Figure 6: Bar chart showing participants' views of the way the marks and feedback were organised in terms of layout and readability

Similarly, almost all the participants (except two for Assignment 2) found the audio feedback on the assignment either 'very good' or 'good'. This indicates the positive value of the audio feedback provided via Talkback®.

6.6 Perceptions on overall impact of the project

The overall experience of the participants seemed to be overwhelmingly positive as seven out of eight respondents stated that the project met their expectations. A number of survey questions were asked to explore the overall experience further.

At the beginning of the project, the participants were asked for their reason for participating in the pilot. Their main reasons were: to improve pronunciation, to improve academic discussion skills and to practise academic presentation skills. Some students also indicated 'to improve listening skills' and 'to explore new technology' as their reasons. Figure 7 summarises the result.

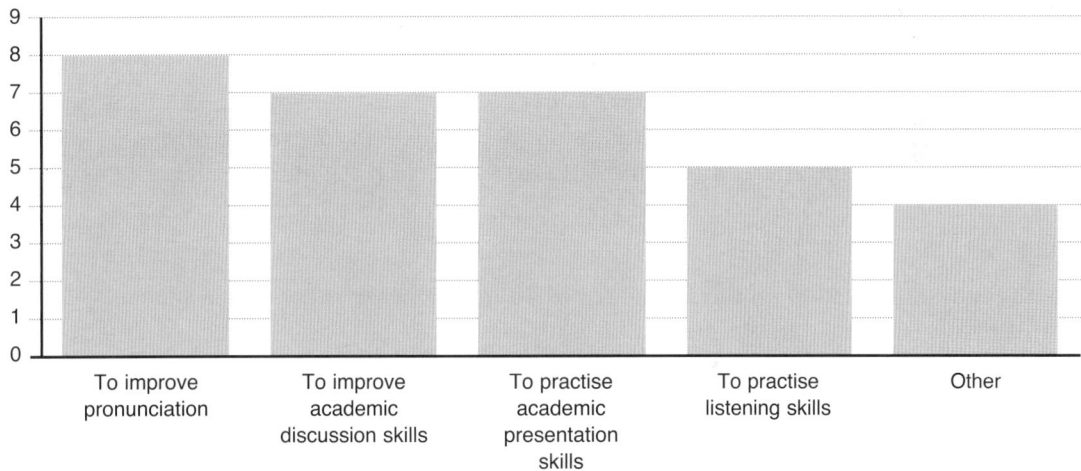

Figure 7: Reasons for participating in the pilot (N=11).

At the end of the project, these participants were asked about their achievement. As Figure 8 shows, this project helped them improve additional aspects of listening and speaking in EAP. The most common four aspects were: 'confidence', 'respond quickly orally', 'respond more appropriately orally' and 'academic presentation skills'. However, there was one participant who was 'frustrated' with the project. The participant was not available for the interview to explore why they felt frustrated.

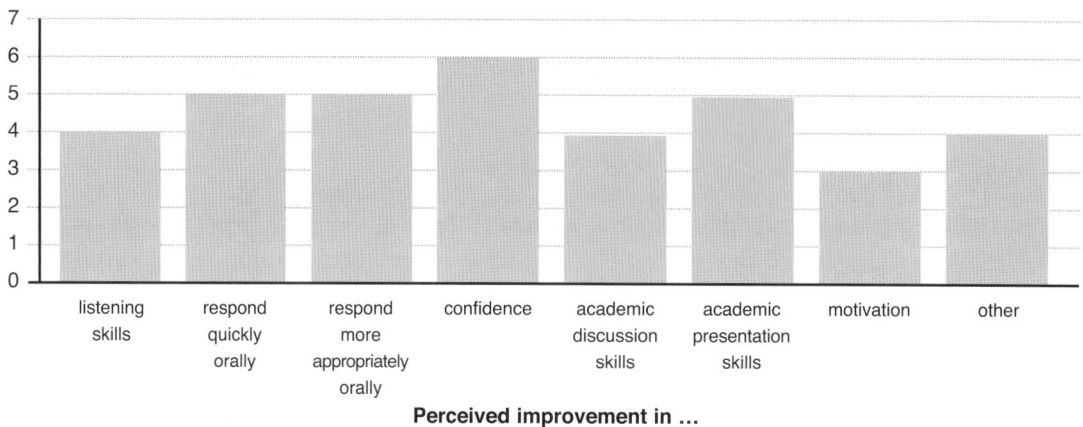

Perceived improvement in ...

Figure 8: Number of participants who thought the pilot had improved specific skills and abilities (number of participants responding to this question = 8)

The participants were also asked to rate the overall usefulness of Talkback® for speaking practice. Almost all the participants said that it was either 'extremely useful', 'very useful' or 'useful'. Only one participant said 'I don't know'. This result suggests that Talkback® is a useful tool for EAP listening and speaking practice. This is reflected in one of the participants' comment: 'It was a very nice addition to L185 [EAP module]. It could have benefitted from a bit more background knowledge, but maybe that comes when it is embedded into a course proper.'

Another question focused on the advantage of Talkback® over other media such as CD ROMs. Most students thought that Talkback® created an authentic interactive situation where one interacts, as suggested by these quotes:

Talkback® allow to listen, to record, to review or to rerecord activities in very easy way. It also allow to do activities anywhere and in any time (access to the computer is not necessary), and submitting assignments is easier without any worries about appropriate recording tool and appropriate file.

The perception of being 'live' was also mentioned: "I am just now doing French, and working with recorded language from a CD is even more 'artificial' than is the phone situation. One advantage is clearly the psychology of direct interaction that is created by using the phone" ...

"I am currently doing the French introductory course. The CD is more like an exercise; the phone is more interactive, more like real life." (Interview)

The participants did not consider that Talkback® had any disadvantage compared to other tools except that it was not integrated with a course in the pilot. Likewise, six out of eight participants said that they would be happy to carry out their speaking assignments via Talkback®. Seven of them also said that they would recommend the module to their friends. Some of the explanations for their recommendations are given below:

This module helps to develop many useful skills which can be transferred to the work place, academic studies and every day communication.

It would help a lot non-native speaker who do not have the possibility to practise their English,

I would recommend the module to anyone, who wants speaking training. It can help to get over shyness and any other feelings that may make speaking difficult and it got me a lot of training and thinking. It also was a nice addition to the EAP course. On its own, however, it would benefit from a bit more theoretical and example input – as I have commented before.

7 Discussion and lessons learned

The findings reported above suggest that Learnosity's Talkback® offers opportunities to EAP students in an ODL context to practise oral skills. These skills can also be assessed by using the same tool. However, the findings also reveal a number of aspects that need consideration if the tool is to be integrated into an EAP module.

It is important to recognise the type of EAP tasks that can be used with Talkback® as this tool is generally used for shorter tasks such as pronunciation (see Demouy & Kukulska Hulme, 2010). It is widely accepted that such tasks are dependent on the purpose and the context of language use (Hyland, 2007). In this respect, we took the view that speaking is a social activity based on a situation (Luoma, 2004). In order to reflect this view, EAP assessment tasks focused on communicative functions for the purpose of academic study rather than general communication skills as noted previously. This meant designing activities that students encounter in academic seminars and workshops in higher education. Likewise, it is common to provide preparation materials in advance of such workshops and seminars. Therefore, activities focusing on seminar discussion skills accompanied reading texts, and audio and video materials. The students had to read, listen to or watch these sources as appropriate prior to the activity. In our view, this aspect of the activity design is an extension of Talkback® which was primarily for short interactions rather than extended ones, as stated earlier. While some students found it difficult to juggle various sources for the activity, others enjoyed doing so without any difficulty. This may indicate the continuous challenge we face while designing listening and speaking materials for EAP in open and distance education.

Talkback® was designed to provide short interaction opportunities to students. Thus, presentation tasks may be at odds with it. Students, however, liked tasks when visual support or more scaffolding was offered. It is not clear yet whether it helped to anchor the task in a more realistic and meaningful situation and therefore, more in-depth analysis is required, but this aspect certainly needs to be looked at more carefully, especially if Talkback® is considered for use with other subjects such as Health or Business.

Talkback®'s flexibility makes the tool available from almost anywhere and at any time for students, offering the potential to switch from one platform to another depending on circumstances or location. So, for instance, it allows students to prioritise landline access at times of high internet traffic or when the only PC in the home is not available. On the project, it gave a few students the choice to do their assignments on the phone as the sound quality was better for them there than on their PC. This also means making the EAP oral tasks suitable for such flexibility.

Unlike the other tools students are used to (e.g., CDs, DVD-ROMs, other web-based interactive tools, etc.), Talkback® does not offer students the option of relying on a transcription of the questions when doing the activities, nor does it allow students to pause to check a word in a dictionary for instance. Though transcriptions of questions were provided (except for assignments) and students could access these via the online review once they had attempted an activity, for several reasons the transcription of sample answers was not made available despite several students asking for them. However, providing transcription of activities at a given point, perhaps once students have completed a set of activities might enhance the learning experience and help students reflect on the progress they have made or consider redoing some activities in view of systematic errors. However, the timing of the release of transcription needs to be considered carefully as it will impact on how students interact with the tool.

A pause facility or an option to repeat the question before answering is not available with Talkback®. Some students felt these options would be useful. The facility to repeat questions already exists in Talkback® but is only available when an answer has been given and the student has indicated that s/he wants to record a new answer. The tool prioritises the immediacy of the response and perhaps makes it less likely that students will access this repeat facility as they have already given an answer and might move on to the next question. Adding those two facilities would actually change Talkback® quite drastically and make it more similar to other existing tools.

Unlike other tools, Talkback® records all responses whether an activity has been completed or not. When a question is answered, the answer is recorded and immediately accessible to the student or their tutor. Students can access their answers immediately after having done the activity on the same platform (phone, Skype, iTunes App). When a sample answer has been provided, they can compare what they have done with it. Both tutors and students can review activities online and as seen before look at the transcription of the questions. This immediate access to generic feedback or answers can be paired with immediate personalised feedback on each answered question by tutors. Nevertheless, a quick response from the tutor is only possible if EAP tasks are short and quick.

From a formative assessment point of view in EAP, Talkback® offers tutors an opportunity to assess their students' specific oral skills and by the same token provide formative feedback on a particular aspect of speaking (e.g., asking for clarification by asking appropriate questions). Such focused feedback is considered effective (Nicol, 2010) as it helps to enhance students' emerging abilities (Shrestha & Coffin, 2012).

The participants pointed out that the tool played a part in their perceived improvement and confidence. For instance, a student remarked that 'Talkback® is much more immediate and pushes a learner to remember more, rather than rely on referring back to dictionaries or verb tables'. Another pointed out that 'it made listening back a more realistic experience' and several emphasised the fact that it helped them to 'respond quicker and get confidence in speaking'. Indeed, confidence is essential for improving EAP oral communication skills (Crosling & Ward, 2002). In the absence of face-to-face immediacy, Talkback® helps ODL students to build their confidence given the semi-authentic environment it creates (i.e., talking to someone at the other end of a phone line/Skype).

It needs to be noted that one technological tool such as Talkback® alone cannot meet the needs of EAP students. Therefore, it is important to recognise how it can be integrated with other tools already in use. For example, if an EAP module uses a VLE site such as Moodle, it is essential to consider how other module materials such as written texts, and multimedia materials can be enhanced by introducing Talkback®.

Though Talkback® has the advantage of offering a variety of access modes and therefore gives users the possibility of switching from one to another if technological glitches occur, one should keep in mind that any technology will come with its share of issues whether it is due to the user's equipment, an unreliable internet connection or simply a power cut. There were syncing issues with the iPhone OU voice app which was tested and under development during the project and these will need to be ironed out and properly tested should the App be offered as a way into the activities.

It is worth noting that this pilot study had a small sample of participants. Therefore, findings from this study cannot generalised and have to be treated cautiously. A further study with a larger sample is desirable.

8 Conclusion and global implications

The result of this pilot study indicated that the project met most of the EAP students' expectations in terms of practising EAP listening and speaking skills in an open and distance learning context. The match between the technological tool, the content and the format was highlighted by numerous comments and results have shown that students perceived that they had improved in skills and confidence. This clearly shows how highly students rate the opportunities to practise listening and speaking skills more intensively and it might be worth investigating how Talkback® can be integrated into mainstream EAP modules which are offered through a VLE site.

The results also demonstrated that the students saw the potential of integrating Talkback® with other technological tools and materials within a distance learning setting where opportunities for oral interaction with a tutor or peers in the target context were few and far between. They commented on how flexible and easy to use it was. They envisaged ways in which this tool could contribute to allowing more personalised and meaningful feedback, how it could enhance interaction with 'real' people when it happened. They saw the potential for more realistic, authentic and meaningful tasks leading to better communicative skills and they enjoyed doing their assignments via the tool.

Opportunities for practising oral skills in EAP offered by Talkback® may not be limited to open and distance learning EAP students. For example, in a traditional face-to-face university, there is a tendency to focus on students' written performance despite the fact that students have to participate in seminars and discussions (Lynch, 2011). Participating in such academic activities can be extremely challenging, particularly to those students who have to operate in English as a second language or a lingua franca (Evans & Morrison, 2011). Spoken skills are often ignored or are limited to presentations even though oral communication is essential for academic communication. Thus, tools like Talkback® and associated mobile technologies can address this kind of gap as students can practise their EAP oral skills outside their regular on-campus EAP sessions.

However, any EAP practitioner or their institution wanting to integrate tools like Talkback® and mobile technologies into their EAP programmes need to make a number of considerations. As suggested by this pilot study, the simple phone and online interface seemed to have posed a few problems to students. For example, some participants thought they needed more instructions on how to get started. So more visual support might very well be needed at the outset to explain how the tool works and what mobile applications the tool can be used with.

Another important point to remember is that given Talkback®'s unique functionality, it would be problematic to use it for assessment only. It needs to be used for practice throughout a module or course. Once used for practice, it would then be logical to use it for assessment, thus providing students plenty of opportunities to 'play' with the technology. Once the technology becomes 'normalised' in students' learning, the tool as a sociocultural tool may pose less threat to the actual learning process (Bax, 2011), which otherwise can cause challenges.

The design of activities using mobile technologies for EAP oral skills deserves careful consideration as well. Activities should be designed with the specificity of the tool in mind, such as various access modes (e.g., ordinary landline, Skype, mobile apps, etc.), potential for quick feedback which may be generic and personalised. As noted previously, shorter interactive activities work better with interactive tools like Talkback®. Longer activities may be demotivating to students.

Technologies such as Talkback® offer options for providing transcriptions of tasks used in the module. It is important to make an informed decision as to whether to provide such transcriptions or not and at what given time in the module. For example, if you make the transcription of a task available from the beginning, the whole purpose of the task may be defeated. On the other hand, if it is provided very late, students may not be able to use it as reference, for example, to check what they heard was correct or not. This is particularly important if students have limited opportunities to hear English language outside their module or course.

Talkback® offers an option for students to make their answers available to all students within the website where the tool is hosted. This facility helps students to engage in collaborative learning and if it is a skill to be promoted through the EAP module then it should be considered. At the moment the tool allows the tutor to make an answer available to all students.

Currently, no practitioner-led mobile technology-enhanced EAP assessment exists unless provided by large commercial organisations (e.g., Educational Testing Services and Pearson). Talkback® or Learnosity's tools appear to be attractive options for assessments designed by teachers which are more context-sensitive and responsive to the needs of EAP students than those provided by commercial providers. Therefore, EAP providers may find Talkback® an attractive cost-effective solution.

Given that the tutor can constantly update EAP oral assessment and practice materials and recycle them, Talkback® resources can be shared among not only the EAP tutors in one institution but also with those working in other institutions if student needs are similar. This also helps to reduce the cost of the tool.

Acknowledgements

The authors would like to acknowledge the generous funding received from the Innovation Office and the Faculty of Education and Language Studies, the Open University. They are grateful for the contributions made by the other project members to the project which provided the data for this chapter: Annie Eardley, Agnes Kukulska-Hulme, Hannelore Green, Felicity Harper and Patrick Andrews.

Note: TalkBack® is no longer available from Learnosity. Instead, a web version is offered (see www.learnosity.com/demos/demos.php)

References

Bax, S. (2011). Normalisation Revisited: The Effective Use of Technology in Language Education. *International Journal of Computer-Assisted Language Learning and Teaching (IJCALLT), 1*(2), 1–15. doi: 10.4018/ijcallt.2011040101

Beatty, K. (2010). *Teaching and researching computer-assisted language learning* 2nd ed. London: Pearson.

Beckmann, E. A. (2010). Learners on the move: mobile modalities in development studies. *Distance Education, 31*(2), 159–173. doi: 10.1080/01587919.2010.498081

Chapelle, C. A., & Chung, Y-R. (2010). The promise of NLP and speech processing technologies in language assessment. *Language Testing, 27*(3), 301–315. doi: 10.1177/0265532210364405

Chapelle, C. A., & Douglas, D. (2006). *Assessing language through computer technology.* Cambridge, UK & New York: Cambridge University Press.

Coffin, C., Donohue, J., & North, S. (2009). *Exploring English grammar: from formal to functional.* London: Routledge.

Crosling, G., & Ward, I. (2002). Oral communication: the workplace needs and uses of business graduate employees. *English for Specific Purposes, 21*(1), 41–57. doi: http://dx.doi.org/10.1016/S0889-4906(00)00031-4

Demouy, V., & Kukulska-Hulme, A. (2010). On the spot: using mobile devices for listening and speaking practice on a French language programme. *Open Learning: The Journal of Open, Distance and e-Learning, 25*(3), 217–232. doi: 10.1080/02680513.2010.511955

Evans, S., & Morrison, B. (2011). The first term at university: implications for EAP. *ELT Journal, 65*(4), 387–397. doi: 10.1093/elt/ccq072

Gilbert, J. (2013). English for academic purposes. In G. Motteram (Ed.), *Innovations in learning technologies for English Language Teaching* (pp. 117–144). London: The British Council.

Hyland, K. (2007). Genre pedagogy: Language, literacy and L2 writing instruction. *Journal of Second Language Writing, 16*(3), 148–164.

ITU. (2013). The world in 2013: ICT facts and figures. Retrieved 17 February, 2014, from International Telecommunication Union http://www.itu.int/en/ITU-D/Statistics/Documents/facts/ICTFactsFigures2013-e.pdf

Kern, N. (2013). 'Technology-integrated English for specific purposes lesson: real-life language, tasks and tools for professionals'. In G. Motteram (Ed.), *Innovations in learning technologies for English Language Teaching* (pp. 87–116). London: The British Council.

Kukulska-Hulme, A. (2009). Will mobile learning change language learning? *ReCALL, 21*(2), 157–165.

Kukulska-Hulme, A. (2012). 'Language learning defined by time and place: A framework for next generation designs'. In J. E. Díaz-Vera (Ed.), *Left to My Own Devices: Learner Autonomy and Mobile Assisted Language Learning. Innovation and Leadership in English Language Teaching, 6* (pp. 1–13). Bingley, UK: Emerald Group Publishing Limited.

Lea, M., & Street, B. V. (1998). Student writing in higher education: An academic literacies approach. *Studies in Higher Education, 23*(2), 157–172.

Lillis, T. M., & Scott, M. (2007). Defining Academic Literacies Research: Issues of epistemology, ideology and strategy. *Journal of Applied Linguistics, 4*(1), 5–32.

Luoma, S. (2004). *Assessing speaking.* Cambridge: Cambridge University Press.

Lynch, T. (2011). Academic listening in the 21st Century: Reviewing a decade of research. *Journal of English for Academic Purposes, 10*(2), 79–88.

Motteram, G (Ed.). (2013). *Innovations in learning technologies for English Language Teaching.* London: The British Council.

Nicol, D. (2010). From monologue to dialogue: improving written feedback processes in mass higher education. *Assessment & Evaluation in Higher Education, 35*(5), 501–517.

Shrestha, P. (2012). Teacher professional development using mobile technologies in a large-scale project: lessons learned from Bangladesh. *International Journal of Computer-Assisted Language Learning and Teaching, 2*(4), 34–49.

Shrestha, P., & Coffin, C. (2012). Dynamic assessment, tutor mediation and academic writing development. *Assessing Writing, 17*(1), 55–70. doi: 10.1016/j.asw.2011.11.003

Stockwell, G. (2007). A review of technology choice for teaching language skills and areas in the CALL literature. *ReCALL, 19*(02), 105–120. doi:10.1017/S0958344007000225

Warschauer, M., & Ware, P. D. (2008). 'Learning, change, and power: Competing discourses of technology and literacy'. In J. Coiro, M. Knobel, C. Lankshear & D. J. Leu (Eds.), *Handbook of research on new literacies* (pp. 215–240). New York: Lawrence Erlbaum.

Xi, Xiaoming. (2010). Automated scoring and feedback systems: Where are we and where are we heading? *Language Testing, 27*(3), 291–300. doi: 10.1177/0265532210364643

Issues in developing ESP courses for dieticians working in 'global communities' in Japan

Akiko Tsuda: Nakamura Gakuen University
Clare Furneaux: University of Reading
Email: atsuda@nakamura-u.ac.jp and c.l.furneaux@reading.ac.uk

1 Introduction

For both immigrants and short-term travellers – especially those who need to have special diets – communication regarding food and nutrition in host countries is critical. This chapter discusses ESP (English for Specific Purposes) for dieticians in Japan. This is a country where food education is heavily promoted by the government as a national policy. The role of English-speaking dieticians and food science specialists is central to maintaining a healthy lifestyle in a globalised community (which, in Japan, mainly consists of immigrants and international students). The purpose of this chapter is twofold: firstly, to explore how decision-makers in curriculum development for dietetic/food science students in Japanese universities perceive English language education for their students and, secondly, to propose possible improvements in ESP programmes for dietetic/food science students in higher education – a context which has scarcely been studied internationally. By way of background, the paper discusses food and the role of dieticians in the Japanese context in some detail.

2 Overview of context

2.1 Comparison of ESP for dieticians in ESL and EFL contexts

Very little research has been done into the language needs of students studying dietetics. One paper that does, however, focus on an ESL (English as a Second Language) context, is Doley (2010). This claims that many ESL students of dietetics living in the US experience similar problems to those of nursing students: academic difficulties, anxiety and depression, and financial hardships. Doley proposes some solutions to these problems, including the need to develop educators' understanding of their students' cultures and the need for fairer treatment in Registered Dieticians, exams for ESL students, by eliminating ethnic biases.

Our focus here is Japan, an example of an EFL (English as a Foreign Language) context, in which English teaching/learning is in a mostly homogeneous foreign-language setting. For dieticians in EFL contexts, specialist teachers teach in the relevant country's first language; therefore, professional English language needs are often not met right away. This is the case in Japan, where student dieticians do not need English while at university but will need it in their future careers.

Table 1 summarises the differences in ESP between ESL (as commonly found in the US/UK) and in EFL (as experienced by the first author in Japan).

Table 1: Comparison of ESP contexts for dieticians in US/UK and Japan

	ESP: ESL (e.g., US/UK)	ESP for dieticians: EFL (Japan)
Language used in ESP classes	Exclusively English	Japanese and English
Students' L1	Heterogeneous (mixed L1s)	Homogenous (L1 Japanese)
English language use outside classroom	Yes	No
Language for National Exams/ professional Licence	English	Local language (Japanese)
Motivation for English language acquisition	Integrative/long term	Instrumental/short term
Long term goals of English language acquisition	To command English for everyday life and future professional needs	To command English for various occupational needs as dietetic specialists
English needs	Immediate	Not obvious. Not immediate. Future needs could include: • communication with patients/clients in hospitals, company cafeterias and schools • needs as researchers • needs as employers/employees in the food industry

In EFL situations, students as well as teachers are rarely exposed to English language outside the classroom, and their learning motivation tends to be instrumental, such as the desire to get higher scores in English proficiency tests, not integration into an English-speaking community.

A CLIL (Content and Language Integrated Learning) approach can be an effective way to motivate students with authentic materials, especially in an EFL setting (Pinner, 2013). In Spain, another context in which ESP is important, Cots and Clemente (2006) reported on a content-based English project in the curriculum of a university degree in Food Science and Technology. In response to an urgent need to offer foreign languages, especially English, to increase the number of multilingual graduates and to offer more accessible courses for international students, they observed not only the relatively low English proficiency of

Spanish students, but also the content instructors' lack of confidence in their communication skills in English. They proposed collaboration for an ESP programme design by 'content instructors' and 'language-teaching consultants'. In their chapter, they describe a two-year pilot study at one of the leading Spanish university departments of food technology.

2.2 Becoming a dietician in Japan

In Japan, becoming any kind of medical specialist is highly challenging – even for Japanese students, who must pass grueling university entrance exams in order to study for several years as undergraduates, and then pass specialist national exams in order to work professionally. There are two tiers of academic qualification for dieticians: a two-year college programme (usually in a junior college or a vocational college) and a four-year university programme. Both follow a national curriculum under the supervision of the Ministry of Welfare and Labor. All dietetics majors commit long hours to lectures, laboratory work and culinary classes, and must also complete internships in hospitals, nursery/primary schools, homes for the elderly and private sector cafeterias. Two-year college graduate 'dieticians' are licensed at prefectural level. Their work is seen as 'nutrition education', as this training is for dieticians who are going to work in nursery schools or company cafeterias; they need to communicate with clients face to face, but do not have to read academic papers. 'Registered dieticians' are those who have the college-level qualification and work-experience as dieticians, or graduates from four-year registered dietician training schools (in universities). They must then pass a national exam, which consists of nine subjects, such as 'Nutrition Science', 'Food and Health', 'Food Education'. The annual pass rate is 30%–50%.

The Ministry of Welfare and Labour curriculum does not specify any English language education for dietetics students and there is no foreign language component in their national exam. In addition, there are no clear guidelines for curriculum development or materials design for EFL in any such vocational higher education context in Japan. Curriculum choices about language education are left to individual colleges and universities, which can choose to omit non-specialist subjects, including foreign languages, from their curriculum.

2.3 Japanese healthcare context: dieticians' needs for English

Japanese dieticians can be required to communicate in English with four categories of people who do not speak Japanese:

1. Other healthcare workers;

2. Foreign workers and their families;

3. Foreign pupils and their parents;

4. Foreign academic colleagues.

In the first group are nurses and caregivers. To cope with the foreseen labour shortage in the healthcare sector caused by the ageing population in Japan, applications for work permits for '*Kaigofukushishi*' (caregivers) for senior citizens and '*Kangoshi*' (nurses) from Indonesians and Philippinos have been accepted as special cases under bilateral Economic Partnership Agreements (EPA) since 2003, and similar applications will be accepted from Vietnam from 2015. These workers' proficiency in Japanese is low, as evinced by the pass rates in national exams for foreign nurses (Guen, 2014).

The second group includes temporary visitors to Japan and foreign nationals working in the country. According to the Japanese Judicial System and Research Department (2014, p. 9), 9,172,146 people entered Japan with residence permits in 2012. The breakdown of their backgrounds is as follows:

- Asia: 7,069,500

- North America: 913,307

- Europe: 828,336

- Oceania: 243,844

Within these groups are people with specific dietary requirements – for example, Indonesian colleagues are usually Muslim and therefore cannot consume any pork or alcohol, both of which are commonly associated with the Japanese diet. A common concept in Japanese cuisine is '*kakushiaji*', which means 'hidden flavour' and includes the alcohol *sake* and *mirin*. In addition, pork-based lard is often used for sweets. Most Japanese people would not be aware of these commonplace ingredients causing problems for some foreign guests. In addition, food allergies are not common in Japan, where nuts and gluten, for example, are not part of the traditional diet. However, these food items are increasingly to be found in Japanese food outlets, but without the necessary labelling. The resulting problems for foreign visitors (and future Japanese consumers) in relation to allergies are not covered in the training of Japanese dieticians.

The third group comprises the 70,000 foreign students in Japanese public schools. In 2012, there were 27,013 pupils who needed Japanese language support. They are returnees from English-speaking countries who need to 'readjust' to Japanese society, pupils with dual nationalities, and children who have foreign parent(s). The pupils' first languages (in descending order of frequency) are Portuguese, Spanish, Korean, Chinese, Vietnamese, Tagalog and English.

The fourth group has relevance for registered dieticians and food scientists who take part in academic activities such as conferences and research projects.

With their expertise and knowledge of food science and nutrition, dieticians and registered dieticians contribute to various sectors, such as medicine, education, industry and academia in Japan. Dieticians work in nursery schools, facilities for senior citizens and company cafeterias in order to supervise the production of nutritious meals (or *Kyushoku*, to be discussed below). Registered dieticians, as specialists in nutrition science, can have much wider employment prospects, such as in hospitals, the food industry or research facilities. With appropriate teacher-training credits, they can become food technology teachers and/or home economics teachers in secondary schools.

As noted above, students and university teachers in Japan see little need for English language teaching in dietetics training courses as they are rarely exposed to English on a daily basis. However, once these students become registered dieticians, they often find that they need to use English in professional contexts.

3 Target situation analysis: Dieticians and their English language needs

Examples of target needs which dieticians/registered dieticians may encounter are given below, based on the first author's observations of students' internships at future workplaces (such as nursery schools, company cafeterias and hospitals) and of faculty members in food technology departments in Japanese and British universities.

3.1 Educational settings

Dieticians who are working for nursery, primary and secondary schools, and secondary school food technology/home economics teachers need to communicate with English-speaking children and their parents, using English as their lingua franca. School dieticians need to translate Japanese menus into English, explain Japanese eating habits and provide nutritional guidance in plain English, without using technical terminology from nutrition/food science.

In Japan, school lunches are mainly *washoku*, Japanese traditional cuisine, and many schools attempt to use locally grown ingredients, some of which might be unknown to some parents from other countries. In particular, dieticians working in nursery schools must also have basic English communicative skills and knowledge about the cultural differences in eating habits of non-Japanese-speaking parents and parents with minimal Japanese skills, as their children will also be eating school dinners and sweets which are prepared by Japanese dieticians.

3.2 Clinical settings

As paramedical staff, registered dieticians in hospitals and public health institutes are required to use English for nutritional guidance for English-speaking patients. Unlike medical doctors and nurses who tend to work in larger groups and can more easily solicit language support from other specialists, hospital dieticians usually work in small groups or alone. They might need to use English without any access to medical translators. In addition, as medical experts, registered dieticians need to update their clinical knowledge through English.

3.3 Business sector settings

As food businesses have become increasingly globalised, a high TOEIC score has become a great advantage for dietetics/food science majors who are looking for work in the food industry. Such positions are keenly sought after by college and university students, and sometimes employers set minimum target scores for job applications and/or employees' promotions. In such companies, the ability to engage in basic business English communication with clients and other employees abroad is expected.

In large, Japan-based companies, *shashoku* (company cafeterias) – where the provision of healthy meals is overseen by company dieticians – are an important employee benefit. To become a company dietician is one career option for dietetic/food science majors. If dieticians are working in cafeterias in multinational companies – for example Rakuten, one of the largest e-commerce companies in Japan – basic knowledge of English food terminology is helpful, since company cafeteria menus are written in English.

3.4 Academic settings

If graduate students want to become full-time researchers in research institutes or universities, they need to read international journals to update their knowledge in their specialties. They also need to be able to contribute to the journals. Further, they need to attend international conferences, which are invariably announced and conducted in English, requiring the use of all four language skills. Even within Asian settings, Japanese dieticians need to speak English to communicate with dieticians coming from other countries. For example, the official language for the Asian Congress of Dietetics is English.

Japanese dieticians can also seek an international arena in which to broaden their horizons, such as to study food science/technology/nutrition science in universities and graduate schools abroad (typically in the United States or United Kingdom). Therefore, their EAP needs are the same as all would-be graduate students, from taking IELTS/TOEFL tests to gain entry, to participating and succeeding as a student in an ESL context.

3.5 As a volunteer in developing countries

Volunteer dieticians in developing countries in Africa, Central and South America and Asia require English-speaking skills for dietetic consultations and presentations to local people. Applying to be a Japan Overseas Cooperation Volunteer (JICA, 2014) requires certification of English proficiency.

4 Food education in Japan

In order to appreciate the need for dieticians to communicate with colleagues and clients in Groups 1–3 above, it is important to understand the central role of food within Japanese education and culture.

In 2013, Japan became the second nation (after France) to have its traditional *washoku* cuisine designated by UNESCO's as an Intangible Cultural Heritage. Demetriou (2013) described the characteristics of *washoku* thus: its emphasis is on harmony and the passing seasons, the minimal use of meat and great use of seafood. He commented that the Japanese government welcomed *washoku*'s designation as recognition of Japan's cultural heritage and of the potential health benefits the diet provides, and in terms of the economic advantages such recognition gives (e.g., food tourism). In addition, he reported on Masanori Aoyagi, the commissioner of Japan's Cultural Affairs Agency, praising *washoku* for its important contribution to feelings of social cohesion.

Food education has always been important in Japanese schools, as exemplified by the Food Education Basic Law introduced in 2005. Dieticians/registered dieticians must take a leading role in food education, including for non-Japanese residents. As already discussed, Japanese workplaces have become more globalised, with increasing numbers of long-term foreign residents who use English (as a mother tongue or second language), and cannot function in Japanese. Their needs must be catered for according to the 'Code of Ethics for Registered Dieticians and Dieticians' established April 27, 2002 (The Japan Dietetic Association website). Provision 2 states that 'Registered Dieticians and Dieticians will not discriminate by nationality, race, religion, belief, principle, lineage, social status, age or sex'.

The long history of the Japanese standardised *Kyushoku* system (which involves school lunches supervised by dieticians) helps form the deep-rooted Japanese mindset towards food culture and eating habits. Based on the 1954 School Lunch Law, school lunches are distributed to elementary schools and junior high schools nationwide. The law stipulates that all public and private elementary and junior high schools in Japan should strive to provide student lunches – that is, *Kyushoku*. Some school dinners are cooked by dinner ladies working in schools, while others are received from school kitchen centres and reheated at schools. Thanks to the *Kyushoku* system, regardless of their family's income, all pupils can enjoy the same dishes with their classmates, in their classrooms, as there are no school cafeterias in typical primary/junior high schools in Japan.

The concept of *Kyushoku* is based on food education. *Kyushoku* are planned by dieticians, who decide on monthly menus; these are sent home to parents with nutritional information to educate them and to avoid having them serve the same dishes for dinner. Pupils serve school lunches for classmates and classroom teachers, wearing special aprons, as part of food education. Japanese schools usually have school dinner committees organised by pupils. Children and teachers eat together in classrooms. Except for the very exceptional student who has a food allergy, students have no choice of food and are encouraged to eat everything, because *Kyushoku* is designed to be nutritious and well-balanced. Fussy eaters are not tolerated. Children in Japan view food specialists with great respect and the first author and her ESP students were very shocked to view a programme about Jamie Oliver's school dinner project in England, with the challenges this project faced in promoting healthy eating in schools.

With a largely homogenous culinary background, Japanese people are mostly unaware of food preferences or dietary requirements associated with belief or religion. As in traditional Japanese diets, pork, *sake* and *mirin* are often used as ingredients. If a non-Japanese pupil, or their parent, cannot explain their dietary requirement in Japanese, they will encounter difficulties. In addition, Japanese adults working in international contexts are also often unaware of religious or personal food taboos. So, for example, in international conventions held in Japan, dietary preferences (such as vegetarian or halal) are rarely catered for.

5 Present situation analysis

5.1 EFL/ESP teachers at tertiary level in Japan

In most Japanese universities, the medium of instruction is Japanese, and textbooks and materials are written in Japanese. Students do not have to use English in their daily academic lives, especially at undergraduate level. In addition, the foreign language curriculum, which includes English, is not regulated by the Ministry of Education. Therefore, not all universities and colleges include EFL as a core subject. However, it is largely understood that students will be offered EFL optional courses during their first two years of study, as this is a common practice in Japanese colleges.

However, that EFL course will not be ESP as understood in most situations – that is, with a focus on discipline-specific content (Paltridge & Starfield 2013b). EFL teachers within the Japanese university system are ill-equipped to handle ESP for a variety of reasons. As this teaching is unregulated (unlike in schools), university-level EFL teachers may have no formal teaching qualification. Individual universities and colleges can employ any EFL instructors and design these courses as they like. No formal language teacher training is seen as necessary, nor is it provided. To be an instructor in this context, an MA degree is the minimum qualification. In practice, this means that many Japanese English literature specialists – with no TEFL/TESOL background or previous ELT experience – are teaching English in universities.

In contrast, tenured professors in science (including dietetics/food science) who are in charge of all curriculum development are mainly PhD holders; many of them have experience of international academia. Therefore, ironically, they are often better informed about and experienced in the international academic arena than the EFL instructors.

Another factor here is the status of many EFL teachers in Japanese universities, where the difference between part-time and full-time teachers is significant. The majority of universities and colleges are highly dependent on part-time EFL teachers/instructors. Private universities, in particular, cannot afford to employ full-time EFL teachers/professors as faculty members on tenure track, because of financial constraints. In many Japanese universities, part-time EFL teachers/instructors teach as many or even more hours than full-time EFL teachers/professors. Part-time teachers/instructors are regarded as adjunct teachers with lower status than full-time colleagues; their responsibilities are limited to teaching, setting exams and submitting grades. Full-time teachers/professors on tenure track, in contrast, have considerable responsibilities, which are divided into teaching, administration and research (Chenoweth & Pearson, 1992; Evanoff, 1992; Nagatomo, 2012).

Part-time EFL teachers/instructors are excluded from the process of curriculum development, even if they have taught within a university for many years. Furthermore, information on classes and students is frequently provided to part-time EFL teachers so late that they have insufficient time to prepare properly or adjust their teaching to their students' needs. These factors have a negative effect on both the quality of teaching and on the teachers' motivation.

In addition, most of the full-time teachers/professors who are in charge of EFL teaching in Japanese universities are not connected to a specific academic department; they belong to a central language teaching centre. This means that they develop no specialist knowledge about their students' disciplines; they also have no support from discipline-specialist colleagues.

5.2 Stakeholders in ESP courses in Japan

Johnston and Peterson (1994) identified four groups of stakeholders in language programmes: learners, teachers, administrators and controlling authorities. It is useful to look at these within the Japanese system:

a. *Learners*: These are mostly young Japanese women who want to work in food-related occupations. In most universities, student evaluations are completed at the end of academic programmes, using questionnaires. This means that current learners have no impact on the programme once it is underway.

b. *Teachers*: these have already been discussed. Considering this specific context, EFL teachers know the actual proficiency of students but do not know their target needs. Specialist teachers know their target needs and have more experience of international academia than EFL teachers, but they have no understanding of the reality of EFL classrooms, nor what ESP is.

c. *Administrators*: These have a major role in programme implementation. As the majority of dietetic training schools are private bodies, the recruitment of students is crucial. This involves screening of applications, for example.

d. *Authorities*: The curriculum for dietetics is strictly supervised by the Ministry of Health and Welfare. It would be difficult to change this curriculum, especially to specify the teaching of optional subjects, such as foreign languages.

5.3 ESP for dieticians' courses and materials in Japan

ESP courses for dieticians are virtually non-existent in Japan because the ultimate goal for faculty members in training schools is to nurture dieticians following the specified national curriculum – which does not include English language courses – and to ensure students pass the annual national examinations. The first author's experience within the Japanese university system suggests that teachers' heavy workloads and a lack of consensus on what English language education for dieticians should be among academic faculty members have hindered the development of ESP for dieticians in Japan. Therefore, ESL/EFL teachers who teach dietetic majors have coped with these issues individually drawing on their own experience without any formal guidance.

6 Nationwide research project

6.1 Introduction

The above issues were the motivating factors behind a national research project, which ran from 2011 to 2013, entitled 'ESP for the training of nutritionists who will contribute to the internationalisation of local communities: needs analysis and teaching materials development', which this chapter draws upon. This research project was funded by a Japanese Ministry of Education, Culture, Sports, Science and Technology research grant. It consisted of: 1) classroom observation; 2) a pilot survey with faculty members and graduates in a university where the first author works; and 3) a nationwide survey.

A needs analysis should underpin any major curriculum development, both in terms of evaluating existing programmes and designing future ones (Richards, 2001; Flowerdew 2013). A strong needs analysis will involve a Target Situation Analysis (TSA) and a Present Situation Analysis (PSA), which have been outlined above. The nationwide survey began with a PSA of the EFL education curriculum for dieticians/registered dietician training schools throughout Japan. As part of this, it surveyed targeted curriculum decision-makers in training colleges and universities for dieticians/registered dieticians.

6.2 Procedure

This survey aimed to identify the attitudes towards EFL education among the teaching staff responsible for developing English curricula for dieticians/registered dieticians across Japan. Drawing on the Japan Dietetic Association websites, and the official websites with university/college prospectuses, the study targeted teaching staff in 300 nutritionist and dietician training institutions across Japan (universities, junior colleges and vocational schools) and asked for their participation in an anonymous, self-reported questionnaire. The language used in the questionnaire was Japanese, and requests for participation and the survey itself were carried out by post. We collected and then analysed 139 responses (a 46% response rate), of which 82 answered the open-ended question focused on here (i.e., 60% of the sample).

6.3 Limitations

It should be noted that the respondents included teachers who were involved in designing the curricula both in two-year college courses for dieticians and four-year university courses for registered dieticians. There is a difference between dieticians and registered dieticians in terms of their postgraduation workplaces; it will thus be necessary in future to conduct separate needs analysis surveys (target situation analysis) in the workplaces for both groups.

Also, to increase the response rate and maintain anonymity, the survey did not ask for detailed academic information about respondents, such as qualifications, publications and overseas experience. However, these characteristics might affect respondents' attitude to the need for English among dietetic students, and thus the lack of this information is also a limiting factor.

6.4 Respondent characteristics

We analysed the 82 answers to the following open-ended question: 'Please give your opinions of English language education in universities, junior colleges or vocational schools which train dieticians or national registered dieticians'. This question was deliberately vague to encourage the widest possible range of answers.

Tables 2 to 5 present the profile of this group of respondents.

Table 2: Place of work

Institution	n	%
Universities	43	52.4
Junior colleges/vocational Schools	39	47.6
Total	82	100

Table 3: Gender distribution

Gender	n	%
Male	38	46.3
Female	44	53.7
Total	82	100

Table 4: Age distribution

Age distribution	n	%
Over 60	28	34.1
50s	31	37.8
40s	16	19.5
30s	7	8.5
Total	82	100

Table 5: Staff role

University/Junior college	n	%
Discipline-specialist teachers (DST)	52	63.4
English teachers (ELT)	27	32.9
Administrators (A)	3	3.7
Total	82	100

7 Findings

To examine the opinions given, text mining was carried out using the clustering analysis software Wordminer (2013), Version 1.1. Keywords were divided into 11 topic clusters based on their relationship in descending order of replies as follows (underlined emphases added by the authors). Topic clusters with a small number of responses (i.e., two) have been kept in here as they add to the overall picture and most fall into one grouping (namely c, see Table 7), giving it a degree of representation.

Table 6: Topic clusters from answers – totals and respondents' professional background

No	Topic cluster	N	ELT	DST/A	Example of answers in this cluster (translated from Japanese by first author) – emphasis is the authors'
1	There is variation in students' English proficiency, and a decline in academic performance.	17	7	10	*"I teach scientific English and because there is <u>a difference in the English reading comprehension of students,</u> I find it difficult to teach. It may be necessary to consider the possibility of streaming classes by level in the future."* (DST) *"I have <u>difficulty in teaching English to students who are not good at or who do not like English.</u> Some students do have knowledge and want an interesting class, so for these students rudimentary English activities are boring. There are also students who are 'allergic' to English."* (ELT)
2	English is only taught as a liberal Arts subject or a general education subject.	11	6	4	*"In our school, English classes are <u>only held as a liberal Arts subject.</u> If we can incorporate ESP (dietetics English) followed by English for General Purposes into the curriculum, student interest will surely increase. However, in that case, it will be necessary to have instructors specialised in the field."* (DST) *"It is unfortunate that <u>general education English classes tend to end in the first year.</u> Students who like English take part in overseas study tours but cannot achieve sufficient proficiency in 2 weeks. English reading comprehension is necessary if students are to go on to graduate school."* (ELT)
3	In the present curriculum, English language teaching cannot be increased.	8	1	7	*"I feel the need for English language education but it always takes a back seat with <u>the presently overcrowded curriculum.</u> Something must be done but a tangible solution has not yet been found."* (DST)

Table 6: continued

No	Topic cluster	N	ELT	DST/A	Example of answers in this cluster (translated from Japanese by first author) – emphasis is the authors'
4	Students need general English.	6	3	3	"*I would like to aim at a higher level of <u>basic language proficiency.</u>*" (ELT) "*I had a hard time choosing teaching materials appropriate for the English level of students at our school. I think that <u>more focus should be put on pronunciation and conversational ability.</u>*" (DST)
5	Globalisation of dieticians is necessary.	5	–	4 (+ 1 A)	"*Even if dieticians are going to be working domestically in one area, I would like to educate students to <u>be workers who act and think with a more global point of view</u>. English is an important tool in achieving this.*" (DST)
6	Students of nutritional sciences give little priority to English.	4	1	3	"*<u>It has low priority</u> because it is not part of the core curriculum. Even if the contents are not of a high level, it is important for students to read dietetics related sources or information and to communicate to them the fact that nutrition and health issues are worldwide concerns.*" (DST)
7	English ability is necessary to gather information via the Internet.	2	–	2	"*If we consider that we will <u>acquire a great variety of information via the Internet</u> in the future, the present English ability of students cannot be said to be entirely satisfactory.*" (ELT)
8	English is necessary for communication for dietetic students/dieticians.	2	1	1	"*Depending on the student, they may want to volunteer or work overseas or to <u>communicate with people from abroad,</u> so it would be good for them to be able to hold a conversation. In the case that they want to invite overseas guests and study cooking, communication ability will be more important than technical jargon.*" (ELT) "*For national registered dieticians, it may be necessary to read English resources such as academic papers, but our school trains students to be dieticians so I believe English should be learned for <u>communication purposes</u>. We cannot expect students to read English materials now.*" (DST)
9	Students have insufficient control of Japanese, their L1.	2	–	2	"*Along with a decline in English education, I feel there is also <u>a decline in Japanese composition skills.</u>*" (DST)

Table 6: continued

No	Topic cluster	N	ELT	DST/A	Example of answers in this cluster (translated from Japanese by first author) – emphasis is the authors'
10	There are few opportunities for dieticians to use English.	2	2	–	*"They do not have as much opportunity as doctors or nurses to use English and we do not expect such opportunities to grow."* (ELT)
11	Students need to read academic papers or other sources in English.	2	–	2	*"It is important at training schools to at least get students accustomed to technical jargon by reading English academic papers. Academic papers cannot be understood with only grammatical knowledge, so it is necessary to give students the reading comprehension ability to read English papers while they are still students. This will be helpful in increasing their knowledge when they are in the job."* (DST)

Key

N: Number of respondents who chose this (Total = 82)

ELT: English Language teachers (Total = 22)

DST: Discipline-specific teachers (Total = 57)

A: Administrators (Total = 3)

There were 19 comments which did not fit into the clusters above, referring to aspects such as:

- bilingual knowledge about terminology (Japanese and English) (1DST);

- development of the standardised ESP textbooks for all training schools (1DST); and

- practical education which is different from traditional type (1DST)

These have been borne in mind in the discussion and suggestions, but the focus is on these 11 clusters, which can be grouped as follows:

Table 7: Topic clusters grouped by issue

Topic cluster grouping	Cluster	Number of respondents
a. Student issues (L1/L2 proficiency)	1, 9	19
b. Curriculum issues	2, 3, 6	23
c. Language need issues	4, 5, 6, 7, 8, 10, 11	23

8 Discussion

8.1 Student issues

It is commonly felt in Japan that academic achievement among Japanese students has been degraded due to the implementation of a policy known as *yutori kyoiku* (which translates as 'relaxed curriculum' or 'education free from pressure') in primary and secondary schools since the 1990s (Wada and Burnett, 2011). A substantial number of professors in Japan feel that, as a result of this policy, students' abilities in numeracy and literacy have plummeted. Programmes in dietetics have many core subjects and the knowledge and skills gained are integral to a dietician's job, so this perceived lowering of standards among school leavers acts as a disincentive to increase curriculum demands in terms of foreign language learning.

In addition, to attract more applicants, many colleges and universities, especially private ones, provide several ways of screening applicants, including 'entrance recommendation only'. This means that applicants do not have to pass written tests, resulting in a wide, unknown range of abilities within one class. Collaboration between secondary and tertiary schools is uncommon and there is no coherence of curriculum across them. As a result of this combination of factors, many teachers, especially part-time ones, are largely unaware of their students' previous education and learning needs.

8.2 Curriculum issues

The ultimate goal for the academic departments is to train students to be dietetic specialists who can achieve certification. A good pass rate in national exams attracts more undergraduate applicants. The curriculum for dietetic majors is so strictly supervised by the Ministry of Health and Welfare and is too full of core subject content to allow enough time for optional subjects, such as EFL/ESP. In addition, students rarely consider continuing their English Language studies in higher education. Because faculty members are basically researchers, their mindset is different from the qualified teachers who have a teaching licence at primary and secondary schools. Therefore, even if students have learned English well at school, they will not find a coherent progression to university language study, if it is offered at all.

8.3 Language need issues

Our respondents list various target needs for their students and they have opposing views. Not all dietetic professors in Japanese higher education have worked as dieticians in local communities; so they may have no idea of the practical English language needs their students will encounter in the workplace, as outlined previously. On the other hand, some respondents, especially discipline-specialist teachers, have progressive ideas for promoting ESP for dietetics, identifying specific needs for the profession. In such an environment, it is difficult to develop a one-size-fits-all curriculum to satisfy all of the relevant institutions in Japan.

The first author's seven-year classroom observation, collaboration with dietetic teachers as a faculty member and the nationwide survey project reported on above indicate that:

1. There is a variety of English language needs among dietetic specialists depending on their workplace; therefore, one should not overgeneralise about the target needs of dietetic students. However, once needs arise at their workplace (for example, giving dietetic advice to English-speaking patients/parents or attending international conferences), dieticians must cope with the situation on their own. Therefore, establishing the foundations for lifelong ESP learning should be promoted. This should include providing a linguistic foundation and developing autonomous language-learning strategies based on both short-term and long-term goal setting.

2. As dietetic majors have wide-ranging English language needs, curriculum developers need to identify and prioritise the most pressing ones. For example, developing cultural literacy in dietetics through ESP is clearly a major priority in the Japanese context because, as we have seen, Japanese people find it difficult to comprehend the culinary needs of non-Japanese people, because of their lack of cultural knowledge. Students should also acquire a familiarity with basic nutritional terminology in English which they can draw upon in their future careers.

3. The national survey identified a lack of consensus among curriculum decision-makers. Without clear aims and objectives, effective teaching/learning is impossible, irrespective of how much is available in the programme. Collaboration among stakeholders grounded in frequent communication and mutual understanding is essential. In addition, continuity of the curriculum between the English for General Purposes (EGP) of secondary schools and the ESP of universities/colleges and cohesion of the college curriculum across core subjects and ESP in dietetics should be developed. By doing this, cohesion of the diachronic curriculum (EGP to ESP) and the synchronic curriculum (ESP and core subjects) could be realised.

9 Pedagogic suggestions for ESP practitioners

9.1 Levels of cooperation

To engage with the disciplines, Dudley-Evans and St John (1998, pp. 15–16, 42–48) suggest three levels of cooperation. In Table 8, below, this framework is used to identify possible cooperation among stakeholders in Japan.

Table 8: Possible cooperation in Japanese 'ESP for dieticians' contexts (based on Dudley-Evans and St John 1998, 42–48)

	Who	Why	How
Cooperation	ESP teachers discipline-specialist teachers administrators students (including previous students) employers	To gather information about students' courses and the priorities of each subject To familiarise each other with relevant target needs	Needs analysis (especially target situation analysis by surveys)
Collaboration	ESP teachers discipline-specialist teachers	To develop ESP programmes/ materials based on the subjects students are learning	Needs analysis (especially present situation analysis: classroom/conference observation) Corpus development and analysis (Nesi, 2013)
Team-teaching	ESP teachers discipline-specialist teachers	To develop Content and Language Integrated Learning programmes to raise students cultural awareness and EAP skills	Following a CLIL approach (Coyle, Hood and Marsh, 2010)

9.2 ESP practitioner roles

Dudley-Evans and St John (1998) provide another useful framework here – that of ESP practitioner roles. This can also be adopted to frame pedagogical suggestions for better ESP programmes for dieticians in an EFL context such as in Japan.

ESP practitioners as teachers

Raising students' and dietetics teachers' awareness about workplace English language needs is essential. Below are examples that the first author has introduced in classrooms (Tsuda, 2012):

- Inviting medical experts and international students who speak English as guest speakers into classrooms: possible topics are food culture from other countries, target needs for dietetic students and religious dietary taboos.

- Assigning students presentations about Japanese food culture, such as *Kyushoku*, local food, Japanese table manners, as part of a simulation, or as an authentic online project, in briefing English-speaking children about *shokuiku* (food education).

- Asking students to write a recipe based on *washoku* (Japanese cuisine) for English-speaking vegetarians in English.

- ESP practitioners as course designers and material providers.

As the market for ESP textbooks in dietetics and food science has not been explored, individual teachers need to develop and provide materials (Barnard and Zemach, 2003).

ESP practitioners as collaborators

As this research project indicates, the development of ESP in dietetics has been hindered by a lack of consensus among stakeholders, a lack of awareness of the need for it at institutional and higher (governmental) levels, and by the lack of space in the current curriculum. To satisfy the students' target needs, the following example of collaboration among stakeholders can be considered, with regard to materials development.

Drawing on principles of second language acquisition relevant to the development of materials for language teaching, Tomlinson (2011, p. 11) notes:

> 'What is being taught should be perceived by learners as relevant and useful. In ESP … materials, it is relatively easy to convince the learners that the teaching points are relevant and useful by relating them to known learners' interests and to 'real-life' tasks, which the learners need or might need to perform in the target language'.

To activate their learners' interest, ESP teachers should raise their awareness of their delayed English language needs, using authentic materials based on the expert knowledge of specialist teachers and cultural insights from English native-speaking teachers. To achieve authenticity in the development of materials, Japanese EFL teachers (who know the learners' linguistic and learning needs), native English-speaking teachers (who know the target language) and specialist teachers (who know the target contexts) should collaborate to produce materials that draw on a dietetics content at appropriate linguistic levels with suitable tasks to promote students' learning of English that will be useful for their specific professional purposes.

ESP practitioner as researchers

As needs analysis is an ongoing process (Long, 2005), detailed analyses of present and target needs are critical for successful curriculum development (Nation & Macalister, 2010), for example, by conducting interviews with:

- English-speaking clients and parents of young children;

- dieticians who need to consult English-speaking patients and their families; and

- graduate students and dietetics researchers.

This analysis can feed into both curriculum development, in terms of informing decisions and into materials design, in terms of providing texts for use in tasks.

ESP practitioner as evaluator

ESP practitioners should become involved in various evaluations including course design, teaching materials and learners. However, common criteria for evaluation of ESP in dietetics programmes or materials do not exist and need to be developed, drawing on insights from ESP teachers, discipline-specialist teachers and practising dieticians. In addition, as test scores will influence students' career prospects, teachers should be accountable for their assessments in designing appropriate language tests for learners. They should consider factors such as practicality, reliability, validity, authenticity and washback (Brown, 1996).

10 Conclusion

Living in an EFL country, Japanese students and teachers do not have to use English on a daily basis. Therefore, current needs for ESP are not perceived by stakeholders in the EFL/ESP curriculum. In addition, institutions currently have to give priority to the requirements of the core curriculum and preparation for national exams, and improvement of English education, therefore, tends to be neglected/postponed. However, because of the globalisation of our communities, even in countries which seem as homogeneous as Japan, we need to develop dieticians who can serve the local communities with English skills as well as scientific ones. These factors may influence other ESP contexts, both within Japan and elsewhere. To explore this, it would be helpful to see a widening of research into and discussion of more EFL/ESP contexts.

Acknowledgements

This chapter draws on the study entitled 'ESP for the training of nutritionists who will contribute to the internationalisation of local communities: Needs analysis and teaching materials development', which was carried out with the support of Grants-in-Aid for Scientific Research, JSPS KAKENHI Grant Number 23520736.

The chapter was completed while Akiko Tsuda was a Visiting Scholar at the University of Reading, UK, working with Clare Furneaux.

References

Barnard, R. and Zemach, D. (2003). In B. Tomlinson (Ed.), *Designing Materials for Language Teaching* (pp. 306–323). London: Continuum.

Brown, D. (1996). *Testing in language programs.* Upper Saddle River, NJ: Prentice Hall Regents.

Cabinet Office, Government Japan. (2006). *Basic program for shokuiku promotion* (Abstract). Retrieved March 7, 2014, from http://www8.cao.go.jp/syokuiku/about/pdf/plan_ol_eng.pdf

Chenoweth, A., & Pearson, E. (1992). Launching a career at a Japanese university. In P. Wadden (Ed.), *A Handbook for teaching English at Japanese colleges and universities* (pp. 3–14). New York, NY: Oxford University Press.

Cots, M., & Clemente, M. (2006). Teaching and learning about food technology in English: an experience of content-based English at university level, *Actas del V Congreso Internacional AELFE, 06*. Retrieved March 7, 2014, from http://www.unizar.es/aelfe2006/ALEFE06/2.%20didactics/43.pdf

Coyle, D., Hood, P., & Marsh, D. (2010). *Content and Language Integrated Learning.* Cambridge: Cambridge University Press.

Demetriou, D. (2013, December 5). Japanese cuisine gets UNESCO heritage status. *The Telegraph.* Retrieved March 7, 2014, from http://www.telegraph.co.uk/news/worldnews/asia/japan/10496326/Japanese-cuisine-gets-UNESCO-heritage-statusj.html

Doley, E. (2010). English as a second language dietetics students: lessons from nursing to facilitate learning experience in dietetics internships. *Journal of the American Dietetic Association. 113*(5), 1806–1809.

Dudley-Evans, T., & St John, M. (1998). *Developments in English for specific purposes: A multi-disciplinary approach.* Cambridge: Cambridge University Press.

Evanoff, R. (1992). Making career of university teaching in Japan. In P. Wadden. (Ed.), *A Handbook for teaching English at Japanese colleges and universities.* (pp. 15–26), New York, NY: Oxford University Press.

Flowerdew, L. (2012). Needs analysis and curriculum development in ESP. In B. Paltridge & S. Starfield (Eds.), *The Handbook of English for Specific Purposes* (pp. 325–346).

Fukue, N. (2009 January). No brown bagging it for students. *Japan Times.* Retrieved March 7, 2014, from http://www.japantimes.co.jp/news/2009/01/27/reference/no-brown-bagging-it-for-students/

Guen, B. (2014, February 2). Give foreign nurses in Japan a boost by treating accord as long-term remedy for labour shortages. *Japan Times.* Retrieved March 7, 2014, from http://www.japantimes.co.jp/opinion/2014/02/02/commentary/give-foreign-nurses-in-japan-a-boost-by-treating-accord-as-long-term-remedy-for-labor-shortages/#.UwrIS2aCj84

Long, M. H. (2005). Methodological issues in learner needs analysis. In M. H. Long. (Ed.), *Second language needs analysis* (pp. 19–76). Cambridge: Cambridge University Press.

JICA. (2014). *Official website.* Retrieved March 7, 2014, from http://www.jica.go.jp/volunteer/

Johnston, B. and Peterson, S. (1994). The program matrix: a conceptual framework for language programs. *System. 22*(1), 63–80.

Judicial System and Research Department, Minister's Secretariat, Ministry of Justice. (2014). Population and households. *Japan Statistical Yearbook*. Retrieved March 7th 2014, from http://www.stat.go.jp/english/data/nenkan/1431-02.htm

Nagatomo, D. (2012). *Exploring Japanese University English Teachers' Professional Identity*. Bristol: Multilingual Matters.

Nation, I. E. E. P. & Macalister, J. (2010). *Language Curriculum Design*. New York: Routledge.

Nesi, H. (2013). 'ESP and corpus studies'. In B. Paltridge and S. Starfield, (Eds.), *The Handbook of English for Specific Purposes* (pp. 407–426).

Paltridge, B. and Starfield, S. (2013a). (Eds.) *The Handbook of English for Specific Purposes*. Chichester: John Wiley.

Paltridge, B. and Starfield, S. (2013b). ESP and pedagogy. In B. Paltridge and S. Starfield, (Eds.) *The Handbook of English for Specific Purposes* (pp. 323–324).

Pinner, R. (2013). Authenticity of Purpose: CLIL as a way to bring meaning and motivation into EFL. *Asian EFL Journal. 15*(4). Retrieved March 7, 2014, from http://asian-efl-journal.com/quarterly-journal/2013/12/03/authenticity-of-purpose-clil-as-a-way-to-bring-meaning-and-motivation-into-efl-contexts/#thethe-tabs-1-3

Richards, J. C. (2001). *Curriculum development in language teaching*. Cambridge: Cambridge Language Education.

The 6th Asian Congress of Dietetics. (2014). *Welcome message*. Retrieved March 7, 2014, from http://www.acd2014.org

The Japan Dietetic Association. (n.d.). *Code of ethics for registered dieticians and dieticians*. Retrieved March 7, 2014, from http://www.dietitian.or.jp/english/infojpndiet/codeethics.html

The Japan Dietetic Association. (n.d.). *Gakko annai (school information)*. Retrieved March 7, 2014, from http://www.dietitian.or.jp/school/index.htm

Tomlinson, B. (2011). Introduction: principles and procedures of materials–development. In B. Tomlinson. (Ed.), *Material development in language teaching* (pp. 1–31). Cambridge: Cambridge University Press.

Tsuda, A. (2012). Developing an ESP course and materials for dieticians. *Professional and Academic English*, Issue 39, pp. 23–24, 29–30.

UNESCO. (2014). *Washoku, traditional dietary cultures of the Japanese, notably for the celebration of the year*. Retrieved 7 March, 2014, from http://www.unesco.org/culture/ich/RL/00869

Wada, M. & Burnett, B. (2011). *"Yutori kyoiku"* and the uncertainty of recent neo-liberal reforms in Japanese Higher Education, *Bulletin of Center for the Research and Support of Educational Practice*, 7, 69–78. Retrieved March 7, 2014, from http://eprints.qut.edu.au/58963/2/

WordMiner Textmining Kenkyukai. (2013). *Seihin gaiyo (Product information).* Retrieved March 7, 2014, from http://wordminer.org/about/15

Language and trade union education in Africa: Developing a critical, transformative approach

Barbara Tully, Northumbria University
Email: barbara.tully@northumbria.ac.uk

1 Introduction

This chapter outlines the context, design, piloting and accreditation of a programme of English for Sierra Leonean trade unionists that brought together the Sierra Leone Labour Congress (SLLC), the University of Sierra Leone (USL) and Northumbria University (NU), UK. The chapter highlights the importance of language as an essential employability skill for trade unionists and their members globally, and draws on a number of initiatives that have led to the development of ESP programmes for trade unionists in Europe. It will go on to present the challenges of adapting a European ESP framework for use in a postcolonial African context using a case study in Sierra Leone in which language and trade union experts were able to develop a critical pedagogy that aimed to address a sociopolitical gap in training needs for workers within the country. The chapter discusses the transformational impact of the project on the key stakeholders and its potential for delivery in other settings. It also argues that by working closely with trade union educators and change agents, the ESP community can harness the global agendas of employability and capacity building to develop language programmes that are critically focused and transformative and that address the sociopolitical needs of workers.

2 Local context

The project rationale was articulated by the SLLC to address a need for their trade union members to develop employability skills within a context of poor local and regional economic opportunities and for trade union representatives to develop leadership and communication skills in order to articulate the needs of their members. Labour market indicators (ILO, 2009) clearly demonstrated the demand for a skilled and literate workforce but just 9% of the working population was in salaried employment and there were major gaps in provision for the employed population in terms of training. Previous projects with the SLLC as well as with the United Mineworkers' Union, the Women's Committee of the SLLC and the Teachers' Union indicated a strong demand for English language training in the context of their employment as negotiators, representatives, writers of policy and reports, presenters of information and as trainers. It was important, however, that the training addressed not only the specific language skills identified by the representatives (or 'reps') but also developed an activist discourse that would empower them as individuals to challenge and represent more confidently and effectively.

In 2012 Sierra Leone featured at 177 out of 186 countries on the United Nation's Index of Human Development and although a relative period of stability since the end of the bloody civil war in 2002 has seen economic growth and the establishment of multi-party elections, considerable inequalities remain. Stirling (2013) describes how trade unions in the country have struggled with a paucity of resources, at times imprisonment and a decimation of membership during the civil war, and have witnessed their main congress building being bombed and offices vandalised. Whilst there has been a decline of some unions such as the mineworkers following multiple closures of mines, the informal sector (i.e., workers without secure incomes, benefits or protection – largely women and youths) has always been dominant and presents major challenges for organising and representing those working in a deregulated market. Nevertheless and despite major resource constraints, Sierra Leone's trade unions are significant civil society actors and are in a continuous process of capacity building at all levels.

It is against this background that trade union leaders in Sierra Leone have sought international solidarity and international training to increase their strength as civil society actors. Some of that support has come from the International Labour Organisation and northern European trade unions including some in Denmark, Sweden and the United Kingdom who have actively promoted an international agenda. As the colonial legacy exists in the trade union movement and its structures as well as in the institutions of Sierra Leone, sharing good practice and education within activism was seen as important and a number of training areas identified by the SLLC had led to programmes being delivered to various sectors and to the leadership. Furthermore, building a skilled workforce is central to underpinning the development of Sierra Leone and, although Krio is used for communication in informal contexts, improving English language skills and competencies is seen as critical for a number of reasons. Firstly, to improve the capacity for the trade unions generally to be able to engage in processes and activities necessary for rebuilding the workforce in Sierra Leone after the civil war; secondly, to develop the representational skills of the unions working with employers; and thirdly, because of the unique potential they have to cascade knowledge and skills to workers through their membership. Such training would also aim to change members' attitudes to their own competencies as many had had limited access to education. The involvement of a higher education institution to accredit and deliver the training was therefore crucial as it legitimised the status of the programme and also raised the ambitions of rank and file trade union members.

Thus the project took shape with myself (an ESP specialist) and an industrial relations expert from NU approaching USL – specifically Fourah Bay College, which is part of the University, to develop a bespoke programme together with the Sierra Leone Labour Congress. The project outcomes would be the design and delivery of a bespoke, accredited English language and trade union programme for representatives designed in response to a skills and needs audit, and a set of learning materials specific to the Sierra Leone context and accredited and delivered by the USL as an innovative model of employability within the curriculum. The programme would also provide a framework for the development of further modules as part of a Continuing Professional Development (CPD) programme route for union members that would improve their career opportunities and open up the opportunity for them to access undergraduate and further study.

3 Engaging with stakeholders

To achieve its outcomes therefore, the project had to meet the needs of a range of stakeholders to deliver some sort of transformational change. For individual participants, the project aimed to build confidence in their communication skills and trade union knowledge therefore changing attitudes to their own competencies. The formal award of university certification would provide a high status qualification valuable both to the individual and to the trade union organisation and its members.

For the University of Sierra Leone, the project fulfilled its need to be engaging in high profile education and training for a wider sector of society. The University of Sierra Leone necessarily has employability and the development of a skilled workforce at the heart of its mission and this was clearly articulated in an initial meeting that the project team held with the Vice Chancellor and senior members of the Senate. However, in practice the university was an 'elite enclosure' (Myers Scotton's 1993 term as referred to by Matsinhe, 2013) and had faced a number of challenges around access programmes and the accrediting of prior experience. It was therefore careful to ensure that appropriate policies were developed to allow access to those without standard entry qualifications without opening the floodgates to an abuse of entry standards. This was a major challenge within the project.

For the government, the project fulfilled a need to promote its commitment to support training for the workforce and specifically in the area of employment relations. As a result, the Ministers of Education and of Labour with whom the project team also met, provided political (though no financial) support throughout and at its dissemination and this helped to raise the status of the training further.

For the SLLC itself, engaging the university in the project was a major breakthrough and endorsed their huge efforts to develop formalised training for its members despite a paucity of resources. It was also a powerful opportunity for them to engage with government and other civil society agencies and to develop opportunities for dialogue on other issues above and beyond the remit of the project.

For the UK team, the project built upon Northumbria University's expertise gained over fifteen years of developing and delivering English language courses and published materials for trade union representative across Europe. Specifically, programmes were designed for many of the major trade union confederations in Europe and for workers in a number of multinational companies (Tully, 2004). In addition to the development of courses and materials, Northumbria had worked closely with the European Trade Union Institute (ETUI) to establish a series of international training seminars to address the development of language and communication in a trade union context across Europe. The challenge then was the extent to which this framework, and its developing and changing European pluralist discourse of trade unionism could, should or would be appropriated by Sierra Leonean representatives. Stirling (2013) presents it as how to avoid a content that 'Is predicated on assumed pluralist ideology despite the difficulties (Sierra Leonean) unions have in gaining institutional legitimacy … in this context the questions are of legitimacy, recognition, status and access to existing power structures rather than challenges to them.' (p. 542). It was also recognised that although addressing the local context was of primary importance, engagement with the global economy was also crucial in view of the growth of international investors (in particular, China) in Africa and the new challenges to trade unions that these investors were bringing. In addition, particular issues such as the priorities of the SLLC to recruit and represent the informal sector and engage and involve more women in activism would inevitably impact on the development of a critical discourse.

The programme was devised with a specific target group in mind. A typical participant would be a union representative (rep) or official who would already be fulfilling a leadership role in their trade union and would have benefitted from trade union education and training programmes. They would be highly motivated to develop their skills and knowledge further although they may lack formal education qualifications and therefore confidence in their own English language abilities particularly in a written context. Whilst likely to use Krio with their members, they may require English to communicate effectively with employers, managers and other civil society organisations beyond the workplace.

Funding was provided through the British Council's Education Partnerships in Africa programme, aimed at establishing university partnerships that would encourage local employers and social enterprises to collaborate in the development of employability skills.

4 Literature review

Hyland and Hamp-Lyons put to language teachers in 2002 the challenge of how to work with, rather than for, disciplinary specialists. This issue was a key pillar upon which the European programmes had been founded and central to the development of both content and methodology in this area was the involvement of industrial relations experts and trade union trainers both as active partners with language tutors in the design of syllabi, tasks and content that understood and responded to power relations (what Benesch 1999, termed 'rights analysis'). In order to underpin this methodology across Europe, course designers had worked with the European Trade Union Institute to establish the principle of delivering annual tutor training seminars at which both trade union trainers and language trainers collaborated. This was to ensure not only that any language development was firmly embedded with a sociopolitical context and that real needs were being addressed but also that the profile and status of language training across Europe was raised with the confederations and acknowledged within training budgets and planning. It was also further underpinned by the production of a language tutor's manual.

In the early stages of development, in the 1990s, a communicative task-based approach was adopted that seemed appropriate to the needs of a multilingual, multicultural group of trade union representatives many of whom lacked confidence – primarily in their spoken abilities in English. Course participants were from a mix of blue and white collar worker backgrounds and had very differing experiences of language learning and of using English as a lingua franca across Europe. The representatives were, however, familiar with models of adult and worker education that recognised the need for active learning promoting a Frierian equality of relationships within the classroom that valued the learners' knowledge and experience. Bridgford and Stirling (2000) describe the development of trade union education in Europe as a move away from a very didactic and teacher-centred approach to one of inclusivity, participation and student-centred, problem-solving learning although Stirling (2013), speculates as to whether the focus on skills comes at the expense of a more explicit political and educational content.

This argument of skills training versus education is all too familiar in the world of ESP and one that if anything is being lost within many universities/education institutions that have come to regard language learning as a skill and language teachers as trainers rather than educationalists. The inevitable consequence of this misconception is reflected in the changing status and power of language staff in many of these organisations. Block (2014) takes the argument into the area of teacher training by commenting that 'The neoliberalism and the marketisation of education have come together to change the meaning of *skill* (his italics) in second language teaching, and how such a development impacts on teachers' and how it becomes a 'discrete package of activity' (p. 166) that is somehow devoid of a sense of self. He also remarks on the need for further research in this area. Nevertheless, the familiarity of the student-centred, task-based approaches to ESP tutors made working closely with trade union trainers an easy collaboration and also fulfilled to a large extent the expectations of the trade unionists themselves who attended the courses and used the materials. What was a new addition into the collaborative methodology was the inclusion of ideological and political input by the industrial relations expert. Once the trade union and language needs had been identified through extensive needs and wants analyses the tasks and exercises were contextualised within a political framework articulated through critical questioning. By co-design and delivery with the language expert, the team was able to develop a critical pedagogy that underpinned the task-based, communicative methodology.

In the European, multilingual context of trade union communication, the focus of language training was very much one of developing spoken fluency in order to exchange information and share good practice to develop a stronger and more interconnected European trade union network. Research conducted on the dynamics of communication within European Works Councils (Stirling & Tully, 2004) found that as well as the obvious linguistic and cultural differences, the development of a solidaristic identity was dependent upon a shared awareness of different priorities and the social and political contexts within which their members were working. Furthermore, whilst linguistic accuracy seemed less important within this context, the issue of the choice of lingua franca (usually English) within the group and the related power of the native speakers and expert users in the group to dominate the agendas was a critical inequality that impacted upon its ability to operate from a position of strength. Discussion of this and other inequalities was therefore seen as a key component of the critical methodology that was adopted for the language training framework. O'Regan's article (2014) on the importance of acknowledging key inequalities in a lingua franca context supports this position as does Pennycook (2001) in his view that language teachers should be engaged in using language to oppose the dominant discourse(s) by challenging the assumptions about the context in which English would be used as opposed to another common language or the native language.

In an African context, however, the key issues were not of language choice and the power implications for the native or expert speaker, nor in the priority to develop oral fluency. As a former British colony, the socio-political remnants of colonialism in Sierra Leone are apparent by the use of English as an official language in legal, political and higher educational settings. In Kachru's Handbook of World Englishes (2009) Ominiyi describes a situation in which, despite the establishment of the Economic Community of West African States (ECOWAS) across the region, there is still an absence of a West African English that would underpin the regional administrative, political and even cultural community (although he alludes to the likelihood of Nigerian English fulfilling this role in the future as it becomes one of the new strong emerging global economies) and describes how English has been the major gatekeeper in the attainment of access to higher socio-economic classes in Sub Saharan Africa. Whilst the arguments for linguistic equality and multilingualism in language planning and policy are well documented (Phillipson, 1992) and the position taken by UNESCO (2003) is one of promoting mother tongue-based multilingual education (MT-MLE), many suggest (Alexander, 2009; Alidou, 2006; Ferguson, 2013; Matsinhe, 2013) that access to English still needs to be democratised. Professor Sozinho Francisco Matsinhe, Executive Secretary of the African Academy of Languages (ACALAN) presents the challenge that:

> The almost exclusive use of former colonial languages as a medium of instruction and for running national affairs in most African countries leads to the exclusion of the vast majority of Africans, as they are kept on the periphery of the political and socio-economic mainstreams, while minority ruling elites and the middle class aspirants enjoy an unfair advantage. (2013, p. 27)

This is a familiar situation faced by many trade unionists throughout the world. Block (2014) argues strongly that such constructs of social class and socioeconomic power should take up a much more central position in applied linguistics research and they are particularly apparent in Africa. In such a context, the development of civil society and a flexible and well-trained workforce, against a background of poor resources and little or no power, is a major issue facing development, democracy and good governance. So for African trade unionists, many of whom would have left school without qualifications (a West African Secondary School Education Certificate (WASSEC) pass in English is part of the standard entry requirement to higher education), improving their confidence to use English accurately and effectively with employers, trade union leaders and in any number of formal contexts was seen as essential for their own empowerment and self-esteem. To be able to access a university course in English and to receive university certification for this was a powerful tool in engaging with those ruling elites to challenge any number of inequalities – including potentially the status and use of English, as is well argued by Canagarajah (1999), Phillipson (1992) and Pennycook (1994) amongst others. Once trade unionists have gained access to the institutions of the elite and developed their self-esteem and status via official accreditation, questions of legitimacy and power flow and it is then that challenges can be made to the status quo particularly around questions of language choice and the status of that language. Mwamadzingo and Dia (2007) acknowledge that labour education in Africa needs to become more responsive to new contexts and challenges by introducing training and education on issues such as democracy, development and political economy for example and to do so, they will need to engage with higher education institutions and experts.

5 Methodology

The project was launched in 2009 and used a well-tried and tested framework in the design of an ESP course, as its methodology included an analysis of needs, an investigation into the specialist discourse and the development of the curriculum (Basturken 2010). An additional important element was the engagement all stakeholders at the outset of the project and the identification of clear objectives to meet their specific political needs (Basturken acknowledges 'focusing the course' under the heading of developing the curriculum but stakeholder engagement is not specifically within the framework). Without a very clear political objective to 'transform' as well as 'perform' (Pennycook, 2007) it is likely to be difficult to engage the content providers and content experts who are needed to support the development of the critical element of the pedagogy.

5.1 Objective setting

The role of the SLLC and in particular their Director of Education was to facilitate the project, to collaborate closely on the initial needs analysis and then as ongoing advisors to the curriculum (as non-participant observers of the pilot sessions) and, crucially, to provide real trade union materials and contexts for the activities and tasks within the curriculum. This also ensured knowledge transfer and capacity building for the English language team and located the project within the real-world needs of the workforce. It also assured the trade union voice within the curriculum of the university and gave them ownership of the course. This was crucial for commitment and face validity as the unions had not always had an easy relationship with the university and indeed during the course of the project, university lecturers were taking intermittent industrial action. The president of the university staff association at the university was also invited to be part of the project team.

The SLLC was also instrumental in engaging government in the project and meetings were held between the project team and the Ministers for Labour and Education in the initial stages of the project. Having such high level personal stakeholder engagement was an important political move as it fulfilled the government's commitment to capacity building, and their recognition of the work of the SLLC in this also ensured the full engagement of the university with the project.

The university engagement was established through formal email contact from NU with the Vice Chancellor of USL, who gave a strong commitment to the project and was supportive throughout. As one of the oldest and most prestigious universities in Africa, Fourah Bay College, (the founding college of the current USL), has delivered English language in higher education since 1827 (Melchers & Shaw, 2011). Over recent years and, particularly, due to the effects of the recent civil war, USL has operated under severe financial and resource constraints. Whilst it has endeavoured to uphold a commitment to teaching quality and research it recognised its responsibility to undertake outreach work in the local community in support of the government's agenda for change and capacity building. As USL had an essentially British quality assurance framework (Fourah Bay College had at one time been affiliated to Durham University), the Northumbria team was able to draw upon its own quality assurance mechanisms to support and inform the discussion around non-standard entry requirements that took place at USL's Senate prior to the validation event. This meant that the programme had a wider impact on USL as this issue needed to be formally addressed by academic registry. It did, however, ensure that the project and its implications on the revision on entry criteria, was acknowledged and discussed at a senior level within USL and this was undoubtedly a driver in its ultimate success.

As well as senior members of USL, two local English language academics were identified to lead the design and development of the curriculum. There was already some expertise in delivering ESP within this team as they had been involved in delivering language training to police officers but they did not have experience of working in such close collaboration with an external organisation to provide meaningful contributions to curriculum design. It was crucial therefore, to establish the objectives and share the intended outcomes of the project and the responsibilities of each of the stakeholders as their contributions were mutually dependant.

The core project team therefore comprised myself as an ESP specialist and project leader and an industrial relations expert from NU; two English language tutors and the Dean of Languages and Social Sciences from USL; three key members of the senior committee of the SLLC, including the Education Secretary. A project administrator was later appointed, who was a postgraduate student from USL.

The project phases and communication methods were set out over eighteen months and involved several phases:

- Phase 1

  Objective setting (Full partner meeting, SL)

  Needs/wants audit, accreditation issues and observation of European trade union language course (Full partner meeting, UK)

- Phase 2

  Curriculum development and materials writing (Distance collaboration between UK tutors and African partners and ongoing liaison between the SLLC and the language tutors in Sierra Leone)

  Pilot delivery, review and evaluation (Full partner meeting plus two-day pilot workshop with trade union representatives, SL)

- Phase 3

  Curriculum development and materials writing two (Distance collaboration between UK tutors and African partners and ongoing liaison between the SLLC and the language tutors in Sierra Leone)

  Pilot delivery, review and evaluation (Full partner meeting plus two-day pilot workshop with trade union representatives, SL)

- Phase 4

  Validation event and dissemination (Full partner meeting, SL)

5.2 Analysing needs and accreditation issue

Having identified and established the stakeholder needs, the team constructed a needs/wants questionnaire that was distributed to 60 trade union representatives (40 male and 20 female) via the SLLC and the data analysed. These reps constituted the full quota of representatives across all trade unions in Sierra Leone and there was a 100% response rate as the questionnaire was distributed and collected at their annual conference. The team agreed to ask reps to respond to a list of trade union areas such as organising and recruiting, labour laws etc., in order of priority on a scale of one to three as to their importance in terms of their own training needs. Respondents were also given a list of communication tasks that they were expected to undertake as part of their union duties such as writing collective agreements, negotiating with employers etc. and were asked to prioritise them in the same way. Both of these lists were compiled by the SLLC in consultation with the reps themselves.

At the same time, the project team met with key staff at the university, including the Director of Quality Assurance, to discuss the requirements of the validation process and the issues that would need to be addressed in order for a successful validation to be achieved. Discussion involved the structure and assessment requirements of the modules, the level of certification, the cost of the programme and the entry requirements. The university had a 'mature age' clause that could be invoked when dealing with students who did not have the usual educational background – that is, the West African Secondary School Examination Certificate (WASSEC). However, in practice this was rarely used and had been open to abuse in the past so USL was eager to find a resolution to the requirements for this particular programme. The terms of these requirements became a crucial area of discussion and negotiation between USL and the SLLC. This in itself was an important outcome of the project as it represented the commitment of the university to seriously engage with the issue of how the workforce could access the institution.

5.3 Specialist discourse and curriculum development

Once the key content areas had been identified via the needs/want analysis, complex discussion took place within the team to identify the specialist discourse through key documents and texts that the SLLC provided. The team also had copies of the European trade union materials that provided some examples of tasks that had been developed around key discourse in Europe. The European materials provided a reference point and a very loose framework from which to initiate the curriculum. Materials were developed and shared across the team and amended. The UK industrial relations expert within the team provided key critical questions to add into the tasks and the materials writers became familiar with including reflective tasks that would critically review the content and the learning.

After six months of drafting and redrafting, phase two of the project culminated in the pilot delivery of a selection of the materials from the first module. The pilot took place at the Fourah Bay College over two days and was attended by 18 trade union reps of which nine were women. The team had agreed a maximum of 18 for the pilot and reps had to undergo an application and interview process run by the SLLC. It had also agreed that as far as possible, 50% of the places would be filled by female reps and this in itself was seen as an important step by the SLLC to promote female worker representation and leadership opportunities. The following unions were represented: Electricity workers (1), Health workers (2), Civil Service (2), Musicians (1), Hotel workers (3), Dock workers (2), Post and Telecommunications (2), Traders (1), Mass Media (1), Fishermen, (1) Construction (1), Artisans (1). Before the pilot training began, participants were given an overview of the aims and objectives of the project and the project activity that had taken place to date. All were aware of the project as they had taken part in initial discussions conducted by the SLLC about their training needs at which they had identified English as being an important issue and they had also contributed to the development of the curricula through the needs analysis questionnaire. Participants were asked to complete an evaluation questionnaire after each session (there were four sessions each day) asking them to rate from 1 to 5 the usefulness, effectiveness, presentation, clarity and objectives of each task. They were also asked how the materials could be improved and to rate the activities in order of which they found most or least useful in terms of developing their communication skills. At the end of the second day, a focus group was held, at which participants were encouraged to share their views of their expectations and experience of the training, its potential value and impact and on how it could be improved.

As non-participant observers, the tutor, the NU language and industrial relations experts and the project team members from the SLLC also evaluated the sessions via a focus group. Objectives for the revision of the materials were then established and findings informed the development of the second module. This process was repeated four months later at a second pilot that was held over two days at which 15 of the original 18 participants attended together with one new participant from the Municipal Workers union. The final project was also evaluated by an independent trade union expert from Njala University who had experience of monitoring and evaluating a number of projects run by the International Labour Organisation (ILO).

The first programme ran from Sept 2011 to June 2012 and follow-up interviews were conducted in 2012 with participants who were available to attend, with the tutor and materials writer and with senior members of the SLLC to gather data on the experience and impact of the course.

5.4 Dissemination and impact

It was crucial for all stakeholders that the results of the project were disseminated as widely as possible. Three final dissemination events were held; one in Freetown (the capital) and two others in the towns of Makeni and Bo to ensure that trade unionists in the provinces were also aware of the project. Over 250 people attended the events and the Ministries of Education and Labour were represented with the Minister for the Southern Region opening the event at Bo. The audiences comprised university staff and students (the Vice Chancellor and Deputy Vice Chancellor of the University of Sierra Leone both made statements), representatives from employers and NGOs, trade unionists, trade union leaders (the President and General Secretary of the Labour Congress both made formal statements), the participants on the pilot programmes (some of whom presented their experience, views and evaluation of the programme, which was an indication of the confidence that even the pilot programme had provided), sixth formers from local schools and their teachers and local dignitaries. The press was also in attendance and as well as print coverage, the project leader was interviewed about the project on national TV and radio news. In addition to the final event, a sensitisation event was held mid-project at the British Council Freetown to which university students were invited to listen to a presentation of the project and to engage in discussion about employability issues and the responsibilities of the university sector. This was an important event that helped to create a positive and inclusive atmosphere for accepting non-standard students onto the campus. During the project, the project leader gave a more in-depth interview about the aims and objectives of the project on Capital Radio, Freetown and members of the project team disseminated the project at conferences in London, Ghana, Senegal and the Gambia and at a number of national and international trade union meetings and conferences. The extent of activity and interest that the project generated reflected the importance of its success to all the stakeholders as a capacity building initiative.

6 Findings

6.1 Curriculum content

The final programme validated was entitled 'Certificate of English and Communication Skills for Trade Unionists' (CETU) and was launched in 2011, the first of its kind in Africa to the author's knowledge. As a two semester part-time programme, it delivers four modules consisting of Language Learning Strategies, Organising and Recruiting Members, Collective Bargaining and Employment Law, Health and Safety. Materials and contexts were provided by the SLLC who were also involved in aspects of the delivery along with guest experts. Criticality was introduced into the syllabus by the use of critical questions on sociopolitical issues and also via reflective activities around life and personal work experiences as well as experiences of studying and learning. The language content of the curricula was developed by the African language tutor by combining his own expert knowledge of the use of English as an official language in Sierra Leone with the perceived needs of the trade unionists themselves and their leaders. Tasks and exercises were also devised by the tutor often with stimulus from the European trade union materials and in discussion with the UK language and industrial relations tutors. Although not a functional-based syllabus, the tutor found it helpful to embed the language development within key contexts such as 'Negotiating with Employers, Addressing and Chairing Meetings, Writing up Grievances etc.' This was also the approach taken in the European materials and participants reported that they found this a useful approach within which to develop their knowledge, confidence and skills. What was initially surprising was the extent to which accuracy was much more important to participants in Sierra Leone than the European trade unionists who were much more focused on developing their fluency. However, as discussed earlier, in a postcolonial context in which a mastery of English often indicates a level of education commensurate with privilege and power, accuracy is likely to take on a greater importance since grammatical errors betray a 'deficit' and this was very much a concern of the participants. It became important therefore to include reflection and discussion of such issues of language and power as integral to the programme. The programme was assessed via a combination of a portfolio of language and communication tasks and summative assessment. All participants found the course valuable and the materials of a high standard. All aspects of the materials were rated quite good or very good with comments that they were 'inspiring' and 'provoking'. Interviewed as a participant of the full programme, Abu Bakrr Kamara from the Sierra Leone Seamen's Union commented:

> For my own personal development as far as this course is concerned, I can say that now, I can communicate more confidently both verbally and in writing to bring out the issues that affect workers, as well as my administrative skills. Also, the course has helped me identify some of the challenges and how to overcome them and, also it is a first step to future academic pursuits in trade union development in Sierra Leone.

6.2 Accreditation and certification

Participants rated highly the experience of locating the training within an HE context. As observers of the pilot delivery, we were struck by the reactions of the trade union participants at being physically in the university. For many of them it was the first time they had been in such an environment, having left school at an early age with few qualifications. To find themselves participants in the design of a university programme specifically aimed at them and their colleagues was considered a great honour. It was this aspect of attitudinal change that was a major objective of the project and ultimately of the programme and it was also an important step for the university. Located on the top of a hill, the university was a remote higher institution to which they would not usually aspire. In focus group interviews after the training, participants said that attendance had and would enhance their personal and professional self-esteem and it would also give their members an aspirational route into higher education and a sense of respect for their leaders. These comments were borne out at the dissemination events at which numerous trade union members expressed their surprise and pleasure that the university had made such concessions to allow them access to a certificated course. Although validation had been a big challenge, as has been previously indicated and there were times when the project team felt that the Senate would not approve it, the final outcome was that participants on the programme should be serving trade union representatives with two substantive recommendations from an appropriate employing authority and from the Labour Congress. Entry requirements had been set so as to allow access to any rep who did not have formal academic qualifications but who had considerable work and life skills – specifically at least five years of relevant work experience in trade unionism and all participants had to be over the age of 25. There is also potential for the development of a Diploma qualification and access to postgraduate study. Indeed one of the female participants has recently applied for a Fulbright scholarship to study an MBA.

Alpha A. Bah from the Motor Driver's Union said:

> It has helped me improve my personal skill in communications and trade union issues. What I'm learning here I am taking to my organisation and teaching my fellow members in the provinces. I tell them what exactly is a trade union and what are the rules and responsibilities of each position. That's what I'm doing now.

For the leadership of the SLLC, the benefits of the course are beginning to show. Jennings Wright (Chair of the SLLC Education Committee and General Secretary of the Hotel Workers Union):

> I see a positive impact. The president of the union has been there and he has been very active in the course and as of now he has been elevated at his place of work to a supervisor. He is still the president of the union. It was the Conference that put him into office. One of my organisers Mr x, who is also on the course, is showing positive signs because, as of now, I see a lot of improvement in the way that he constructs his letters. There are times that I give them various things to handle and I read the drafts of what they do. I see the positive side. I believe that by the end of the course it will have created a lot of impact among the students that are there.

The Director of Education at the SLLC, Max Conteh, also expressed how the course fulfils some of its aims for capacity building and succession planning:

> I see it as a very good course that is geared towards building the capacity of a real, professional, trade unionist. A trade unionist who is engaging with day-to-day affairs ... I would like to see how we can promote more to our colleagues and see how we can discuss with our affiliates and also employers. It has a return benefit for employers if people are properly trained to represent their members.

7 Conclusions and global implications

This project highlights the opportunities for the ESP community to engage with trade unions and worker education organisations to present English language as a key employability skill that is set within the context of industrial relations and workers rights. Employability and capacity building are issues high on the political agenda of governments and education providers, particularly in development contexts. ESP providers therefore have an opportunity to engage with them to develop transformational training programmes that will fulfil the needs of these stakeholders by addressing key skills but more importantly will also fulfil the genuine sociopolitical needs of the workforce. Rather than simply producing linguistically competent workers through neutral ESP workplace training, there are opportunities (and some might argue a responsibility) to develop transformative adult education and training programmes that will not only develop linguistic competency but also provide workers with opportunities to make a difference to their own lives and to influence and affect change for others.

In addition, by working closely with trade union educators and other change agents, there are valuable CPD opportunities for ESP practitioners to engage with critical pedagogy that can challenge not only socioeconomic and political inequalities but also the discourse of the elite. Furthermore, we have seen that developing English language skills within an activist framework and within an elitist institution helps to build confidence to use the official language to serve the interests of working people. This may even open up debates that challenge the status and use of English in both postcolonial settings such as Sierra Leone and in multilingual contexts such as Europe. In the former, the challenge is to enable stakeholders to promote their own critical agendas in a situation where English is still the preserve of an elite. In the latter, the challenge is to enable stakeholders who are less than expert users to promote such agendas in a situation where English is the lingua franca often by default. Developing new curricula and pedagogy appropriate to adult learners that is recognised by the award of formal qualifications also requires universities and colleges to review their access policies for students with non-standard qualifications and opens up campuses not only to the presence of a different type of student but also opens up debates about inequalities, access and activism. One of the unexpected outcomes of this project was that trade union leaders were being invited onto campus to deliver lectures about the history and politics of trade unions while some students were choosing to write dissertations about such topics, visiting the labour congress and interviewing activists to collect data. This is transformational education in which those traditionally on the periphery or excluded can challenge inequalities including that of language choice and access.

The biggest challenge, however, is funding and sustainability. In contexts where resources are severely limited, capacity building projects may not be prioritised within a range of competing and pressing demands. In Sierra Leone, for example, neither the university nor the Labour Congress has funds to sponsor students and the onus is placed on the unions or even on members themselves to finance such training. Government policies and laws are needed to ensure that employers are held responsible for supporting the development of safe and fair working conditions and appropriate training; and Western unions need to look at how the limited support that they provide to African unions, for example, can be best deployed. As an ESP community, we can work with a range of stakeholders to try to influence policy and funding decisions to support such capacity building projects. The challenges that were overcome in the design and validation process in this project could provide a model for trade unions in other countries. There are also great opportunities for ESP professionals to engage in the research and development of critical pedagogies and to research the impact of such programmes. Stirling concludes that '[l]earning to communicate more effectively in English both empowers individuals and opens access to dominant hierarchies but leaves aside the more radical questions raised by Afrocentric approaches which might ask why collective bargaining, for example, might not be done in Krio or an indigenous language' (2014, p. 548). Only by opening up worker access to contexts in which such debates are taken seriously can real change and transformation take place.

Acknowledgements

I would like to acknowledge the enormous contribution of all members of the team involved in this project. In Sierra Leone, I am indebted to Muluku Tarawally, Max Conteh, Jennings Wright, Arthur Smith, Osman Gbla and, in particular, the materials writer and tutor Kenneth Osho. The enthusiasm and dedication of the trade union representatives who participated in the piloting of the programme, together with their feedback, was invaluable. In the United Kingdom, I am indebted to John Stirling, whose commitment to the development of trade union education in Sierra Leone is always inspiring.

References

Alexander, N. (2009). 'The impact of the hegemony of English on access to and quality of education with special reference to South Africa'. In Herbert, W. (Ed.), *Language and Poverty* (pp. 53–66) Clevedon: Multilingual Matters

Alidou, H., Boly, A., Brock-Utne, B., Diallo, Y. S., Heugh, K. & Wolff, H. E. (Eds.) (2006) *Optimising Learning and Education in Africa – the Language Factor*. Paris: Association for the Development of Education in Africa (ADEA).

Basturkmen, H. (2010). *Developing Courses in English for Specific Purposes*. Basingstoke: Palgrave Macmillan.

Benesch, S. (1999). Rights analysis: Studying power in an academic setting. *English for Specific Purposes, 18*, 313–327.

Block, D. (2014). *Social Class in Applied Linguistics*. New York & London: Routledge.

Brigford, J., & Stirling, J. (2000). *Trade Union Education in Europe*. Brussels: European Trade Union College.

Canagarajah, A. S. (1999). *Resisting Linguistic Imperialism in English Teaching*. Oxford: Oxford University Press.

Ferguson, G. (2013). The language of instruction issue: Reality, aspiration and the wider context. In H. Mcllwraith (Ed.), *Multilingual Education in Africa: Lessons from the Juba Language-in-Education Conference* (pp. 17–20). London: British Council.

Freire, P. (2004). *Pedagogy of the Oppressed*. NY & London: Continuum.

Hyland, K., & Hamp-Lyons, L. (2002). EAP: Issues and directions. *Journal of English for Academic Purposes, 1*(1), 1–12.

International Labour Office. (2009). Employment Sector and Social Protection Sector. *The informal economy in Africa: Promoting transition to formality: challenges and strategies*. Geneva: ILO.

Kachru, Y., Kachru, B. B., & Nelson, C. L. (2009). *The Handbook of World Englishes*. Oxford: Blackwell.

Matsinhe, S. F. (2013). 'African languages as a viable factor in Africa's quest for integration and development: The view from ACALAN'. In H. Mcllwraith (Ed.), *Multilingual Education in Africa: Lessons from the Juba Language-in-Education Conference* (pp. 23–35). London: British Council.

Melchers, G., & Shaw, P. (2011). *World Englishes*. Oxon: Hodder Educational.

Mwamadzingo, M., & Ben Said Dia, I. (2007). Trade Union education in Africa – Challenges and Future Prospects. *Labour Education, 146–147*, 49–56.

O' Regan, J. (2014). English as a Lingua Franca: An Immanent Critique. *Applied Linguistics, 35*(1), 1–21.

Pennycook, A. (1994). *The cultural politics of English as an international language*. London: Longman.

Pennycook, A. (2001). *Critical applied linguistics: a critical introduction*. London: L. Erlbaum.

Pennycook, A. (2007). *Global Englishes and transcultural flows*. London: Routledge.

Phillipson, R. (1992). *Linguistic Imperialism*. Oxford: Oxford University Press.

Stirling, J. (2013). Power in Practice: Trade Union Education in Sierra Leone. *McGill Journal of Education, 48*(3), 531–549.

Stirling, J., & Tully, B. (2004). Power, Process and Practice: Communications in European Works Councils. *European Journal of Industrial Relations, 10*(1), 73–89.

Tully, B. (2004). 'Organising across borders: developing trade union networks'. In I. S. Fitzgerald & J Stirling, (Eds.), *European Works Councils: Pessimism of the Intellect, Optimism of the Will* (pp. 165–177). London: Routledge.

UNESCO. (2003). Education Position Paper. *Education in a multilingual world*. Paris: UNESCO.

Academic reflections: Disciplinary acculturation and the first-year pathway experience in Australia

Donna M Velliaris: Eynesbury Institute of Business and Technology
Craig R Willis: The University of Adelaide
Paul B Breen: Greenwich School of Management
Email: dvelliaris@eynesbury.sa.edu.au, craig.willis@adelaide.edu.au and paul.breen@gsm.org.uk

1 Introduction

Although the increasingly multicultural composition of cohorts within Australian higher education (HE) campuses has brought much social and financial benefit, the situation remains 'beset by a number of challenges' (Bodycott & Walker, 2000, p. 80). Prime among those challenges is the ability of international students to acculturate to norms of Australian HE, which may be characterised as peer-assisted, problem-based, real-world, self-directed and student-centred. These academic discourse patterns may contradict any expectations previously encountered by international students who often arrive in this new context with 'misperceptions' about academic study (Bryson, Hardy, & Hand, 2009, p. 1) and a lack of skills required to make a successful transition (Kantanis, 2000). The challenge of switching between/among different institutional cultures is accentuated in many cases by students using English as a Second (ESL) or Additional Language (EAL), which carries with it 'a particular kind of vulnerability' (Hellsten, 2002, p. 10).

International students transitioning to Australian HE – particularly at the undergraduate level – are expected to adjust to discipline-specific language without yet having had exposure to the discipline in question and to demonstrate academic proficiency whilst situated on the periphery of the Australian academic community (Velliaris & Warner, 2009). While there is an English language level below which students could be at risk of failing, achievement of a minimum score on a proficiency test is only a starting point. It is not always an 'appropriate model' for university preparation (Moore & Morton, 2005, p. 43) and students' readiness to cope with tertiary studies should be judged against a range of contributing factors 'other' than English. There may be a gap concerning international students': (a) expectations of the language level needed for academic success and integration into the HE community (as evidenced by their English language proficiency score); and (b) the reality of the complex academic skills required in a lecture theatre for example. A large body of research in Australia has focused on issues such as 'connectedness' (McInnes & James, 1995), 'institutional belongingness, social involvement, alienation' (Williams, 1982) and 'negotiated engagement' (McInnes, 2001).

Throughout this chapter, the term 'international students' or simply 'students' is specific to individuals enrolled at 'Eynesbury' (pre-university institution) on temporary student visas and who are non-English-speaking background (NESB). This chapter is centred on qualitative and 'narrative' data gathered from an internally-administered Eynesbury staff evaluation of a specially designed 'Mixed Programme' (MBTH). The MBTH unites English for Academic Purposes (EAP) and English for Specific Purposes (ESP) in an integrated manner, thus enabling international students to accelerate their way into Australian HE. The survey findings presented in this work elucidate both positive and negative features of the MBTH for improving educational attainment given the growing importance of 'partner' institutions amidst the rising number of international students seeking HE in Australia. This examination makes a valuable contribution to the scant body of knowledge on Australian 'pathway' programmes.

2 EAP and ESP: Moving beyond language provision alone

EAP is a relatively young field, 'emerging as an entity distinct from English Language Teaching (ELT) in the 1960s, with the first usage of the name occurring in the 1970s' (Alexander, 2010; Jordan, 2002). Originally, EAP was a branch of ESP (Jordan, 2002, p. 73), but it has gradually evolved as a discipline in its own right, due to the numbers of international students venturing to English-speaking countries to study within HE. It was a subject created out of the practical demands of the era in which it was conceived and one that was largely situated within the domain of HE; particularly language centres within HE.

In those earlier decades, there was greater emphasis on language support rather than subject specificity. Amongst the organisations at the forefront of this were British universities such as Birmingham, Leeds, Newcastle and Manchester (Alexander, 2010, p. 2). Historically, EAP – though best embedded in the broader context of other disciplines being studied (Sloan & Porter, 2010) – has been the 'poor relation' of more 'specific' subjects in HE (Hamp-Lyons, 2011, p. 91). In recent times, however, it has developed considerably and into what Hamp-Lyons (2011, p. 89) defined as the 'linguistic, sociolinguistic and psycholinguistic description of English as it occurs in the contexts of academic study and scholarly exchange'. This has also meant that, in some ways, it has returned to its ESP roots and become more 'goal driven' (Alexander, Argent, & Spencer, 2008; Martin, 2014).

Kirk (2013) raised the question, 'Are we, as EAP professionals, "just" language teachers?' He added that recent changes have emphasised that it is EAP teachers' 'responsibility to provide for our learners an induction, of sorts, into the practices of the Academy'. As Gilbert (2013, p. 120) expressed, '[p]reparing Non-Native Speakers (NNS) for the demands of academic study in an English language environment requires a dual focus of helping students to develop both the language competency and study skills which will help them to succeed'. By doing so, EAP teachers are helping to 'demystify the road that lies ahead' and better enable students to concentrate not only on language, but also on a broad range of academic competences (Kirk, 2013).

Hyland and Hamp-Lyons (2002) referred to this duality as 'general English' and 'study skills' encompassing tasks such as listening to lectures, academic writing and oral presentations. This approach can be called English for General Academic Purposes (EGAP), aimed at preparing students for general academic studies across disciplines. In cases where more specific needs are identified, the teaching approach may be focused and developed based on conventions of discipline-specific language use. This approach is known as English for Specific Academic Purposes (ESAP) and is built on 'an understanding of the cognitive, social and linguistic demands of specific academic disciplines' (Hyland & Hamp-Lyons, 2002, p. 2). 'EGAP isolates the skills associated with study activities such as listening to lectures, participating in supervisions, seminars and tutorials' whilst 'ESAP integrates the skills work of EGAP with help for students in their actual subject tasks' (Blue, 1988, p. 41).

In summary, throughout the four to five decades of its history, EAP has been an 'eclectic and pragmatic discipline' (Hamp-Lyons, 2011, p. 89), often having to adapt in order to survive and sometimes forced into being compromised by the 'fads' of the day (Maddux & Johnson, 2011, p. 1). Jordan (2002, p. 73) stated that 'since the early days of language support for international students in Britain, the US, Australia and elsewhere, there have been many changes, not least in materials, methods, technology, expectations and finance'. He added that changes were emphasising 'academic culture' as opposed to a solely linguistic focus. This academic culture was defined as the 'higher education system, subject specialist conventions regarding staff and student relationships and expectations and writing' (Jordan, 2002).

3 Local context: Eynesbury

Eynesbury consists of three schools: Eynesbury Senior College (ESC); Eynesbury College Academy of English (ECAE); and Eynesbury Institute of Business and Technology (EIBT). Eynesbury 'international' students are generally young (between 15–23 years) and over 2013 have represented more than 20 different nationalities/ethnicities. In alphabetical order: Bangladesh; Cambodia; China (mainland, Hong Kong and Macau); Colombia; Egypt; France; India; Indonesia; Iran; Kenya; Lebanon; Libya; Malaysia; Nepal; Nigeria; Oman; Pakistan; Saudi Arabia; Singapore; South Korea; Sri Lanka; Taiwan; Turkey; Venezuela; Vietnam; and Zimbabwe.

Eynesbury students follow a variety of career and study pathways. Some intend to enter ESC to complete Years 10–12 of high school. Some intend to enter the Eynesbury Foundation Studies Programme (FSP), which has direct entry arrangements with two South Australian universities. Some students will enter the International College of Hotel Management (ICHM) or Le Cordon Bleu Adelaide, both of which have transition arrangements with Eynesbury, while others will enter Flinders University, most notably in the Diploma of Nursing or Paramedic programmes after an ECAE recommendation has verified their level of English language proficiency. Finally, some students enrol in the Certificate IV in Tertiary Preparation (C4TP) or a Diploma in Business (DB), Information Technology (DIT) or Engineering (DIPE) in EIBT.

- Students who enter at the 'Upper-Intermediate' level have an IELTS or ECAE equivalent average of 5.0 in all sub-skills and 5.0 in both reading and writing. They will enrol in English for Business, IT and Health Sciences (MBTH_UI) and *one* course from their diploma programme; and

- Students who enter the MBTH at the 'Advanced' level have an IELTS or ECAE equivalent average of 5.5 in all sub-skills and 5.5 in both reading and writing. They will enrol in English for Business, IT and Health Sciences (MBTH_AD) and *two* courses from their diploma programme.

Notably, students are exposed to themes, vocabulary and concepts related generally and specifically to 'business' within an 'Australian' context.

The MBTH requires students to demonstrate achievement in all EAP learning outcomes and tasks are timetabled throughout the course to allow for regular evaluation and discussion of student progress. The student learning outcomes include:

- to *analyse* and *apply* a range of individual and team learning strategies;

- to *analyse, plan* and *compose* an academic research report that includes interpreting and presenting data in diagrammatic form;

- to *analyse, plan* and *present* a researched and referenced oral presentation, together with a formal group discussion;

- to *participate* in a range of formal and informal assessments, both individually and in groups;

- to *plan* and *compose* six academic essays across a range of genres;

- to *pass* all assessments in reading, writing, listening and speaking midway through and also at completion; and

- to *operate* within the cultural context of Australian HE.

Students will 'Pass' with an aggregate score of 50% including a pass in all assessments and examinations, whilst simultaneously maintaining an 80% attendance record.

As noted above, in addition to the EAP component, MBTH students are required to enrol in one or two diploma courses led by an EIBT lecturer with ESP credentials. In this way, students are 'apprenticed' into the Australian academic environment in a supportive and staged fashion. Only the Diploma of Business lecturer(s) who have a background in TESOL are able to teach EIBT's component of the MBTH. Yet, all MBTH students are integrated into the 'mainstream' and so the lecturer is faced with a multitude of English levels. Currently, there appears to be little to differentiate 'so-called' ESP courses from other business courses.

4 Collaborative action research

While 'student' evaluations have been conducted at the end of each trimester, an evaluation of ECAE and EIBT 'staff' perceptions of the MBTH has never been performed. The fact that the academic calendar comprises trimesters that do not coincide between these two schools, and that most lecturers were sessionals, empirical exploration of staff perceptions has been a complex undertaking. With this in mind – and as a means of testing the ground for a more expansive study – exploratory research on the MBTH was conducted in accordance with guidelines from Neuman (2004, p. 15). This involved becoming familiar with this programme and its particular features, gathering survey data from staff and creating a preliminary picture of the situation to be able to generate ideas for future research.

A fundamentally collaborative 'action research' methodology was considered best suited to this study as it involved critical enquiry by practitioners and researchers into their own practice and had the ability to combine 'action and reflection, theory and practice' (Reason & Bradbury, 2001, p. 1). Although it is not the purpose of this chapter to present an elaborate discussion of the essential features of action research, it is important to validate the genesis of this research framework and provide readers with a basis from which to engage with this work.

Action research is an iterative process involving practitioners and researchers collaborating together on a particular cycle of activities, including: (a) problem diagnosis, (b) action intervention, and (c) reflective learning (Avison, Lau, Myers, & Nielson, 1999). According to Altrichter, Posch and Somekh (2000, pp. 204–205), action research makes an important contribution to:

- curriculum development and improvements in the practical situation under investigation by enhancing the quality of teaching and learning through new and successful action strategies;

- the professional development of teachers to improve their practical theories and competence in action through reflection;

- the collective development of the profession by means of opening up individual practice to scrutiny and discussion and thus broadening the knowledge base of the profession; and

- the advancement of educational research.

Altrichter et al., (2000, p. 4) further stressed that action research directs attention to one of the most essential motives for doing research. That is, to improve the 'quality' of teaching and learning as well as the conditions under which staff and students work in educational institutions. Action research is intended, therefore, to support educators in coping with pedagogical obstacles. Thereafter they may relay new insights to others for the purpose of advancing the knowledge base of the profession.

In early 2014, persons involved with the delivery of the MBTH were invited to respond via the Portal (Eynesbury's intranet) to one open-ended question:

- *From your own personal perspective, how do you evaluate the MBTH programme?*

In first-person narrative form, five respondents contributed to this study; three past/present teachers, one ECAE administrator and one EIBT administrator. The overarching aim was to utilise the qualitative data to gain primary perceptions – positive and negative – pertaining to the MBTH for future improvement. The objectives specific to this study included:

- to *acknowledge* staff reflections as a rich source of description;

- to *communicate* different perspectives;

- to *share* the findings with Eynesbury colleagues (ECAE and EIBT and other internal departments) for teaching and learning improvement; and

- to *gain* insight(s) into areas for future empirical exploration.

No narrative style or way of articulating the content of participants' responses was established or agreed on. This was motivated by a desire for the writing to be a trial process.

Elliott (1991) considered action research to be essential in the development of schools as flexible and dynamic learning environments and crucial to 'genuine' school improvement. Similarly, Carr and Kemmis (1986) viewed action research as empowering practitioners to take control of the development of educational practice(s) themselves. In other words, action researchers are not prepared to heedlessly accept problems they may face from day-to-day, but choose to reflect upon them and search for strategies to better thrive in the face of adversity. In addition, action researchers build upon strengths and overcome weaknesses by experimenting with new ideas and approaches rather than letting pedagogical practices petrify over time.

5 Personal experience narratives

The recorded narratives presented herein – in full and random order – are based on respondents' personal experiences and do not offer any generalisable claims. They provide an insight into five participants' experience(s) with the MBTH programme; conceived as a subjective process realised in a specific historical context. Readers should, therefore, make their own judgments about the extent to which commonalities/dissimilarities may potentially inform their own practices.

Respondent 1:

The MBTH is a 'unique' Eynesbury offering designed to provide students with the opportunity to enrol in EIBT courses while further developing their English skills. This is especially valuable for students with weaker language skills who may not be able to handle a full academic load.

Throughout the 13 weeks, the curriculum provides many opportunities for students to improve their macro-skills (reading, writing, listening and speaking). There are a variety of assessment tasks, which include seminars, research reports, essays, interviews, debates and examinations. Furthermore, each of the assignments and topics are business-related, so students are given exposure to a wide variety of vocabulary to help facilitate their learning in other EIBT courses.

There are, though, a couple of challenges to consider. First, there is little/limited opportunity within the MBTH's structure to make it more practical. It would be ideal for the research and writing components to be completed through real-life interaction with people in the business world, instead of just using material derived from books or magazines. The schedule needs greater flexibility so that educational field trips are incorporated to make the work more practically-based.

One other notable difficulty is having students who have already completed and failed an ECAE course who then enrol in the MBTH. They tend to have a negative attitude, which implies they *'know it all'* or *'have done it all before'*. It is better to have a class of students who come in 'fresh'. In spite of this, it is a good course. Many of my previous students provided positive feedback on things they had learned, while also giving constructive criticism on things that could be changed/improved. Many changes happened as a result of that feedback. I think there is still room for improvement, but I see the value of offering this programme to prospective students.

Respondent 2:

The MBTH has many commendable features, including a clear structure and assessment regime, tests of each of the four main English skills and a variety of written genres recycled into the research report and that have a range of models for analysis; a mix of skills/sub-skills are practised in listening, reading and kinaesthetic (e.g., jigsaw) modalities. It is possible and recommended that auxiliary materials to cover deficiencies in a particular student or class. As mentioned in *Learner English*, with the Chinese, one can take nothing for granted.

Peter Armstrong's explication of Chinese authoritarian rote-learning, teaching and supervision methods contrasts with the Western communicative approach in which student autonomy and self-discipline is key. Similarly, there is a lacuna of academic skills deemed essential for progress in the Western educational system, namely: questioning; brainstorming; researching from credible sources; note-taking rather than plagiarising; critically assessing evidence and logical argument; categorising individual examples into main points for a structured plan; and editing written work before submission. Clearly, much of the above is what Chinese students come here to learn, however, as experience and learning take place retrospectively, only exceptional students tend to pick up and run with the high volume of requirements, as well as fine-tune the accurate language and style demanded of quality academic writing for example. The same may be said of seminar requirements.

The Chinese competitive ranking model inculcated by students is also at odds with the communicative model favoured in the Western education system; so too is their generally low appreciation of Western contemporary history, politics or culture. Admittedly, not many Westerners could recite a list of recent political leaders from any Asian nation, but

Asian students learning English as the international language of business, academia and world affairs, seem to be ignoring how intimately and intricately the language is bound up in the culture.

There are further problems of motivation and capacity that stem from the previously mentioned authoritarian and traditional culture. First, some MBTH students privately confided that they really wanted to study other (sometimes more creative) programmes such as 'design' rather than the finance, management or international business that they had been sent to Australia to complete. Second, many students become overwhelmed by the high volume input and exacting course requirements of the programme. Some of these problems may be addressed by incorporating more (explicit) learner training into the programme, its courses and its assessment, to convince students that 'product' (such as a plagiarised translated essay) is of less pedagogic value than 'process' in the Western educational model. More evidence-based entry requirements for admission (i.e., on-arrival testing) may also help to avoid student distress and floundering in class that can compound motivational problems.

Respondent 3:

Today, the dominance of English in international business contexts is seemingly beyond dispute. English is an intrinsic part of communication in multinational settings and a fact of life for many business people. Oftentimes, I feel fortunate that my native language is English and I try to imagine if it were something far less familiar like Punjabi or Danish, or even the totally unfamiliar 'Sentinelese'.

In addition, I ponder the situation whereby my entire primary and secondary schooling was in English, but then in order to increase my employment prospects, my parents had encouraged (or directed) me to study abroad a Diploma of Business with courses such as (e.g., Mongolian) *Foundations of Business Law* with a skill level equivalent to IELTS 5.0; partial command of the language, coping with overall meaning in most situations, though likely to make many mistakes. That is, a moderate user of (e.g., Mongolian) who is able to handle 'basic' communication.

As a pathway provider, EIBT offers flexible entry, smaller class sizes with an average of less than 30 students and extended contact hours (i.e., diploma students receive an additional 2–3 hours per week per course over and above that provided at university). The premise of 'pathway' programmes is to offer a soft landing, as well as a sheltered environment where foreign students can simultaneously address weaknesses in their English language proficiency, make progress toward their degree and acculturate socially and educationally to Australian HE.

Conceptually, therefore, the MBTH would seem to be a safer and smoother option for low English-level Eynesbury students to transition into the Diploma of Business. The overwhelming majority of our students, however, envisage and strive to complete their studies in the shortest and fastest way possible and believe that an additional six months – or even one trimester – is a 'lifetime'. Generally speaking, they do not realise that once they commence the diploma, their Grade Point Average (GPA) starts calculating and it is more beneficial for them to take an extra trimester (or two) to guarantee university entry.

Anecdotally, the MBTH has received 'mixed' reviews and realised fluctuating results. Discussion has been based primarily on the English language proficiency of students entering HE. It could be seen as problematic that EIBT sets an IELTS requirement for diploma entry that is lower than for university entry and then chooses to accept students at an even lower-level again. Not surprisingly, ECAE students who attain the minimum English language score – and gain entry into the MBTH – often mistakenly believe that they possess the linguistic resources to complete their diploma studies. And, this belief is often reflected by EIBT lecturers who are expecting them to be able to handle their course content.

Questions then arise such as: *If a student does not have the required English skills for a full diploma programme, how do we justify allowing them to take two academic courses? If they fail those course(s) due to poor English levels, where do we stand ethically in making them pay to repeat the course(s)? Should we only offer the MBTH to students who are transferring to diploma study from ECAE, but have marginally failed to meet requirements, as it is understandable that these students do not want to return to further ECAE study?*

Specifically within EIBT, there is a 98% international student population with the remaining 2% being international students who have gained Australian Permanent Residence (PR) or citizenship. Undertaking a diploma course(s) requires acquisition of a substantial amount of high-order and discipline-specific vocabulary as would be delivered to local first-year students. Indisputably, English is the *Lingua Franca* (ELF) of our student body. Hence, our students face the challenge of learning English and using English to learn, with few exemplars other than those provided by lecturers. And, despite being consistently reminded to *'Please speak English'*, students may associate almost entirely with others of the same ethnicity.

Accomplishing educational goals, as opposed to economic goals, requires more than merely increasing the number of overseas students. Appropriate information, services and support mechanisms are critical in helping them have a positive experience(s), fulfil their educational goal(s) and return home as satisfied customers.

Respondent 4:

The MBTH was originally a transition programme for offshore Chinese students with an overall IELTS score of 5.0–5.5 and an EIBT offer. The MBTH cohorts were unique, i.e., students originated from the same institute in China and were to study together at the same institute in Australia. Students were typically high achievers whose English language skills required some support while they 'transitioned' into Australian HE. A 'standard' English language programme runs for 10 weeks, but the MBTH was designed for 15 weeks to enable students to simultaneously undertake one EIBT diploma course and intensive English language classes to maximise opportunities for their academic advancement.

The success of students in the MBTH was variable – as one would perhaps anticipate – and especially in relation to language acquisition which is, by and large, based on a range of considerations including: learner motivation; Target Language (TL) input; and rehearsal/practice, etc. The early aims of the MBTH were to assist students incrementally to develop the language and self-study requirements for university in a more supported language-learning environment than they may otherwise encounter, i.e., in a certificate or diploma course there would be no language-learning component because it is expected that students already *know* and *understand* the language.

Somewhat paradoxically, over time, the MBTH has become a programme of study that has offered onshore students the chance to study an EIBT course as well as English language at the same time as providing them with additional language support (in stark contrast to the original aims of the course which was developed for higher achievers). There is little doubt that enhancements and adjustments to the MBTH could potentially improve student outcomes, but it may also be worth considering that a number of other factors contribute to learning. Learner motivation is a significant factor in success, whether academic or language-related and no amount of tweaking around the edges or input from lecturers will enhance performance unless a learner is capable, motivated and willing to work towards passing and graduating.

Respondent 5:

There is a common expectation amongst international students, that studying in an English-medium university should automatically produce a significant improvement in their English language skills. This is certainly not always the case. At Eynesbury, it is widely understood that the reasons why students perform poorly are many, varied and complex. Personal factors (e.g., age, gender, personality, attitude and motivation), cultural factors (e.g., family pressures), academic factors (e.g., previous studies), teaching and support factors (e.g., English language support, general study advice and the interest and ability of lecturers) all have a role to play in influencing how successful students will be at the tertiary level.

The IELTS is best regarded by Australian universities and the Australian government. Essentially, an IELTS score between 6.0–7.0 is commonly accepted by Australian universities as the 'minimum' English language score necessary for admitting (undergraduate) international students. However, as those scores may be up to two years old at entry, they may not always provide an accurate measure of the 'current' status of the student's English language proficiency. These IELTS entry scores are set at what is considered to be the minimum level necessary to cope with HE. Thus, a score of IELTS 7.0 is sufficient to gain entry to most HE courses, but NESB students at this level are still likely to require and benefit from further English language support.

In setting minimum language requirements, we (ECAE and EIBT) need to better consider the degree of academic and/or language support we are able to provide MBTH students. While support is offered, staffing is perhaps, too limited to deal with all the problems. And, the decision to raise a language threshold would not necessarily attract a more successful cohort of international students and may, at the same time, deny entry to suitable students. Importantly, we need to better understand the 'root causes' of students' language learning problems, by familiarising ourselves with their prior experiences and beliefs about learning. In turn, this will enable us to design a higher-quality MBTH programme.

6 Findings and discussion

While it is acknowledged that the number of participants involved in this research was small, the information sourced from their comments provided pertinent points with which to advance the MBTH. This following section reiterates the: (a) positive attributes of the MBTH; (b) constructive criticisms related to the MBTH; and (c) recommendations for future improvements to the MBTH.

Positively, the MBTH is a 'unique' Eynesbury offering designed to provide students with the opportunity to enrol in EIBT while further developing their English skills. It offers a soft landing, as well as a sheltered environment, where international students can simultaneously address weaknesses in their English language proficiency and make progress toward their degree. Conceptually, this programme would seem to be a safer and smoother option for low English-level students to transition into the Diploma of Business. The MBTH has many commendable features including for example: a clear structure; a variety of academic genres; and tests of each of the four English skills. Crucially, embedded topics embrace 'business-related' issues, so students are given exposure to discipline-specific vocabulary that will help facilitate their learning experience in EIBT. The MBTH offers a variety of assessment tasks including: debates; interviews; research reports and essays; seminars; and examinations. Last but not least, previous MBTH students provided feedback that led to improvements over earlier trimesters.

Critically, the MBTH has received 'mixed' reviews and realised fluctuating results since its inception. For example, students envisage completing their studies in the shortest/quickest way possible without consideration of language-related barriers. There is a common expectation among international students – and many times staff – that studying in an English-medium HE environment should automatically produce a significant improvement in fluency. Relatedly, students mistakenly believe that they possess the linguistic resources to complete their diploma studies with an IELTS of 5.0, which equates to a moderate user who is able to handle 'basic' communication. Consequently, MBTH students seem quite overwhelmed by the high volume input and exacting requirements of the programme and although support is offered, staffing is perhaps too limited to deal with all the problems. Additionally, learner motivation (academic or language-related) is a significant factor in achieving success and no amount of input from lecturers will enhance performance unless a student is prepared and capable of passing. Indeed, all MBTH students face the challenge of learning English and using English to learn, with few exemplars other than local Eynesbury staff. And, despite being consistently reminded to 'Speak English', they may associate almost entirely with others of the same ethnicity.

Subsequent 'action' stemming from this 'action research' will endeavour to take on board recommendations such as those listed below:

- Auxiliary materials (e.g., vocabulary consolidation and extension) should cover deficiencies in a particular student and/or class;

- Increased learner training should be focused on convincing students that 'product' is of less pedagogic value than 'process' in the Western educational model;

- Lecturers need to better understand the 'root causes' of language learning problems, by familiarising themselves with students' prior educational experiences and beliefs about learning;

- Research and writing components should be completed through real-life interaction with 'professionals' in the business world;

- Students need to be reminded that once they commence diploma studies, their GPA starts calculating and it is better to take more time to complete their programme than jeopardise university entry;

- The programme schedule should call for greater flexibility so that educational field trips and events can be embedded (e.g., Work-Integrated Learning (WIL)); and

- Students who have already completed and/or failed an ECAE course should be interviewed/restricted as they often bring a negative attitude to the MBTH.

Traditionally, data collected in schools have been used to assess student performance and educational researchers proclaim various practices as either 'effective' or 'ineffective'. Eynesbury educators, however, face unique sets of students (over 10 different backgrounds at any one time) who may respond variably to a range of teaching and learning strategies. By acknowledging and utilising data stemming directly from ECAE and EIBT staff involved with the MBTH, academic findings can be brought down to earth and judgments about what works within specific MBTH classes can be shared and addressed. Moreover, when targets/goals for improvement are clearly defined, the teaching community may be more likely to understand and support future initiatives.

7 Conclusion

International students face a range of problems related to their adjustment to a new social, cultural and educational environment. The role of Australian 'preparation' programmes is certainly crucial, not only in terms of developing English language skills, but also in fostering the vital academic skills required for effective integration into HE life. Eynesbury is adopting a more practical and pragmatic response to its role and its potential to enhance the first-year student experience, through taking special account of the academic and English language vulnerabilities of its population. By enhancing the student experience, EIBT will be better able to address issues that may lead to academic anxiety and withdrawal; transition and retention concerns.

As part of EIBT's self-reflection for advancement, the learning needs of international students enrolled in the MBTH programme has been a factor for consideration. It should be acknowledged, however, that the observations shared in this chapter are one small part of the complex process of creating effective HE pathway programmes. With reference to the 'recommendations' listed above, improving strategies that encourage autonomy, reflection and performance success, together with appropriately integrated language and learning support, may aid in augmenting the potential of every student transitioning to HE. Significantly, what this experience achieved was to plant the seed for further empirical investigation into the engagement of persons involved with the MBTH, in addition to the many other programmes delivered by Eynesbury. Contemplation and planning for that data collection has not been addressed here, but the possibilities abound and the future certainly looks brighter.

References

Alexander, O. (2010). *The leap into TEAP: The role of the BALEAP competency framework in the professional development of new EAP teachers.* Paper presented at the Joint Conference IATEFL English for Specific Purposes SIG, Bilkent University.

Alexander, O., Argent, S., & Spencer, J. (2008). *EAP essentials: A teacher's guide to principles and practice.* Reading, UK: Garnet Education.

Altrichter, H., Posch, P., & Somekh, B. (2000). *Teachers investigate their work: An introduction to action research across the professions.* New York: Routledge.

Avison, D. E., Lau, F., Myers, M. D., & Nielson, P. A. (1999). Action research. *Communications of the ACM, 42*(1), 94–97.

Blue, G. (1988). 'Individualising academic writing tuition'. In P. C. Robinson (Ed.), *Academic writing: Process and product [ELT Documents 129]* (pp. 95–99): London: Modern English Publications.

Bodycott, P., & Walker, A. (2000). Teaching abroad: Lessons learned about inter-cultural understanding for teachers in higher education. *Teaching in Higher Education, 5*(1), 79–94.

Bryson, C., Hardy, C., & Hand, L. (2009). *An in-depth investigation of students' engagement throughout their first-year in university.* Paper presented at the UK National Transition Conference, University College London.

Carr, W., & Kemmis, S. (1986). *Becoming critical: Education, knowledge and action research.* London: Falmer Press.

Criper, C., & Davies, A. (1988). Research Report 1(i) ELTS Validation Project Report. Cambridge: British Council/UCLES.

Elliot, J. (1991). *Action research for educational change.* Buckingham: Open University Press.

Gilbert, J. (2013). 'English for academic purposes'. In G. Motteram (Ed.), *Innovations in learning technologies for English language teaching.* London: British Council.

Gillett, A. (1996). What is EAP? *IATEFL ESL SIG Newsletter (6)* (pp. 17–23). Kent, UK: International Association of Teachers of English as a Foreign Language (IATEFL).

Gillett, A. J., & Wray, L. (2006). *Assessing the effectiveness of EAP programmes.* London: BALEAP.

Hamp-Lyons, L. (2011). 'English for academic purposes'. In E. Hinkel (Ed.), *Handbook of research in second language teaching and learning* (Vol. 2, pp. 89–105). New York: Routledge.

Hellsten, M. (2002). *Students in transition: Needs and experiences of international students in Australia*. Paper presented at the 16th Australian International Education Conference, Macquarie University, Australia.

Hyland, K., & Hamp-Lyons, L. (2002). EAP: Issues and directions. *Journal of English for Academic Purposes, 1*(1), 1–12.

Jordan, R. R. (2002). The growth of EAP in Britain. *Journal of English for Academic Purposes, 1*(1), 69–78.

Kantanis, T. (2000). The role of social transition in students' adjustment to the first-year of university (online). *Journal of Institutional Research, 9*(1).

Kirk, S. (2013). Progress and plausibility [The TEAPing Point Blog]. Retrieved September 12, 2013 from http://theteapingpoint.wordpress.com/2013/01/13/progress-plausibility/

Maddux, C. D., & Johnson, D. L. (2011). Technology in education and the concept of cultural momentum. *Computers in the Schools, 28*(1), 1–4.

Martin, P. (2014). Teachers in transition: The road to EAP. In P. Breen (Ed.), *Cases on teacher identity, diversity and cognition in higher education* (pp. 287–317). PA: IGI Global.

McInnes, C. (2001). Signs of disengagement? The changing undergraduate experience in Australian universities. *Centre for Studies in Higher Education*, 175–189.

McInnes, C., & James, R. (1995). *First-year on campus: Diversity in the initial experiences of Australian undergraduates*. Canberra, Australia: Australian Government Publishing Service.

Moore, T., & Morton, J. (2005). Dimensions of difference: A comparison of university writing and IELTS writing. *Journal of English for Academic Purposes, 4*(1), 43–66.

Neuman, W. L. (2004). *Basics of social research: Qualitative and quantitative approaches*. MA: Pearson Education Incorporated.

Reason, P., & Bradbury, H. (Eds.). (2001). *Handbook of action research: Participative inquiry and practice*. London: Sage Publications.

Sloan, P., & Porter, E. (2010). Changing international student and business staff perceptions of in-sessional EAP: Using the CEM model. *Journal of English for Academic Purposes, 9*(3), 198–210.

Velliaris, D. M., & Warner, R. (2009). *Embedding 'learning guides' in a flexible delivery mode: Improving academic acculturation for international students at an Australian university*. Paper presented at the 20th ISANA International Education Conference, Hotel Realm, Canberra, Australia.

Williams, C. (1982). *The early experiences of students on Australian university campuses*. NSW, Australia: University of Sydney.

Research-based perspectives for teaching Asian graduate student writers

Yalun Zhou: Rensselaer Polytechnic Institute
Donna Bain Butler: American University
Michael Wei: University of Missouri – Kansas City
Email: zhouy12@rpi.edu, dbbutler@wcl.american.edu and weiyou@umkc.edu

1 Introduction

In the past thirty years, Asian students have been flocking to Western countries for academic purposes. Statistics abound (GHK, & Renming University, 2011; Institute of International Education [IIE], 2013; Organization for Economic Co-operation and Development [OECD], 2013). These Asian students comprise up to 53% of foreign students enrolled worldwide (OECD, 2013). Geographically, Europe is the top choice of foreign students enrolled outside their country of origin, followed by North America and Oceania. The dramatic fivefold increase of foreign student enrolments in the last three decades (from 0.8 million in 1975 to 4.3 million in 2011) has been accompanied by discussions in the fields of English for Specific Purposes (ESP), English for Academic Purposes (EAP) and Writing Across Curriculum (WAC) about imposed challenges on non-native English-speaking (NNES) student writers (e.g., Casanave & Hubbard, 1992; Scheneider & Fujishima, 1995). ESP/EAP teachers and researchers advocate more effective instruction for NNES students writing academic English papers at the undergraduate and graduate levels without simply conforming to Western conventions and disciplinary requirements (e.g., Bain Butler, 2010; Cox, 2011; Fu & Townsend, 1998; Jordan & Kedrowicz, 2011).

When reviewing ESP/EAP scholarship, however, we found a paucity of research investigating Asian student's cultural roots for learning academic English writing. Students' views on writing in foreign-language academic English are not generally known or understood – in the East or in the West. While there is research ongoing that includes Asian perspectives on second language (L2) writer competencies and difficulties in writing academic English papers and articles (e.g., Hu, 2001), perspectives of L2 academic writers themselves are few (Bitchener & Basturkmen, 2006; Braine, 2002; Zhou, 2010). Even more scarce is research disclosing cultural views toward academic L2 writing in the context of English as a Foreign Language (EFL). This chapter explores Asian EFL graduate student writers' perspectives on EAP writing. Researching these students' linguistic, educational and cultural perspectives – that is, their ways of looking at and thinking about academic English writing – helps us understand the interrelation of academic literacy and L2 writing.

Specifically, this chapter investigates Asian graduate student writer perceptions and metaphors for academic English writing, with implications for a process approach to writing instruction that includes revising and editing. By exploring how academic English writing is perceived by Asian graduate student writers (Chinese N=50 and Thai N=50), cultural influences related to EAP students' writing knowledge and academic literacy emerge (Braine, 2002). The purpose is to help EAP/ESP professionals understand Asian students' background knowledge that may contrast across cultures, disciplines, languages and educational systems. This is important because prior (background) knowledge is the basis for L2 academic writer learning and development.

2 Literature review

Internationalisation is 'a pressure no one who teaches can be unaware of' (Holliday, 1999, p. 99). In the 2005 *IAU Global Survey Report*, Knight (2006) reported that 73% of higher education institutions ranked internationalisation as a high priority. International education has become a marketable and profitable enterprise. Currently, both international students and their host institution faculty and staff face challenges associated with internationalisation in higher education. International students may struggle with content knowledge and linguistic growth, and administrators and faculty may rethink their management, curricula and pedagogy (Knight, 2006). Despite all efforts, tensions and confusions exist. One overarching attitude of some university professors is reflected in their views on the presence of international students and their English proficiency (Turner & Robson, 2008). 'The challenge of teaching students from vastly different cultural backgrounds with questionable language skills drives me crazy at times', a faculty member remarked (Douglas, 2005, p. 168). From the NNES students' side, a Chinese student, for example, learned nothing from a content professor's feedback: 'Once I got a comment on my paper like this: "You have written very beautifully, but presented nothing"' (Fu & Townsend, 1998, p. 130). Since academic writing plays an important role in graduate studies for non-native English-speaker students (Braine, 2002) and for the purpose of this article, we focus our discussion of the research literature from two perspectives: faculty attitudes toward L2 academic writers and challenges of L2 academic writers. First we address faculty and student L2 academic writer perspectives, then we address the English language teaching (ELT) context in China and Thailand.

2.1 L2 writers and L2 writing from the perspective of faculty

Regardless of discipline or students' first academic language (L1), all English-medium university professors utilise writing assignments as a means of assessing students' mastery of disciplinary knowledge and expect skills for disciplinary appropriate description, argument and critical thinking. University programmes require students to write within disciplinary conventions (Hyland, 2013). While native English-speaking students may feel challenged in writing English academic papers, NNES students may suffer more because of contrasting background knowledge. NNES students may have both local problems (e.g., grammar and sentence structure) and global problems (e.g., organisation, convention and rhetoric) in academic disciplinary writing. The higher the level of the programme, the more writing problems encountered because of higher expectations from faculty regarding L2 English written language use and content analysis (Casanave & Hubbard, 1992).

Over-emphasising English proficiency in the admission process, furthermore, falsifies professors' expectations and reinforces negative stereotypes of NNES students (Turner & Robson, 2008). Faculty members may complain about grammar mistakes and grammar competency of NNES graduate student writers. They may think such mistakes distract their time and energy from critiquing NNES students' scientific ideas and research methods (Jordan & Kedrowicz, 2011). The following comments of faculty toward NNES students are typical in the authors' personal and professional experience:

> My philosophy is that it's not my job to teach them how to write, I'm not a writing instructor. If they have major problems, they should take a writing course, hire a tutor or get an editor …

> I had falsely assumed that the students had [the knowledge of how to write] and I never even asked myself how and where they've got it. (Angelova & Rizantseva, 1998, p. 24)

Knowledge of writing and L2 academic writers is lacking among those responsible for assessing academic research papers of NNES students.

2.2 L2 writers and L2 writing: Challenges and frustrations of NNES students

In a study about L2 students in graduate engineering programmes, Jordan and Kedrowicz (2011) found that NNES students were challenged by extended technical writing combined with challenges of writing in unfamiliar cultural, linguistic and rhetorical contexts (see also Cope this volume). High TOEFL scores do not mean these students are proficient in writing discipline-related papers or articles. This mismatch in gauging the gap between general language and L2 writing proficiency is particularly apparent to Asian students who comprise the majority of international students in the US.

After being admitted to English-medium institutions, NNES students need to use English to a point adequate enough to pursue university-level study (Constantinides, 1992). These NNES students might be fluent readers of English but not proficient writers of academic English. Their challenges are twofold – they need to: (a) write in English fluently and accurately in accordance with academic standards, and (b) learn to write in language specific to their discipline's conventions – impossible to achieve within a single composition or writing-intensive course (Patton, 2011). Learning to write is a developmental process.

The demanding requirements of academic writing for NNES students to succeed in English-medium programmes are daunting. Faculty members want to see L2 students write with disciplinary-approved ways to demonstrate their 'acculturation into the field' (Hyland, 2013, p. 250). To meet this requirement, NNES students are disadvantaged because '[academic] discourses are complex and often different from those in their home cultures, shortcomings in their written texts are all too clearly visible to assessors and competence is essential for academic success' (Wette, 2014, p. 60). Once they have started their academic learning, NNES writers experience 'a totally new writing style in the university.' (Evans & Morrison, 2011, p. 203). Unlike English composition that Asian L2 writers are used to doing, writing assignments expected from native English-speaking faculty include: (1) summary of/reaction to a reading, (2) annotated bibliography, (3) report on a specified participatory experience, (4) connection of theory of data, (5) case study, (6) synthesis of multiple sources, and (7) a research project (Horwitz, 1986), to name a few. Different rhetorical organisation and conventions often characterise academic English writing from sources with often implicit criteria for what is considered good writing. Interrelated linguistic and academic requirements are factors that cause L2 writers to struggle in their use of English (Zhou, 2010). Academic writing challenges may become even more intense as NNES student writers move beyond the first-year adjustment period. Lack of exposure to, and familiarity with, using English for academic purposes contributes to the hardships faced by NNES student writers (Zang, 2007).

The dilemma for NNES students overall is that the writing they felt good about as undergraduates may not be well received by their Western professors, and the kind of writing they did not like might get them good grades (Fu & Townsend, 1998). NNES student writers often have difficulty organising ideas and argument, for example, especially over an extended stretches of discourse. They also have difficulty using the appropriate (objective) style of writing and expressing their thoughts clearly in English (for example, writer positioning). The cause of their confusion and frustration is that they remain bound by their native cultural traditions and do not know the criteria for good writing in the new language and culture (Fu & Townsend, 1998). They may feel out of control and almost helpless when they try to write in English. They want to be taught explicitly and be corrected with grammar, phrasing, word choice and native English-speaker prose construction (Snively, 1999). In addition to micro feedback relating to cohesion of ideas and stylistic requirements, macro level feedback for overall structure of academic genre is needed for L2 academic writers (Bitchener & Basturkmen, 2006). Explication of genre without corrective feedback may not be enouugh for learners.

3 Local context

Harmer points out that, 'the social context in which learning takes place is of vital importance to the success of the educational endeavour' (as cited in Hayes, 2009, p. 2). Among Asians studying in North America, Chinese students are the leading group of international students, with Thai students the second largest group from South East Asia (IIE, 2011). Therefore, in this next section, we provide the sociocultural and sociolinguistic local context of EAP/ESP instruction in China and Thailand. This section serves as cultural context for participants in our study who have their own culturally based ideas of what constitutes good writing and good English language teaching (ELT) in China and Thailand.

3.1 Cultural perspectives of good writing

There are distinctive criteria and different views for what counts as 'good writing' (Li, 1996; Reichelt, 2003). NNES students often bring with them culturally different strategies when writing academic or professional papers, and research suggests that these strategies often conflict with discipline-specific conventions (e.g., Connor, 1996, 2002; Jordan & Derowicz, 2011).

In Chinese culture, for instance, students read to memorise and write to imitate. When they revise their writing, they tend to spend more time polishing their language than working on the content. Good writers in their view use metaphors to enhance writings. The more metaphors they use the more effective and convincing the writing is (Xu, 2012). If the Chinese say a person can write well, they do not refer to the ability to express ideas clearly, but rather to knowledge of the classic literature and the ability to manipulate artistically its forms and language in writing (Fu & Townsend, 1998).

Influenced by Chinese literacy practices, Chinese students view 'memorisation, repetition and imitation of authoritative texts as legitimate learning strategies for acquiring a canon of privileged knowledge' (Hu & Lei, 2012, p. 837); therefore, they do not perceive plagiarism as a violation of citing authentic texts. Researchers like Fu and Townsend (1998) and Snively (1999) found that their L2 graduate students transfer the Chinese criteria for good writing into academic writing in English. For them, a major purpose of writing is to show mastery of the established form and demonstration of knowledge of literary tradition through their artistic ability. This Chinese perspective is in line with Confucian literary tradition that emphasises using idioms, proverbs and an indirect approach in essay writing (Liu, 2009).

When Chinese students try to utilise the same principles in academic English writing, however, they may receive criticism from their English-speaking professors. Li (1996) vividly described her literacy shock when writing English in America: 'In my American classes, I soon found myself struggling aimlessly … the problem was not with grammar or the lexicon … It was comments beyond the sentence level in my writing that left me in endless speculation' (p. ix). With respect to revising, Chinese students tend to emphasise the language forms more than anything else in their writing. To make one's writing 'rich with beauty and taste' is a standard for good writing held by all. In their Chinese education, the students were rigorously trained to strive for this aesthetic standard in their writing and frequently used it in their written and oral speech (Fu & Townsend, 1998). They were not trained in technical writing.

For Thai students, Thai language interferes with their English writing in three aspects: structure, lexicon and rhetoric cohesion (Bennui, 2008). In contrast to Chinese views of good writing, Thai teachers of English think the most important factors for good writing are idea development, overall structure and cohesion (Bennui, 2008; Khongput, 2010). When grading student English papers, Thai L2 writing teachers also care about students' ability to consciously suppress negative transfer from Thai, the students' L1 (Khongput, 2010). However, they do think positive transfer (e.g., Thai proverbs and cultural elements) from Thai to English or Thainess in English writing enriches L2 English writing (Bennui, 2008; Buripakdi, 2012; Watkhaolarm, 2005). Watkhaolarm (2005) even pointed out the legitimacy of keeping Thainess in English writing because some cultural elements such as Thai society collectivity, seniority, humility and religion are impossible to transfer into English writing. For Watkhaolarm (2005), English writing teachers should view Thai English as a variety of World Englishes and respect the originality of students' English writing.

Cross-cultural perspectives on good writing reveal that culturally embedded training of criteria for good writing in EFL students' L1 has extensive impact on EFL students' L2 writing processes. Teachers of NNES students in English-medium countries should be aware of cultural differences and the culturally rooted conceptions for 'good writing' that NNES students bring into their monolingual English-medium classrooms. Consciously or unconsciously, NNES students translate L1 criteria for 'good writing' into their L2 composition and academic writing. Knowledge of NNES students' cultural understanding and perceptions of good writing helps native English faculty evaluate NNES students. To date, uninformed native English-speaker perceptions prevail.

3.2 ESP/EAP instruction in Asia

Local context is defined in this article as the English education of China and Thailand, English education in general and English writing instruction in particular. ESP/EAP research has emerged in Asia only within this decade (Cheng & Anthony, 2014). NNES English teachers outnumber native-speaking teachers worldwide and ELT situations in China and Thailand are not an exception (Bolton 2004; Hayes, 2009). Understanding ESP/EAP instruction in China and Thailand helps clarify how students in these countries are trained in English language education, especially in ESP/EAP classrooms.

3.3 ESP/EAP in China

ESP/EAP is a new concept for English education in China (Lee & Chen, 2009). Although in recent years there have been some changes in the College English Curriculum Requirements and the focus of ELT in China does include listening and speaking (Jin & Yang, 2006), writing academic English papers in one's discipline is still not the focus of English instruction (Hu, 2005). EAP instruction to non-English major students has been viewed as feasible and necessary only in the last decade (Xu, 2012). However, with most ELT teachers trained only in literature and Applied Linguistics, it is understandable that ESP/EAP course materials rarely touch scientific and technological texts; ESP/EAP teachers may be unable or unwilling to explain discipline-specific texts and writings in English (Cargill, O'Connor, & Li, 2012).

With respect to ESP/EAP pedagogy, Western concepts of English writing such as the process approach, genre-based approach and writing for academic purposes have been introduced to China's ELT teachers, but disciplinary writing is not required until the senior year of college English. As Townsend's (2005) research participant described regarding her experience with English writing, '… teachers look for language use, a real point, grammar, figures of speech, compound sentences. Chinese teachers do not pay attention to creativity and original thought …' (p. 146).

You's (2004) study on China's English writing classrooms disclosed that English writing instruction in current Chinese ELT classrooms is predominantly 'teach to the test'. Emphasis on English instruction is given for preparation of CETB-4 (College English Test Band 4), a national English test for college non-English majors to take for graduation. A typical English writing class involves students copying a 'model essay' from a list that fits into the three-paragraph structure required by the CETB-4 examination. Weekly topics for the three-paragraph essay practice centre around daily lives or popular topics in newsletter headlines. Both the CET syllabus and College English syllabus indicate that the writing section of the English test values correct form more than well-developed thoughts.

Thus, Chinese students are trained to write from models and memorised phrases. They learn to write in English more as a subject for linguistic forms. Although they are required to write extensively in their native language, in their English language classes they focus solely on drills in language structure. They do little purposeful writing in English and hence, they have no experience with Western concepts of style, function and structure (Fu & Townsend, 1998). Due to the emphasis of examination in College English, Chinese students have limited opportunities and academic training in composing extensive academic writing that complies with Western accepted conventions (Hu & Lei, 2012). The end result is that Chinese students enter English-medium degree programmes without prior systematic instruction or experience with writing academic papers in English (Hu, 2007; Zhou, 2010). Consequently, they face great difficulty when they compose in English for their studies in English-medium institutions (Fu & Townsend, 1998).

3.4 ESP/EAP in Thailand

According to Kachru's (1998) categorisation, Thailand belongs to the expanding circle of English in terms of English use, which means that English is used as a *lingua franca* in business and is a mandatory foreign language course. Due to cultural reasons (Khongput, 2010; Tangpermpoon, 2008; Wichadee, 2013), research papers concerning ESP/EAP in Thailand are not prolific. On reviewing ELT and language use in Thailand, Baker (2008) observes that the 2002 National Education Curriculum mandates 12 credit hours of English for college English: 6 for general English and 6 for academic English or English for specific purposes. Implementing this National Education Curriculum was not ultimately successful, however. Thai students' English proficiency is still very low, with writing skills below average (Foley, 2005). When investigating the factors for this failure, several studies (e.g., Baker, 2008; Geringer, 2003; Wichadee, 2013; Wiriyachitra, 2002) attribute it to unqualified English teachers. In a survey to Thai English teachers, the teachers themselves listed teaching English writing as their top problem (Noom-ura, 2013).

With regard to ELT in Thailand, Thai students are used to waiting for a teacher's hierarchical and top-down methods of teaching. They rarely take initiatives for critically thinking in learning activities such as learning to write in English. It is not uncommon that Thai students never learn how to write in English, even if they have already finished their masters level of education or if they are non-English majors (Tangpermpoon, 2008). Also important to note is that current Thai teachers were once EFL students. The way these teachers were taught about writing in English very much influences the way they teach their students to write now (Dueraman, 2012). It is natural that their writing instruction focuses on surface level grammar and sentence structure only. Without professional development, it is unlikely that they will value the process approach to writing and incorporate it into their writing classrooms because they would not understand its purpose. In addition, non-English major Thai students seldom have opportunity to receive training in English writing due to the fact that English education in Thailand does not prepare students to write in English at postgraduate levels (Tangpermpoon, 2008).

Since English will be used as a medium of communication in ASEAN countries in 2015, this pressing situation urges ELT professionals in Thailand to improve Thai students' and Thai teachers' English proficiency, especially speaking and writing at professional levels (Dueraman, 2012). To effectively teach English writing, Tangpermpoon (2008) proposed using an integrated approach that teaches Thai students both a cognitive approach for grammar structures and a social constructionist approach that utilises peer review and writing teacher feedback. This combined cognitive interactive approach may work well with Thai students in their educational context.

3.5 ESP/EAP issues needing to be addressed

One cause of Asian students' confusion and frustration is that they remain bound by their native cultural tradition and do not know the criteria for good writing in the new language and culture. They may feel out of control and almost helpless when trying to write in English (Matalene, 1985). The heavily cherished cultural traditions of respect for authoritative opinion and producing 'beautiful writing' (*mei wen* in Chinese) cause Asian students to crave correction and guidance (Snively, 1999).

Two ESP/EAP issues worth exploring in the research literature are: (1) the mismatch of NNES student perceptions of academic English writing and expectations of faculty in English-medium classrooms, and (2) a pedagogical model for effectively teaching NNES students about academic English academic writing that informs ESP/EAP professionals in both ESL and EFL settings.

On the one hand, Asian students, as non-native English speakers, can get lost between native writing conventions and discipline-specific writing conventions and therefore expect to receive explicit or continuous feedback on their writing as they develop their academic literacy. On the other hand, L2 writers' native language and culture are neglected (Bennui, 2008). Western faculty who teach or advise them may not have training or knowledge in intercultural communication or second language acquisition or writing (Jordan & Kedrowicz, 2011). Such a mismatch calls for more widely published research, knowledge and recognition of Asian students' cultural roots in academic English writing to help them learn more effectively and efficiently. To date much L2 writing research focuses on comparison of linguistic features rather than cultural factors and correlation of content and thinking of Chinese EFL learners (Xu, 2012). Although some scholars (Kaplan, 1966; Xu, 2012) have raised the importance of understanding L2 writers' cultural thinking in writing academic English papers, such voice comes from scholars researching patterns of L2 writers' academic English writing or thinking (e.g., intercultural rhetoric). Authentic voices of L2 academic writers themselves, detailing why they think or write in a certain way, is missing in the scholarship of L2 writing research and pedagogy.

NNES student challenges in academic writing concerns faculty calling for proficiency in academic English writing and scholarship. This concern applies to both the ESL context (e.g., in the United States) and the EFL context (e.g., continental Europe and East Asia). As Evans and Morrison (2011) noted, NNES students are worried about stylistic refinement or linguistic features (e.g., vocabulary and grammar) whereas professors are concerned about

NNES students' ability to articulate their understanding in disciplinary writing. It is therefore especially important that L2 writers be exposed to writing in their disciplines (Zhu, 1992). The L2 writing literature indicates, however, that general purpose ELT does not provide sufficient preparation for students wishing to study in English-medium higher education abroad. A well-designed generic EAP class may be helpful for NNES students' institutional and disciplinary acculturation (Evans & Morrison, 2011). However, NNES learners must be taught explicitly about L2 academic English writing with strategies successful writers use for improved performance. Strategies can help students adapt to the target discourse community fairly quickly (Bain Butler, 2010/2012; Braine, 2002; Manchón, Roca de Larios & Murphy, 2007; Mu & Carrington, 2007). Without intensive training in academic English writing or any explanation of culture-specific concepts and values in scholarly writing, L2 writers can be very distressed by feelings of inadequacy (Fu & Townsend, 1998; Li, 1996). Their identity as competent learners may be compromised.

As a research team consisting of ESL and EFL L2 writing instruction scholars, we explore the following research questions from two perspectives: (a) Asian graduate student writer perceptions and metaphors for academic English writing; and (b) an approach for teaching ESP/EAP writers that connects EFL writing culture and ESL writing conventions for students in, or preparing for, English-medium institutions. Background knowledge is a significant factor for L2 writer learning and development, with new knowledge of writing conventions built on prior knowledge. The research questions (RQ) we discuss and report on in this chapter are the following:

1. What are Asian graduate writers' perceptions of native academic culture?

2. What are Asian graduate writers' perceptions of academic English writing?

3. What are Asian graduate writers' perceptions of strategies for academic English writing?

4. What are Asian graduate writers' perceptions of composing for academic purposes?

5. What is an effective approach that builds on L2 writers' cultural roots in EFL academic writing and promotes their academic literacy in ESL academic writing?

4 Methodology

Through a quantitative approach, this research explores 100 Asian graduate students' perspectives of academic writing (Chinese N=50 and Thai N=50). A questionnaire investigating key issues in writing that influence academic writing literacy for the participants was used. Key issues under investigation were: (a) native academic culture, (b) academic English writing, (c) strategies for academic English writing, (d) composing for academic purposes, and (e) metaphors for academic English writing. The purpose was to disclose cultural influences related to EAP students' writing knowledge and academic literacy. Considerations for choosing graduate students rather than undergraduate students are twofold: (1) our extensive literature review revealed almost no undergraduate English writing across the curriculum courses in China and Thailand, and (2) graduate students in both university research sites have academic English requirements as a component for graduate studies, although forms and requirements differ.

4.1 Data collection procedures

Two of the authors – Wei and Zhou – have direct access to participants through their former colleagues in China and Thailand. After orienting and training their colleagues about research instruments, colleagues administered data collection in their respective universities among graduate students who had written academic papers in English. The data collection took place at one sitting, lasting approximately 30 minutes. Participants in each country volunteered to complete one questionnaire in their English class or in their leisure time through research colleagues. The authors' Academic English Writing Questionnaire (Bain Butler, Zhou, & Wei, 2013) allowed graduate student writers to reflect on their academic culture and to identify actions intentionally employed ('strategies') for writing academic English assignments and papers. All questionnaire items included definitions, and research colleagues did not interpret questionnaire items or definitions for research participants.

4.2 Participants

One hundred graduate students (50 in China; 50 in Thailand) whose major is not English participated in this study. Chinese participants were law students studying academic English in east coast China. They ranged in age from 24–33 and were first- or second-year graduate students. Thai participants were aged 23–52 and were mixed majors at a national university in lower northern Thailand. The range of majors of Thai participants extended across Educational Research and Evaluation, Social Development, Communication Management, Curriculum and Instruction, Educational Administration and Art Education.

Table 1: A comparison of the age ranges of the study participants from China and Thailand

Country	Male	Female	Youngest (age)	Oldest (age)
China N=50	20	30	24	33
Thailand N=50	18	32	23	52

At the time when data were collected, all participants were engaged in writing academic paper summaries ('abstracts') for their research in L2 academic English.

4.3 Instrument

As previously mentioned, the Academic English Writing Questionnaire (Bain Butler, Wei, & Zhou, 2013) was used to collect the data. It is a 50-item survey instrument comprised of 48 closed items and two open-ended items. It evolved from a 100-item Preliminary Writing Strategies Questionnaire adapted from Bain Butler's (2010) dissertation research with permission from Mu & Carrington (2007) in Australia. This concise, reliable survey instrument was intended to discern perceptions among graduate student writers across academic cultures in a second academic language, with a view to enhanced critical thinking in academic writing and advanced language use when writing research from printed and electronic sources.

4.4 Validity and reliability

Procedures were implemented to ensure the validity and reliability of the study. For content validity, we consulted with a variety of teachers, the research literature and target group members for relevance, representativeness and exactness of wording. A validity check with our Thai and Chinese colleagues disclosed 'no objections' about questions or results (personal communication, 13 December 2011). After data collection, we used the Statistical Package for the Social Sciences (SPSS) 21 to analyse the reliability of the questionnaire. The Cronbach's Alpha was .832 for the questionnaire indicating the questionnaire was very reliable.

5 Findings and discussion

Our questionnaire aimed to investigate five key issues related to academic culture and L2 writing culture. These issues were: (a) native academic culture, (b) academic English writing, (c) strategies for academic English writing, (d) composing for academic purposes, and (e) metaphors for academic English writing.

With respect to research question (RQ) #1, Asian graduate writers' perceptions of native academic culture, both Chinese and Thai participants strongly agreed that academic writing is very important in their native culture and that good writing means citing authoritative sources. What counts as borrowing 'other writers' ideas' remains unclear, however; qualitative research is needed to probe student understandings further. Participants acknowledged the importance of academic writing and were aware of criteria for 'good academic writing' (e.g., convention, structure and process) in their native culture. This result echoes other researchers' findings regarding 'good writing' (e.g., Fu & Townsend, 1998; Li, 1996).

With respect to research question (RQ) #2, Asian graduate writers' perceptions of academic English writing, participants overwhelmingly agreed that writing English well is important for both academic studies and career or profession. Not all students thought they were taught citing from sources for academic writing, even though more than 80% of them agreed that academic writing in English involves learning from source text and communicating learning to highly educated readers.

With respect to research question (RQ) #3, Asian graduate writers' perceptions of strategies for academic English writing, most participants said they revised several times from first draft to final draft. Most participants saw themselves as 'conscious, goal-oriented and strategic' in academic writing. However, student responses indicated that L2 academic writing instruction in China and Thailand could put some emphasis on interaction strategies for getting feedback in writing from professors and peers and also from teachers at different stages of writing, especially when writing from source texts.

With respect to research question (RQ) #4, Asian graduate writers' perceptions of composing for academic purposes, 56% of the participants said they write by listing, repeating, or paraphrasing sources when writing academic papers in English. They also said they write to critique, persuade, or interpret evidence selectively and appropriately in English. More than 60% of the participants agree or strongly agree with the value of writing with higher levels or purposes for academic English.

With respect to research question (RQ) #5, an effective approach that builds on L2 writers' cultural roots in EFL academic writing and promotes their academic literacy in ESL academic writing, most participants agree or strongly agree with the metaphor of being an architect or an artist when composing academic papers in English. The perception of writing English as an artist echoes the result of Fu and Townsend (1998). Such students prefer to plan, draft, edit and re-work/revise their drafts during writing. A little less than 50% of the participants agree or strongly agree with the metaphor of labourer for correcting language use. The overarching metaphors that emerged from the two open-ended questions are: (1) L2 writing as composer, cook, scientist, or engineer; and (2) L2 writing as difficult and complex.

Overall, the results of our survey underscore cultural perceptions of Chinese and Thai graduate student writers with regard to strategies and processes of academic writing in English. While research findings open a window for readers to understand Asian-trained graduate students' perceptions of L1 and L2 academic writing, they also call for more research, collaboration and proficiency-based academic English writing instruction. The most notable findings in this study are those related to writing from sources with higher levels of citation and writing purposes. Results also reveal the importance of encouraging Chinese and Thai graduate L2 writers to seek feedback and communicate with professors and peers during the writing process.

Researchers and policy makers have been overlooking academic culture as a factor that contributes to the success or hindrance of NNES students in English-medium institutions (Cheng & Fox, 2008). Faculty members' expectations of L2 academic writers and their L2 writing production point to reader-centered writing in ESP/EAP instruction. This means that L2 writers need to understand and incorporate an audience for their texts (Hyland, 2011; 2013). Explicit teaching of revision and multiple drafting is not practiced in most ESP/EAP classrooms; if taught, students would make more gains in L2 academic writing basics and discourse-related language skills (Sengupta, 2000).

Based on the findings of this study, and the gap in L2 writing/L2 writer research literature, a process approach for teaching NNES academic writers is called for (e.g., Hyland, 2003; 2006). The process approach is a teaching approach to writing which emphasises the development of good practices by stressing that writing is done in stages of planning, drafting, revising and editing that are recursive, interactive and potentially simultaneous (Hyland, 2006). 'The process orientation also implies a strong concern for the learner's strategies for gaining language skills' (Oxford, 1990, p. 5). With more knowledge and understanding of composing, text development and written language use, NNES writers aiming for academic success in English-medium academic writing would thereby advance their language skills and writing proficiency (competence).

6 Global implications

Student writer perspectives are important for ESP/EAP writing instruction that advances proficiency by building on student writers' existing competences. Understanding how students are grounded in language and literacy contributes to an empowering L2 writing pedagogy that is 'process-oriented, autonomous and experiential' (Canagarajah, 2006, p. 15). When NNES students study at English-medium institutions, challenges are daunting and painstaking as students work on transforming from EFL learners to ESL users (Johnson, 2008; Zhou, 2010). NNES are challenged as writers due to the lack of familiarity with disciplinary writing and with writing in another language: that is, L2 academic English.

With the unprecedented increase of NNES students studying at English-medium institutions worldwide, the tension and conflicts between L2 academic writers and readers grows exponentially. Research and problem-solving endeavours in fields such as Second Language Acquisition, ESP/EAP classrooms, Intercultural Communication and International Education, to name a few, are ongoing. Cross border educational pursuits of NNES at English-medium institutions pose challenges to all stakeholders globally. The ongoing issues under discussion are: (a) the mismatch of NNES students' assumptions and faculty expectations (e.g, Fu & Townsend, 1998; Hu, 2007; Jordan & Kedrowicz, 2011; Li, 1996); (b) the fact that L2 English writing teachers are mainly language teachers without proper writing instruction or training (e.g., Leki, 1992; Stuart, 2012); (c) the separation of Writing Across Curriculum and ESP/EAP practitioners (e.g., Geller, 2011; Todd, 2003); and (d) the existence of writing centres incapable of making a difference for international graduate students writing for academic purposes (e.g., Zhou, 2010).

7 Conclusion and recommendations

As graduate students who have crossed cultures and who have lived through the transformation process from EFL to ESL academic English writers and now to ESP/EAP professionals in US higher education, we are concerned with learning and development and what it means to teach writing to NNES writers. We propose five recommendations to all gatekeepers involved in the academic success (or failure) of NNES students in English-medium institutions. Gatekeepers include ESP/EAP educators, academic writing programme faculty and staff, and discipline faculty assessing Asian-trained students.

First, get the facts about L2 academic writing and instruction to understand who you are teaching and assessing. More research like the current study disclosing NNES writer perspectives should be conducted, and research findings should be widely disseminated. Empirical research informs academic writing instruction across cultures and disciplines, opening possibility for writing more kinds of texts in academic English. The imbalance of L2 academic writing research (for example, abundant contrastive research on syntactic or rhetoric comparison of Chinese L2 writers and the infertile research on their academic writing culture and perspectives) is a call for action to ESP/EAP scholars and practitioners. The more L2 writer cultural profiles are made available in the field, the more ESP/EAP writing pedagogy would be identified, and the more successful NNES student writer transformation would be.

Second, L2 writing teachers should help students identify L1 writer strategies and compare rhetorical conventions in both languages so that L2 writers are aware of the differences (Mu & Carrington, 2007). The research findings and process pedagogy suggested in this chapter can serve as a starting point for ESP/EAP writing instruction in the East, closing the gap with the West. For teachers, reflective approaches with questionnaires could help identify student writer needs and help develop a learner-centred pedagogy, connecting student native culture and practice with transformation that would be well received in Western academic writing convention. Helping linguistically and culturally diverse student writers discover what is appropriate and conventional when writing in their native academic language, and disclosing contrasting cultural ideas about academic writing and written language use, would make a difference for Asian graduate student writers and professionals working in English-medium institutions globally.

Third, a combination of process-based, learner-centered pedagogy (Hyland, 2002/2009) and genre-based, systematic assessment in ESP/EAP curriculum (Hu, 2007) should help Asian-trained graduate students meet academic writing criteria at higher university levels. Best practices focus on 'producing entire papers – not on grammar, parts of papers, or rhetorical modes, such as comparison/contrast and definition' (Williams, 2014, p. 223). Such curricula could bridge the gap between the East and the West in L2 academic writing instruction, meeting Asian student writers' cultural criteria for beauty and accuracy, as well as faculty expectations for writing across the disciplines. Perspectives of Asian NNES student writers in this research reveal a need to emphasise training of writing from source text and getting sociocultural-interactive feedback from their Asian readers.

Fourth, the aforementioned separation among professionals in ESP/EAP writing, WAC and writing centre services points to the need for institutional collaboration and professional development – in the East and in the West. The advantages of collaboration among faculty members in ESP/EAP, WAC and the academic units, as well NNES and NES writing faculty (e.g., Cox, 2011; Geller, 2011; Hall & Navarro, 2011) are multi-faceted. Collaboration would do three things to support L2 academic writer learning and development: (1) inform ESP/EAP writing teachers who have not had professional training in the type of writing products faculty members expect, (2) strengthen ESP/EAP curriculum and pedagogy from both L1 and L2 writer perspectives, and (3) enlighten academic teaching faculty and staff with an informed view of L2 student writers so they can teach them more effectively and assess them more fairly.

Last but not least, ESP/EAP writing professionals need to network institutionally – that is, not only across cultures, but also across disciplines. Institutional information exchange should include student writer perspectives of academic English writing, L2 writing practice in EFL context, and teaching L2 writing convention in ESL context. This conversation would help ESP/EAP/disciplinary writing teachers better prepare NNES student writers to meet academic language and literacy standards in English-medium institutions and in professional, disciplinary communities. Professional academic exchange is mutually beneficial to students, to teachers, and to institutions of home culture and host culture (Townsend, 2005). Facilitating NNES students' familiarity with, and transformation from, EFL academic writer to ESL academic writer is essential to Asian students' academic success and professional development in English-medium institutions and every professional educator has a role to play.

Acknowledgements

We would like to thank our Thai and Chinese colleagues for their assistance in data collection: Dr Arunee Onsawad, Associate Professor and Vice President for Quality Assurance, Naresuan University, Thailand; and Mr Liejun Tang, Associate Professor, in charge of Master's and doctoral English teaching, Department of College English Teaching and Studies, Qingdao University, China. Without them this study would not have been possible. In addition, we are very grateful for the reviewer's insightful comments that motivated our revision.

References

Angelova, M., & Rizantseva, A. (1998). "If you don't tell me, How can I know": A case-study of four international students learning to write the US way. ERIC Education Resources Information Centre, ED 423696.

Bain Butler, D. (2010). *How L2 legal writers use strategies for scholarly writing: A mixed methods study.* (Doctoral dissertation), University of Maryland, College Park.

Bain Butler, D. (2012). The use of language and literacy strategies in L2 academic legal writing context. In T. Austin & R. Erguig (Eds.), *Language and literacy: A socio-cultural perspective* [Special issue]. *Languages et Linguistique [Languages and Linguistics], 29–30,* 111–132.

Bain Butler, D., Zhou, Y. & Wei, M. (2013). When the culture of learning plays a role in academic English writing. *ESP Across Cultures, 10,* 55–74.

Baker, W. (2008). A Critical Examination of ELT in Thailand: The Role of Cultural Awareness. *RELC Journal, 39*(1), 131–146. doi: 10.1177/0033688208091144

Bennui, P. (2008). A study of L1 interference in the writing of Thai EFL students. *Malaysian Journal of ELT Research, 4,* 72–98.

Bereiter, C., & Scardamalia, M. (1987). *The psychology of written composition.* Hillsdale, NJ: Erlbaum.

Bitchener, J., & Basturkmen, H. (2006). Perceptions of the difficulties of postgraduate L2 thesis students writing the discussion section. *Journal of English for Academic Purposes, 5*(1), 4–18. doi: 10.1016/j.jeap.2005.10.002

Bolton, K. (2004). 'World Englishes'. In A. Davies & C. Elder (Eds.), *The Handbook of Applied Linguistics* (pp. 367–396). Oxford, UK: Blackwell.

Braine, G. (2002). Academic literacy and the non-native speaker graduate student. *Journal of English for Academic Purposes, 1,* 59–68.

Buripakdi, A. (2012). On professional writing: Thai writers' views on their English. *International Journal of Applied Linguistics, 22*(2), 245–264.

Canagarajah, S. (2006). TESOL at 40: What are the issues? *TESOL Quarterly, 40*(1), 9–34.

Cargill, M., O'Connor, P., & Li, Y. (2012). Educating Chinese scientists to write for international journals: Addressing the divide between science and technology education and English language teaching. *English for Specific Purposes, 31*(1), 60–69. doi: 10.1016/j.esp.2011.05.003

Casanave, C., & Hubbard, P. (1992). The writing assignments and writing problems of doctoral students: Faculty perceptions, pedagogical issues and needed research. *English for Specific Purposes, 11,* 33–49.

Cheng, A., & Anthony, L. (2014). ESP research in Asia. *English for Specific Purposes, 33,* 1–3. doi: 10.1016/j.esp.2013.07.002

Cheng, L., & Fox, J. (2008). Towards a better understanding of academic acculturation: Second language students in Canadian universities. *The Canadian Modern Language Review, 65*(2), 307–333.

Connor, U. (1996). *Contrastive rhetoric: Cross-cultural aspects of second-language writing.* New York: Cambridge University Press.

Connor, U. (2002). New directions in contrastive rhetoric. *TESOL Quarterly, 36*(4), 493–510.

Constantinides, J. (1992). Academic challenges and opportunities. In D. McIntire & P. Willer (Eds.), *Working with international students and scholars on American campus* (pp. 1–25). Washington DC: National Association of Student Personnel Administrators.

Cox, M. (2011). WAC: Closing Doors or Opening Doors for Second Language. *Cross the Disciplines, 8*(4). http://wac.colostate.edu/atd/ell/cox.cfm

Douglas, A. A. L. (2005). *Still in transition: An ethnographic case study of the academic and cultural adjustment experiences of Kuwaiti students enrolled in a formal agreement partnership between an American university and the State of Kuwait.* (Doctoral dissertation), University of Missouri-Kansas City.

Dueraman, B. (2012). Teaching EFL writing: Understanding and Re-thinking the Thai Experience. *Journal of Alternative Perspectives in the Social Sciences, 4*(1), 255–275.

Evans, S., & Morrison, B. (2011). Meeting the challenges of English-medium higher education: The first-year experience in Hong Kong. *English for Specific Purposes, 30*(3), 198–208. doi: 10.1016/j.esp.2011.01.001

Foley, J. A. (2005). English in ... Thailand. *RELC Journal, 36*(2), 223–234. doi: 10.1177/0033688205055578

Fu, D., & Townsend, J. S. (1998). Cross-Cultural Dilemmas in Writing: Need for Transformations in Teaching and Learning *College Teaching, 46*(4), 128–133.

Geller, A. E. (2011). Teaching and Learning with Multilingual Faculty [1]. *Cross the Disciplines, 8*(4). http://wac.colostate.edu/atd/ell/geller.cfm

Geringer, J. (2003). Reflections on professional developments: Toward high–quality teaching and learning. *Phi Delta Kappan, 84*(5), 373–380.

GHK Consulting, & Renming University. (2011). EU-China Student and Academic Staff Mobility: Present Situation and Future Developments. Joint study between the European Commission and the Ministry of Education in China.

Grabe, W., & Kaplan, R. (1996). *Theory & Practice of Writing.* Essex, UK: Addison Wesley.

Hall, J., & Navarro, N. (2011). Lessons for WAC / WID from Language Learning Research: Multicompetence, Register Acquisition and the College Writing Student. *Cross the Disciplines, 8*(4). http://wac.colostate.edu/atd/ell/hallnavarro.cfm

Hayes, D. (2009). Non-native English-speaking teachers, context and English language teaching. *System, 37*(1), 1–11. doi: 10.1016/j.system.2008.06.001

Holliday, A. (1999). Small cultures. *Applied Linguistics, 20*(2), 237–264.

Horwitz, D. M. (1986). What professors actually require: Academic tasks for the ESL classroom. *TESOL Quarterly, 22*(3), 445–462.

Horwitz, E. K. (2008). *Becoming a language teacher: A practical guide to second language learning and teaching.* Boston, MA: Pearson Education.

Hu, G. W. (2003). English language teaching in China: Regional differences and contributing factors. *Journal of Multilingual and Multicultural Development, 24*(4), 290–318.

Hu, G. W. (2005). Professional development of secondary EFL teachers: Lessons from China. *Teachers College Record, 107*(4), 654–705.

Hu, G. (2007). Developing an EAP Writing Course for Chinese ESL Students. *RELC Journal, 38*(1), 67–86. doi: 10.1177/0033688206076160

Hu, G., & Lei, J. (2012). Investigating Chinese university students' knowledge of and attitudes toward plagiarism from an integrated perspective. *Language Learning, 62*(3), 813–850. doi: 10.1111/j.1467-9922.2011.00650.x

Hu, J. (2001). *The academic writing of Chinese graduate students in sciences and engineering: Processes and challenges.* (Unpublished doctoral dissertation), University of British Columbia, Vancouver, British Columbia, Canada.

Hyland, K. (2002/2009). *Teaching and researching writing*. 2nd Ed. New York: Routledge.

Hyland, K. (2003). *Second language writing*. New York: Cambridge University Press.

Hyland, K. (2006). *English for academic purposes: An advanced resource book*. New York: Routledge.

Hyland, K. (2011). 'Learning to write: Issues in theory, research and pedagogy'. In R. M. Manchón (Ed.), *Learning-to-Write and Writing-to-Learn in an Additional Language* (pp. 17–35). Amsterdam: John Benjamins.

Hyland, K. (2013). Faculty feedback: Perceptions and practices in L2 disciplinary writing. *Journal of Second Language Writing, 22*(3), 240–253. doi: 10.1016/j.jslw.2013.03.003

IIE. (2011). Open Doors 2011 Fast Facts: International students in the U.S. Retrieved September 6, 2012, from www.iie.org/en/Research-and-Publications/Open-Doors

IIE. (2013). Open Doors 2013 Fast Facts. Retrieved January 20, 2014, from http://www.iie.org/Research-and-Publications/Open-Doors/Data/Fast-Facts

Jin, Y., & Yang, H. (2006). The English proficiency of college and university studies in China: As reflected in the CET. *Language, Culture and Curriculum, 19*(1), 21–36.

Johnson, E. M. (2008). An investigation into pedagogical challenges facing international tertiary-level students in New Zealand. *Higher Education Research & Development, 27*(3), 231–243.

Jordan, J., & Kedrowicz, A. (2011). Attitudes about graduate L2 writing in engineering : Possibilities for more integrated instruction. *Cross the Disciplines, 8*(4). Retrieved from http://wac.colostate.edu/atd/ell/jordan-kedrowicz.cfm

Kachru, B. (1998). English as an Asian language. *Links & Letters, 5*, 89–108.

Kaplan, R. B. (1966). Cultural thought patterns in inter-cultural education. *Language Learning, 16*, 1–20.

Khongput, S. (2010). EFL writing assessment practices: Teachers' perspectives. Retrieved January 14, 2014, from http://www.iaea.info/documents/paper_4d32ee9a.pdf

Knight, J. (2006). *Internationalization of higher education: New directions, new challenges (2005 IAU global survey report)*. Paris: International Association of Universities.

Lee, D. Y. W., & Chen, S. X. (2009). Making a bigger deal of the smaller words: Function words and other key items in research writing by Chinese learners. *Journal of Second Language Writing, 18*(4), 281–296. doi: 10.1016/j.jslw.2009.07.003

Leki, I. (1992). *Understanding ESL Writers: A guide for teachers*. Portsmouth, NH Boynton/Cook.

Leki, I. (1995). Coping strategies of ESL students in writing tasks across the curriculum. *TESOL Quarterly, 19*(2), 235–260.

Li, X.-m. (1996). *Good writing in cross-cultural context*. Albany, NY: State University of New York Press.

Liu, Y. (2009). The impact of cultural factors on Chinese and American college students' rhetorical choices in argumentative discourse: A contrastive study. *International Communication Studies, 18*(1), 128–142.

Manchón, R. M., Roca de Larios, J., & Murphy, L. (2007). A review of writing strategies: Focus on conceptualizations and impact of first language. In A.D. Cohen & E. Macaro (Eds.), *Language learner strategies* (pp. 229–250). Oxford: Oxford University Press.

Matalene, C. (1985). Contrastive rhetoric: An American writing teacher in China. *College English, 47*(8), 789–808.

Mu, C., & Carrington, S. (2007). An investigation of three Chinese students' English writing strategies. *TESL-EJ, 11*(1), 1–23. http://tesl-ej.org/ej41/a1.html

Noom-ura, S. (2013). English-Teaching Problems in Thailand and Thai Teachers' Professional Development Needs. *English Language Teaching, 6*(11). doi: 10.5539/elt.v6n11p139

OECD. (2013). *Education at a Glance 2013: OECD Indicators*: OECD Publishing.

Oxford, R. L. (1990). *Language learning strategies: What every teacher should know*. Boston, MA: Heinle.

Patton, M. D. (2011). Mapping the gaps in services for L2 writers. *Cross the Disciplines, 8*(4). http://wac.colostate.edu/atd/ell/patton.cfm

Reichelt, M. (2003). Defining "good writing": A cross-cultural perspective. *Composition Studies, 31*(1), 99–126.

Schneider, M. L., & Fujishima, N. K. (1995). 'When practice doesn't make perfect: The case of a graduate ESL student'. In D. Belcher & G. Braine (Eds.), *Academic writing in a second language: Essays on research & pedagogy* (pp. 231–265). Norwood, NJ: Ablex Publishing Corporation.

Sengupta, S. (2000). An investigation into the effects of revision strategy instruction on L2 secondary school learners. *System, 28*, 97–113.

Snively, H. (1999). *Coming to terms with cultural differences: Chinese graduate students writing academic English*. (Doctoral dissertation), Harvard University.

Stuart, C. (2012). Succeeding through uncertainty: Three L2 students in a first-year composition class. (Unpublished dissertation), University of Washington.

Tangpermpoon, T. (2008). Integrated approaches to improve students writing skills for English major students. *ABAC Journal, 28*(2), 1–9.

Todd, R. W. (2003). EAP or TEAP? *Journal of English for Academic Purposes, 2*(2), 147–156. doi: 10.1016/s1475-1585(03)00014-6

Townsend, M. (2005). Writing in/across curriculum at a comprehensive Chinese university. *Language and Learning Across the Discipline, 5*(3), 134–149.

Turner, Y., & Robson, S. (2008). *Internationalizing the university*. London: Continuum.

Watkhaolarm, P. (2005). Think in Thai, write in English: Thainess in Thai English literature. *World Englishes, 24*(2), 145–158.

Watson Todd, R. (2003). EAP or TEAP? *Journal of English for Academic Purposes, 2*(2), 147–156. doi: 10.1016/s1475-1585(03)00014-6

Wette, R. (2014). Teachers' practices in EAP writing instruction: Use of models and modeling. *System, 42*, 60–69. doi: 10.1016/j.system.2013.11.002

Wichadee, S. (2013). Factors related to professional development of English language university teachers in Thailand. *Journal of English for Teaching, 38*(5), 615–627.

Williams, J. D. (2014). *Preparing to teach writing: Research, theory and practice*. New York: Routledge.

Wiriyachitra, A. (2002). English-language teaching and learning in Thailand in this decade. *Thai TESOL Focus, 15*(1), 4–9.

Xu, X. (2012). Cultural factors in EAP teaching – Influences of thought pattern on English academic writing. *Cross-Cultural Communication, 8*(4), 53–57. doi: 10.3968/j.ccc.1923670020120804.2307

You, X. (2004). "The choice made from no choice": English writing instruction in a Chinese University. *Journal of Second Language Writing, 13*(2), 97–110. doi: 10.1016/j.jslw.2003.11.001

Zang, S. (2007). *Chinese students' later-year experiences in Canadian universities* (Masters Thesis), Lakehead University.

Zhou, Y. (2010). *The lived experiences of L2 Chinese graduate students in American higher education: A phenomenological narrative inquiry*. (Dissertation), University of Missouri, Kansas City.

Zhu, L. (1992). *The adaptation of Chinese engineering students to academic language tasks at the university of Calgary*. (PhD. dissertation), University of Victoria.

Contributors

Jennifer Cope

Email: jen.cope@sydney.edu.au

Jennifer Cope has been teaching ESP and General English to international and migrant language learners in Sydney, Australia for over 15 years. Jennifer is also an Academic Tutor on the Masters of Education in TESOL program at the University of Sydney, where she is completing her PhD research.

Kevin Knight

Email: krknight1@hotmail.com

Kevin Knight (doctoral candidate in Linguistics, MBA, MPIA) has worked for private, public and academic sector institutions including Sony and the Japan Patent Office. He teaches English for Specific Purposes (ESP), business and organisational leadership at Kanda University of International Studies (KUIS) in Japan. His doctoral research is on leadership communication and development.

Christopher N. Candlin

Email: christophercandlin@gmail.com

Christopher N. Candlin is Senior Research Professor Emeritus in the Department of Linguistics at Macquarie University, Sydney. His current research is in applied linguistics particularly in the field of professional and organisational communication. He has over 150 publications and has successfully supervised 65 doctorate students. He also edits or co-edits eight international book series.

Alice Lawrence

Email: a.lawrence@sheffield.ac.uk

Alice Lawrence has taught ESP/EAP/ESAP in industry and higher education in the United Kingdom since early 1990s and is currently responsible for the provision of in-sessional English language support services at the University of Sheffield, UK.

Jane Lockwood

Email: lockwood@cityu.edu.hk

Jane Lockwood has been working in the area of English for Specific Purposes for the last 30 years. Her practical and research focus has mainly been in the area of English for occupational purposes and she has most recently been working in the business processing outsourcing industry in Asia.

Saba Mansur

Email: sbahareen@comsats.edu.pk

Saba Mansur is an Assistant Professor at the Humanities Department COMSATS Institute of Information Technology, Islamabad, Pakistan, and has over ten years' experience of teaching ESP courses at university level as well as over four years of teacher education experience. She earned her Master's in TESOL from the University of Leeds on the British Council's Hornby Scholarship.

Prithvi Shrestha

Email: prithvi.shrestha@open.ac.uk

Prithvi Shrestha is Senior Lecturer in ELT at The Open University, UK. He has published a number of books, book chapters and refereed journal articles in the areas of EAP, ESP and mobile language learning and teaching. He is currently a Joint Coordinator of the IATEFL ESP SIG.

María Ángeles Martín del Pozo

Email: maryange@dlyl.uva.es

María Ángeles Martín del Pozo has taught English and Spanish as a second language since 1997 (Dublin City University, Ireland; Universidad de Valladolid, Spain). In 2014 she completed her thesis at Universidad Complutense (Madrid) in the field of CLIL teacher training. In 2000 she was awarded the European Label for Innovative Language Teaching and Learning.

Neil Matheson

Email: nj.matheson@auckland.ac.nz

Neil Matheson teaches at the University of Auckland. Neil has taught EAL, EAP and TESOL in various contexts for 25 years. Currently he is teaching and researching academic writing, Pasifika student success initiatives and online learning.

Helen Basturkmen

Email: h.basturkmen@auckland.ac.nz

Helen Basturkmen lectures on undergraduate and postgraduate courses in Language Teaching at the University of Auckland. Her research interests include the study of discourse features of written text in research reports, feedback on student writing in dissertations and theses, pragmatics, ESP/EAP course development processes and disciplinary differences in academic writing.

Jo Fayram

Email: jo.fayram@open.ac.uk

Jo Fayram is Staff Tutor for Languages and co-chair of an online EAP module at The Open University. She has extensive experience of teaching and managing EAP and ESP courses in higher education in the UK. Her main research interest is the impact of presence on language learning in asynchronous and synchronous contexts.

Valérie Demouy

Email: valerie.demouy@open.ac.uk

Valérie Demouy is Lecturer of French at The Open University. She has carried out several projects related to technology and language learning with French language learners at the university. She is interested in researching the role of mobile technologies in language learning.

Akiko Tsuda

Email: atsuda@nakamura-u.ac.jp

Akiko Tsuda is an Associate Professor at Nakamura Gakuen University, Japan, where she teaches EGP and ESP to dietetic students. She has an MEd from Temple University (TESOL) and an MA and a PhD in Social and Cultural Studies from Kyushu University.

Clare Furneaux

Email: c.l.furneaux@reading.ac.uk

Clare Furneaux is Associate Professor in Applied Linguistics at the University of Reading, UK. She teaches on undergraduate and postgraduate programmes in English language and ELT and supervises research into second language writing.

Barbara Tully

Email: barbara.tully@northumbria.ac.uk

Barbara Tully is Director of Collaborative Partnerships and Principal Lecturer in EAP at Northumbria University. She has worked for many years on the development of language courses, materials and tutor training for international trade unionists and on communication training for workers in multinational companies and European Works Councils.

Donna Velliaris

Email: dvelliaris@eynesbury.sa.edu.au

Donna Velliaris is Academic Advisor at the Eynesbury Institute of Business and Technology, a specialist pre-university institution where international students work towards the goal of Australian tertiary entrance. She holds graduate certificates in Australian Studies and Religious Education, graduate diplomas in Secondary Education, and Language and Literacy Education, as well as three Masters degrees in Educational Sociology, Studies of Asia and Special Education. In 2010, she graduated with a PhD in Education focused on the social and educational ecological development of school-aged transnational students.

Craig Willis

Email: craig.willis@adelaide.edu.au

Craig Willis is Academic Coordinator at the Eynesbury Institute of Business and Technology and Senior Lecturer in the School of Civil, Environmental and Mining Engineering at the University of Adelaide. Teaching classes of up to 550 students, he has developed innovative ways of providing continuous formative feedback using interactive teaching techniques, peer instruction and professional engineering processes. In the space of two years he was recognised with seven awards for excellence in teaching and learning at faculty, university and national levels.

Paul Breen

Email: paul.breen@gsm.org.uk

Paul Breen is a Senior Lecturer and scholar at Greenwich School of Management, London, and a graduate of the University of Manchester. Originally from Ireland, he has worked in a number of contexts both in the British Isles and overseas. His research interests are primarily in the areas of identity (professional, personal and cultural), teacher development, educational technology and studies conducted in researchers' own workplaces.

Yalun Zhou

Email: zhouy12@rpi.edu

Yalun Zhou is Assistant Professor at Rensselaer Polytechnic Institute. Her research interests are applied linguistics and instructed second language acquisition. Her recent work involves technology uses in language teaching and learning, and teaching language and culture in immersive, intelligent learning environments.

Donna Bain Butler

Email: dbbutler@wcl.american.edu

Donna Bain Butler is a Fulbright Specialist in Applied Linguistics/EFL at American University in Washington DC. She designs and teaches ESP/EAP courses for international graduate students and visiting scholars as an adjunct professor at the law school. Her research focus is on developing international graduate student writers.

Michael Wei

Email: weiyou@umkc.edu

Michael Wei is Associate Professor and Program Director of TESOL program at School of Education, University of Missouri – Kansas City. His research interests include learning English to near native-like proficiency, reading/writing English as a second or foreign language, learning environments, early second language development and second language acquisition.